PATCHWORK AMONG FRIENDS
FROM PATTERNS TO POTLUCKS

BY JUDY MARTIN

CROSLEY-GRIFFITH PUBLISHING COMPANY, INC.
P.O. BOX 512, GRINNELL, IA 50112

Page 13

Page 25

Page 37

Page 47

Page 57

Page 71

Crosley-Griffith Publishing Company, Inc.
www.judymartin.com (800) 642-5615
Photographs by Dean Tanner, Primary Image
Photographs by Anne Geissinger, Pixeldust & More
Printed by Acme Printing, Des Moines, IA

Contents

Page 81

Page 93

Page 105

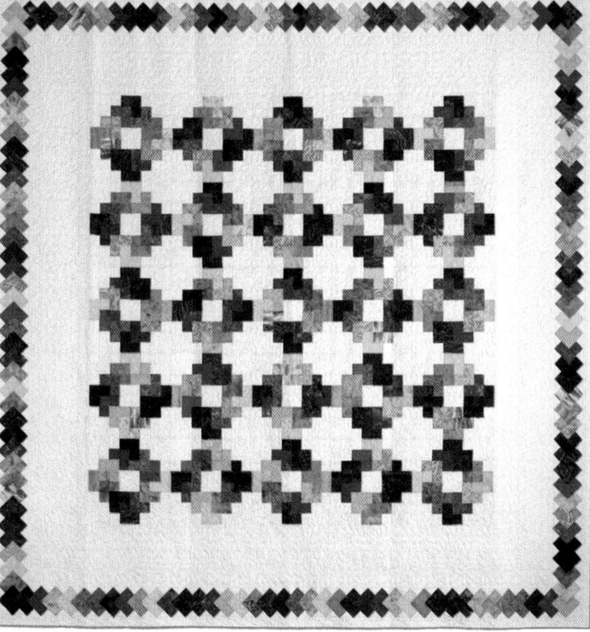

Page 119

Special thanks to Lana Corcoran, Debbi Treusch, Lee Plisch, and Jenise Antony for quilting; to Doris Hareland for piecing Rolling Hills Log Cabin and Summer Holiday; and to Tami Hemmer for piecing Boston Beauty. Thanks, as always, to Steve Bennett and Chris Hulin for proofreading.

Quilters' Get-Togethers

Since the days of the first quilting bee, quilting has been a social activity. Bees are less common now, though many churches and some quilt guilds still have a frame filled and ready for any who care to sit awhile and stitch in the company of friends. When most people lived in rural areas, catching up on news of one's friends was at least as important as the task of completing the quilt. When an impending wedding or the birth of a baby called for a quilt, many hands helped meet the deadline.

Quilters today still enjoy social contact with other quilters. Many attend classes or participate in a guild where they find support, expertise, encouragement, companionship, appreciation, and more. Others find what they seek by participating in an online forum.

If you have a specific project in mind, you may enjoy sharing the challenges and successes with others. Find like-minded individuals online or at your local guild or ask your local quilt shop for a specific class. Or take it upon yourself to initiate a class without a teacher or organize a strip exchange or fat quarter split with others who are interested in the same project.

Here are some ideas for activities that you may enjoy sharing with other quilters.

Quilt Classes

Quilt classes seem to provide many quilters with the same companionship and deadline that a quilting bee once did. Generally, each student works on her own quilt, and some of the work is done independently at home. An ongoing class brings people together on a regular basis, and assignments keep at least some of the students progressing apace. A class can also provide expertise, as the teacher takes on the role of experienced mentor to the students. Some quilters take classes more for the social aspect and the assignments or deadlines than for the help with skills and methods.

The quilts in this book are ideal for class projects. Several quilts, such as State Fair Star, Boston Beauty, or Morning Glory, are challenging quilts covering new ground. A teacher can provide the expertise to bring everybody up to speed.

Some quilts in the book involve basic skills, but require perserverance due to the many patches involved. Sun Valley Log Cabin and Thanksgiving are two such examples. An ongoing class can provide the assignments, deadlines, and encouragement to keep going.

A couple of the patterns in this book are ideal for one-session classes where a small project is completed or nearly finished during the session. Thanksgiving and Rolling Hills Log Cabin are offered as table runners. A class allows the students to set aside the time to complete a small project and feel a sense of accomplishment for doing so.

Online Groups

Far-flung groups in online forums serve much the same purpose as a class. Sometimes the "list mom" offers advice or gives assignments, and sometimes she simply establishes a place to ask questions or share experiences as each member tackles the same project. A certain amount of hand holding and encouragement is expected in one of these forums, but it comes naturally when everyone in a forum is supportive. Someone needs to take charge at least enough to announce plans. Participants can agree on the assignments and deadlines. As each participant completes her quilt, she can share a photo online, and everyone can celebrate her achievement.

A Class Without a Teacher

Assembled friends and spinoffs from a local guild can meet physically in members' homes to share the experience of making a specific project, as well. This is a good way to get to know your fellow guild members better. Several friends can decide to do the same quilt project or they can provide each other support and encouragement as they tackle different ones. Classmates can jointly decide on assignments and deadlines. Regular meetings keep everyone on target and allow less experienced classmates to seek assistance or advice from more experienced ones. The class can culminate in a reveal party to show off the finished quilts. If several class members have not finished in time for the reveal, you might schedule a one-month reunion to allow a second chance to complete the quilts and share them with the group. The reunion is a perfect opportunity to discuss the next project for the group to undertake.

The class without a teacher can serve much the same purpose as a class. It provides a social outlet, assignments, and deadlines that many quilters crave. In many cases, it can provide mentoring of less experienced quilt makers, as well.

However, when a project is challenging and ventures into unfamiliar territory, or when the disparity of skills in the group is great, an experienced teacher is invaluable.

Reveal Parties

Show-and-tell sessions and reveal parties can provide the push needed to get a project done in a timely manner. A party is the perfect way to celebrate your accomplishment with good food and good company. Most commonly, a reveal party would be attended by others making the same project, but friends who share a deadline for diverse independent projects will enjoy them, as well. Even non-quilters can share in the fun. If you have a special friend or family member with whom you share news of your progress, by all means, include him or her. Go out to eat at a favorite restaurant or prepare a special meal at home. Go ahead and get out the good dishes and make it an event. Display your quilt for all to see, then sit back and bask in the compliments!

If your social group is online, share a photo of your quilt as your "reveal party." Do this on your favorite quilt forum or your own blog. If you blog, announce your deadline to help you commit to finishing your quilt on time. Share a favorite recipe, as well, for a party atmosphere.

Setting Parties

Setting parties are perfect for Log Cabin projects where you can choose one of several block arrangements. Everyone loves a second opinion, and here you can get third and fourth opinions, as well.

So what constitutes a setting party? The star of the party is a set of completed blocks. A design wall is ideal for arranging the blocks, but a clean floor will do in a pinch. A digital camera will record the sets so you can preserve them, choose your favorite, and follow it when you assemble the blocks into a quilt top. Also use the camera to capture the festive atmosphere as you celebrate completing your blocks and looking forward to the completed quilt. Put on your favorite music to keep things lively.

If everyone is making a similar quilt, only one person needs to have her blocks completed in time for the party. Be sure to take digital photos of each setting and e-mail these to the other participants so they can reconstruct their favorite set with their own blocks later. Setting parties also work among non-quilting friends. Non-quilters may have some very creative ideas for arranging blocks once they see how Log Cabin sets work.

Ice Cream Socials & Potluck Suppers

What complements a social event better than good food? Whether you are involved in a reveal party, an exchange, or other get-together, why not incorporate a potluck or an ice cream social?

When what you seek is face time with other quilters, why not invite some friends to join you for an ice cream social? If eating ice cream with all the fixins' doesn't float your boat, how about a chocolate-themed extravaganza where everyone brings a chocolate treat to share? Or a salad-only potluck could be just the ticket if you are not into sweets.

In this book, I offer several recipes for potluck or other party fare. You will find desserts and salads as well as entrees. These are favorites at my house that you will enjoy making for your family or taking along to a meeting and a luncheon or dinner with your friends.

If you plan to serve food at a meeting, be sure to keep warm dishes appropriately warm and cold dishes suitably cold until serving time. This is most easily accomplished if you plan to eat first and have your meeting later.

Exchanges

Exchanges are an excellent excuse for a get-together. You can swap blocks or split fat quarters and give half away in exchange for half of someone else's fat quarter. This adds scrap variety to your quilt, and the fabric pieces will remind you of the friends who provided them. Another possibility is to exchange strips of a width needed for a shared project. A strip exchange is especially appropriate when a pattern calls for many strips of the same width in different colors. The 1½" strips of Rolling Hills Log Cabin or the 2¼" strips of Rainbow's End are good examples.

Though exchanges can be a fun way to add variety to your quilts and celebrate friendships, they are not for everyone. There will likely be different skill levels among participants. If you won't be happy with mixed results, don't sign up for a block exchange or a strip swap. Instead, opt for a fat quarter split. For a block or strip swap, it is helpful to agree on whether all fabric will be prewashed or all will not be. Dissenters may want to opt out or have a separate exchange.

Friendship Quilts

Autographs or favorite sayings can be exchanged for friendship quilts. These are often organized by family or friends for a gift quilt to commemorate an occasion, such as an anniversary or retirement. Participants may make a block or simply sign a patch of plain fabric, depending on their sewing skills. The blocks may be of each maker's unique design or all blocks may be the same pattern. Often, a unifying fabric is supplied. Friends Forever, Summer Holiday, Rainbow's End, and Thanksgiving all have center patches suitable for signing.

The organizers usually assemble the blocks into a quilt top and get the quilting done.

When many participants are non-quilters, one person often makes the blocks, incorporating patches signed by each participant. A party is the easiest and most fun way of collecting signatures. A Pigma pen is a good choice for an enduring signature. Freezer paper ironed onto the back of the patch will stabilize the fabric for ease in signing. You can also gather some or all of the signatures through the mail. Be sure to include the patch, a permanent pen, and a return envelope.

A signature quilt need not be made as a gift. You can gather signatures of friends, relatives, or even celebrities for a quilt you intend to keep yourself.

Quilts for a Cause

Charity quilts are often made at retreats, where assembly-line work is done by a group, or individuals simply make quilts in the company of others. These are often quilts of simple designs. Rainbow's End is ideal for a quilt to be donated to a charity. Summer Holiday is a little more involved, but would make a stunning Quilt of Valor for a deserving recipient.

Raffle quilts are typically organized by a committee that provides pattern and fabric packets (and sometimes cut patches) for participants to sew at home. The committee completes the quilt when blocks are returned. A good raffle quilt has simple blocks that make a stunning quilt. Thanksgiving is a perfect pattern for such a project. For this quilt, each packet should contain instructions and fabric for a single leaf. The leaves can be assembled into the larger blocks and pieced borders by the committee.

Occasionally, a handful of friends will get together to make a quilt to be raffled or auctioned as a fund raiser. A retreat is perfect for such a project. Some may cut and press while others sew. A challenging and exceptional quilt such as State Fair Star, Boston Beauty, or Morning Glory is a good choice in this case.

Make Your Event Memorable by Playing Quilt Show, the Game

Whether you are splitting fat quarters, setting Log Cabins, showing off your newly completed quilts, making charity quilts at a retreat, or enjoying an ice cream social, add to the fun by playing the new game designed by Judy Martin and her husband, Steve Bennett: Quilt Show. In this game, you collect fabric to your heart's content and convert your fabric to quilt blocks and quilts. When the quilt show arrives, you had better be ready with prize-worthy quilts if you want to win the game!

Quilt Making Skills

All of the quilts in this book are within your grasp. If you have doubts, realize that it is not a matter of perfection, but of skills. Whether the mere idea of perfection stresses you or the slightest imperfection causes stress, having the right skills will go a long way toward making your quilt making more satisfying and enjoyable.

When I began pondering my most recent book, *Stellar Quilts,* which featured not-exactly-your-average quilts, the first thing I did was to recruit a beginner. My neighbor Anne, who loves quilts and had made only one or two baby quilts of basic squares, was the ideal candidate. I spent a few minutes showing her how to rotary cut unusual shapes using paper templates taped to a ruler. Then I gave her some fat quarters and a pattern. A short time later Anne showed off her perfect block, proclaiming it the most beautiful thing she had ever made! She had no idea she was capable of this.

Anne did not have enough experience to have preconceived notions. She trusted me, used my methods, and got the desired results. People ask me all the time how I achieve such good points and joints. I am convinced the method has everything to do with the results.

That said, it doesn't matter to me what method you use. I simply want you to enjoy making quilts and make the kind of quilts you enjoy. If improving your skills will improve your enjoyment, read on for some suggestions.

The Right Seam Allowance Makes Everything Fall into Place

Anne had a leg up when she made her perfect block because she was using my sewing machine. My machine already had a tape guide in place for a perfect scant ¼" seam allowance. I have always maintained that you can sew anything once you master the seam allowance. Mastering your seam allowance will take a half hour of your time and serve you well for the rest of your quilt making years. If your patchwork results have been less than stellar in the past, deal with your seam allowance before you start your next project.

The perfect seam allowance has nothing to do with measuring your seam allowance. Instead, you determine it by sewing a sample with several seams and comparing that sample to an unstitched patch. Start by rotary cutting nine 1½" squares and a 1½" x 9½" rectangle. Join the squares end to end. Finger-press seams to one side. Place the rectangle and squares face to face. If the seamed squares turned out smaller than the rectangle, your seams are too deep; if the rectangle is smaller, your seams are too shallow. Say your seamed unit is ¼" too small. You have taken eight seams, with each seam affecting the finished size of two squares. That means your seam allowance is too deep by $\frac{1}{64}$" (¼" ÷ 16). If you even have a ruler with $\frac{1}{64}$" rulings, your eyes are better than mine if you can keep the marks from running together. This line is $\frac{1}{64}$" thick: ______________________

You can see that your adjustment will probably be very small, just the width of a thread or two.

I mark my seam allowance with a piece of black electrical tape on the throatplate of my sewing machine. It leaves a slight ridge to follow, and it doesn't get as gummy as masking tape. My machine has a line etched on the throatplate that is supposedly a ¼" seam allowance. It provides a nice line parallel to which I can run the tape. Make a second sample with the adjusted seam allowance. Repeat until your sample is perfect.

Take a few moments to master your seam allowance. Get it right, and save time and aggravation later when you don't have to struggle with ill-fitting parts.

The Lengthwise grain is Less Stretchy Than the Crosswise Grain

The lengthwise grain is parallel to the selvage. It is the least stretchy grain. It is more stable than the crosswise grain, and it follows the printed pattern more closely. While squares and half-square triangles will have sides on both lengthwise and crosswise grains, starting with the lengthwise grain yields the optimal results, both in stability and in following the printed motif. For rectangles and other long shapes, you want the longer sides on the lengthwise grain. For diamonds, where two sides are on the straight grain and two are on the bias, you want to follow the lengthwise grain rather than the crosswise grain for a more stable edge. Borders are also best cut on the lengthwise grain.

The Point of Point Trimming

The main point of trimming points is to help you align the ends of neighboring patches with each other before stitching. Eliminating bulk and dog ears in the seams is just a bonus. For 45° angles, such as those in some diamonds, trapezoids, and ¼- and ½-square triangles, my Point Trimmer tool works perfectly. Many templates in this book call for the "C" trim of the tool. Align the tip of the patch with one edge of the tool and the line at that corner of the tool. Cut off the fabric that extends beyond the tool.

Sometimes, when you align the ends of the trimmed patches for sewing, only one of the two trims at a point aligns with the neighboring patch. Use that trim as your guide and ignore the other.

For unusual shapes, you will need to use the paper template or tape it to the back of a rotary ruler to make a custom point trimmer.

Lose Your Anti-Bias Bias

Many of the quilts in this book have triangles or diamonds and bias edges. The bias grain is really no big deal. You are not likely to stretch it as long as it is flat against the bed of your sewing machine. Actually, bias is nothing to fear once your seam allowance is right. Most stretching comes from overhandling fabric, especially when you rip seams. You won't have nearly so much seam ripping when you have mastered your seam allowances.

Here are the big ifs that will help you neutralize the bias threat. If you trim points, you can see exactly how patches are supposed to align with their neighbors. If your seam allowance is perfect, you can trust the fit. If you pin seams and joints, you can be sure that you keep things properly aligned. If you finger press rather than pressing with an iron, you can avoid stretching bias edges. And if you don't push or pull fabric as you stitch, but gently guide it along your seam guide as the patches lay flat on the sewing machine bed, you are not going to stretch anything out of shape. Repeat after me: "Bias is no big deal." So stop worrying and make the quilts you really want to make. No ifs, ands, or buts about it.

Press for Success

It is not necessary to press after each seam. It is better to simply finger press the seam allowances to one side from the right side of the fabric, at least until all bias edges are sewn. When you do press with an iron, be careful not to stretch bias edges out of shape. Use a dry iron and press straight down or in the direction of the straight grain.

Use common sense when deciding which way to press seam allowances. You don't want dark seam allowances to show through light patches; you don't want too much bulk in any one place; and you don't want a patch to billow because all of its seam allowances are pressed toward the patch. Furthermore, you do want seams to oppose at joints. That is, you want the seam allowance pressed to one side for one unit and pressed to the opposite side on the other unit. Each seam will form a ridge, and when you slide one unit next to the other, you can feel the two seam allowances locking together when they are precisely aligned. The first rule of pressing is to press away from the bulk. That is, if you are sewing a single patch to a seamed unit, press the seam allowances toward the single patch. Where many points come together, press all seam allowances clockwise (or all counterclockwise) so that they will oppose each other. In general, try to press at least one seam of every patch away from the patch.

As you sew the patches together for your quilt, crease the seams to one side using your thumbnail rather than using an iron. I lay the unit, right side up, on my thigh. I run my thumbnail along the seam line to train the seam allowance in the right direction. This is finger pressing. I prefer my thumbnail to a pressing stick. It lets me feel the seam to make sure it is fully open. I press my fabric before cutting patches, and I don't press again with an iron until the blocks are complete. Careful finger pressing won't stretch bias edges. It also prevents tucks and preserves the ridges of the seam allowances to make perfectly matched joints a breeze.

A Point Well Taken

Sharp points define a good star. Don't miss the point by cutting yours off with less-than-stellar sewing. Mastering your seam allowance will go a long way towards assuring good points. Realizing that the points are supposed to be ¼" in from the raw edge will help, as well. You don't want your points at the edge of the block until the last seam has been taken. At a point, your seam allowances should cross in an "X," the center of which is ¼" in from the cut edge. If your stitching line goes across the intersection, perfect joints are assured. Your star points will be sharp and precisely on the edge of the finished block after it is stitched into the quilt top.

Pin-Point Accuracy

For precise sewing, rely on pins. Most sewing machines do not feed the top and bottom fabrics evenly. Pins can keep joints aligned as you stitch. I pin at every joint and at intervals of 3" or closer on long seams when joining rows of blocks, attaching borders, attaching binding, or stitching together backing panels. Pinning also helps when you are working with bias edges.

If you have trimmed points, it is easy to align the ends of the seam. Pinning the seam at both ends will give you results you can count on. Laying your work on a bed or a table helps you keep it flat and even while you pin.

I like short, fine pins with small heads. I leave the pins in place at the joints and stitch over them. Larger pins make a bigger hump to waddle over. The fine pins bend easily, but they are inexpensive, and I keep an extra box on hand.

Make Note of Reverses

Most of the common patches, such as squares and rectangles, are symmetrical; that is, they look the same face up or face down. These can be cut right- or left-handed, with fabric folded in half or not, with the same results. Some other patches, such as long triangles, parallelograms, and half trapezoids, are asymmetrical. Take care to cut these asymmetrical patches according to your quilt plan.

Here are some helpful guidelines:

1. Some quilts call for asymmetrical patches and their reverses in equal quantities. These are mirror images; cut both at the same time from fabric folded in half.

2. Mirror images can also be cut from stacked fabrics, half of them face up and half face down.

3. Sometimes all asymmetrical patches in a quilt are alike. In such a case, you must not fold the fabric. Furthermore, care must be taken to keep stacked fabrics all facing the same side up.

Use fabric that is face up to cut patches that do not have an "r" after the patch letter. Use fabric that is face down to cut their reverses, indicated with an "r" following the patch letter. This also applies to rotary cutting with paper templates. Tape paper templates to a ruler so that you can read the letters on the template through the ruler.

For traditional templates, place them face down on the back of the fabric to mark around them with a pencil. (Place traditional templates face up on the back of the fabric for reverses.)

Partial to Partial Seams

Partial seams are used when a joint is crossed by a straight seam, but you need to make the seam in two passes because one of the two segments you are joining extends beyond the other. These seams are easy to do. You simply start sewing at the end of the seam where the segments are the same length, but you stop sewing before you get to the uneven end. Often, the partial seam will allow you to take regular seams next. When you get further along, and the two segments are now even, you may complete the partial seam, stitching from where you stopped before to the end of the seam.

The only hard thing about partial seams is knowing when to use them. I make it easy for you: A partial seam is called for when you see a pink line between two pink dots. Simply start stitching at the pink dot at the end of the patch. Stop stitching approximately at the other pink dot. Complete the seam line later, after adding patches to make the neighboring segments the same length.

Y-Seams: Why Not?

Set-in seams or Y-seams (indicated by a pink or green dot in the diagrams) are nothing to fear. If you cut and stitch accurately, your set-in patches will fall into place naturally. The important thing to remember about set-in patches is that you must not stitch over the seam allowances at the joint. The seam allowances need to be free to pivot in order for the joint to lie flat. You will have to stitch a Y-seam in two passes: from the joint to one side and from the joint to the other side. I usually put a pin where I need to start the first line of stitching. For the second pass, the first line of stitching marks my starting point. Most set-in seams involve two like patches and one different one. I usually sew both of the matching patches to the different one first. The final seam joins the two matching patches. Because they match, it is easier to align these patches perfectly for the final seam.

If you chain piece, you can alternate starting and ending the seam at the Y-joint. This will allow you to leave the presser foot down and continue stitching in a chain half of the time. You may need to change to a shorter stitch length as you approach the Y-joint. The small stitch will permit you to end your seam precisely at the end of the previous line of stitching.

Backing a Winner

The sizes listed in my patterns allow the extra 8" of length and width required for mounting on a longarm quilting machine. Unless your quilt is very small or you are using extra-wide backing material, you will have to join two or three lengths of material to make your backing. Trim the selvages off the yard goods before cutting out the panels. Cut out the quilt panels as listed in the pattern. Make a fresh cut at the end of the length of backing fabric to square it up. Use a square ruler or a long, wide one to make sure the corners are square. Cut each panel precisely the same length and width. Pin and stitch panels together with ¼" seam allowances. Press seam allowances to one side. Press the quilt top and backing well. Pick off or snip any stray threads.

Preparation & Quilting

You are now ready to quilt your top or deliver it, along with the backing, to your trusted longarm quilter. Take this book along to show the quilter the quilting suggestions, if you like.

If you plan to quilt the top yourself, I cannot teach you hand or machine quilting in the space of a few paragraphs. If you do not know how to quilt, I suggest you take a class or get a book devoted exclusively to that subject. If you are already well-versed in quilting, I suggest you study the quilting detail photograph of the pattern in question as well as other patterns in this book to give you some ideas. Some of the motifs were digitized commercial motifs. Some were based on my own sketches. Most of the feathers were quilted free-hand. Gridwork and stripes were ruler-aided. I had many stars and other patches quilted in the ditch around the shape to add definition.

Bound for Glory

In preparation for binding, use a rotary cutter and ruler to trim the batting and backing even with the quilt top. Take special care to achieve right angles at the corners. Cut the binding fabric into straight strips (or bias) 2" wide and in sufficient quantity to go around the quilt's perimeter with several inches to spare. Trim the ends of the strips at a 45° angle, with all ends parallel to one another when the strips are all right side up. Trim the points using my Point Trimmer to help you align the strips for seaming. Pin and stitch the strips end to end with ¼" seam allowances to make one long strip. Press these seam allowances open. Fold the strip in half lengthwise with right sides out. Press the fold for the full length of the binding strip.

Lay the quilt face up on a flat surface. Starting on one edge of the quilt (and not near the corner), lay the folded binding strip over one edge of the quilt. Start about 4"–6" from one end of the binding. Align the raw edges of the two layers of binding with the cut edges of the quilt top, and pin through both layers of binding plus the quilt top, batting, and backing. Pin and stitch the binding to just one edge of the quilt, stopping ¼" from the raw edge at the corner of the quilt. Wrap the binding around to the back of the quilt at the corner so that it is even with binding on the front. Crease the binding crosswise at the quilt's raw edge. Now bring this creased edge to the front of the quilt and

align the crease with the raw edge of the part you just stitched. Pin at the corner, then pin along the entire next side. Stitch from ¼" from the crease in the binding at one corner to ¼" from the raw edge at the next corner. Back tack the ends of the seam.

Repeat this process until the binding is stitched to all edges and around all corners. Stop stitching 8"–10" short of your starting point. Lay the starting end of the binding strip over the quilt top, and pin it to the edge of the quilt ¼" from the binding's starting end.

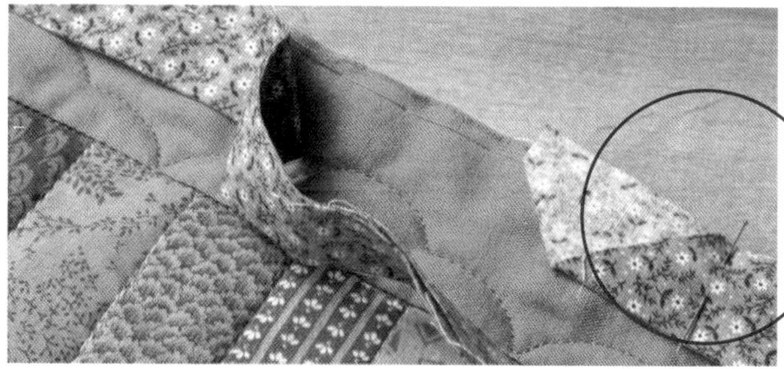

Lay the final end of the binding strip over it. With a pin, mark the point where this strip meets the pin at the end of the first strip. I always position this pin to follow the angle at the end of the first strip. This pin marks the seam line joining the two strip ends.

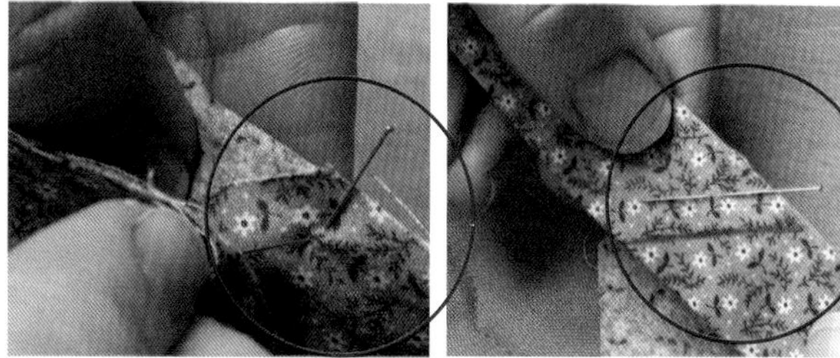

Unfold and cut off the end of the strip ¼" outside the pin at a 45° angle. Trim the point using the A trim of my Point Trimmer. Pin the two binding strip ends together and stitch with a ¼" seam. Press the seam allowance open. Refold the binding in half lengthwise and pin it to the quilt. Stitch from the point where you left off to the starting point, back tacking at both ends.

Wrap the binding around the perimeter of the quilt to the back side as you hand stitch. Align the crease with the stitching line that attached the binding strip. Hem stitch by hand to secure the binding to the back of the quilt. Take a tiny back stitch every so often. At the corners, stitch to the end of the stitching line. Position the binding for the beginning of the next side. Take a stitch to secure the binding for the next side to the corner, and use your needle to tuck under the excess at the miter. Continue in this manner until the binding is hand stitched all around the perimeter of the quilt. Then celebrate because your quilt is finished!

Important Pattern Information!!!

Please read this one small page before you go on to use the patterns. It may save you time and aggravation. Some of my presentation and methods may differ from patterns you have used in the past.

Size Matters

Quilts are presented in two or three sizes, with yardage and diagrams for each size. Block and quilt sizes are finished sizes, not including seam allowances. I do not allow any extra for trimming down to size. Border measurements include ¼" seam allowances, but they do not include extra beyond that. Rotary cutting dimensions include ¼" seam allowances all around. Backing panels include 8" extra length and width. All yardage and fat quarter requirements allow for 4–5% shrinkage.

Yardage and specifications list patches in alphabetical order. Rotary Cutting Details show strips in size order, starting with the widest strips of each color. Templates show seamlines (dashed), cutting lines (solid), grain arrows, and point trims.

Rotary cutting dimensions are shown for basic shapes. When a "+" follows a number, it means that the measurement falls halfway between the listed number and the next higher ⅛".

I show how to rotary cut unusual shapes by taping the paper template to a rotary ruler. Free downloads of these templates in pdf form are online at www.judymartin.com/templates.cfm. Be sure to print them at 100% scale.

The Method to My Madness

My patterns are written for your choice of rotary cutting and machine piecing or traditional template cutting and hand sewing. My rotary cutting directions call for lengthwise strips, parallel to the selvage. Feel free to use your favorite shortcuts, where applicable, but realize that some of the patterns do not lend themselves to shortcuts. My instructions call for cutting out strips, then cutting strips into patches of various shapes. Nonetheless, it is not necessary to cut out the entire quilt before you begin sewing. In fact, I recommend making a test block as soon as you have cut out enough patches for one. In my own quilt making, I alternate a bit of cutting with a bit of sewing to keep up my interest in a project. Feel free to follow suit if you think you would prefer some variety.

A Picture is Worth 1000 Words

I use visuals more than words to guide you in making the quilts in this book. I show blocks and construction units in exploded diagrams. These are labeled with patch letters. You may find it helpful to lay out your patches as shown in the diagram. The block diagram is exploded more in the upper left corner than it is in the other corners. Start by referring to the upper left corner of the diagram. The patches that are touching are the first ones you should stitch together. Repeat this step for all similar parts of the block. As you proceed, look to the other corners of the block, as they show more clearly what to do in the later steps. In general, note that patches that are shown closer together are joined before you attach more distant patches.

In some cases, where exploding the block does not reveal the piecing order very well, I present a diagram with a numbered piecing sequence. Join the patches having the same number to each other first. Then join patches in numerical order.

In the block diagrams, ">" means you should press seam allowances toward the tip of the arrow.

I used my stash, so my quilts are scrappier than would result from the number of fat quarters listed.

The quilt diagrams show blocks and individual patches. Blocks are named using the last letters of the alphabet. Patches are named using the first letters of the alphabet. Borders are labeled with dimensions as well as a number indicating piecing sequence. Attach them in numerical order.

In most cases, the quilting for the photographed examples was done freehand or using commercial digitized motifs on a longarm machine. I show close-up photos of the quilting. Feel free to show the photos in the book to your longarm quilter to give her ideas for the quilting.

State Fair Star

Looking for a pattern for a masterpiece? Look no further. State Fair Star combines impressive Feathered Stars in two sizes. It is a challenging quilt with a number of set-in seams and several uncommon shapes.

This original quilt was designed and pieced by Judy Martin and quilted by Lana Corcoran.

State Fair Star is a good candidate for a class or a class without a teacher. The finished quilts should be so glorious that you really must have a reveal party to celebrate their completion. Fat quarter splits or strip exchanges can add scrappy variety to your fabrics for the red feathers.

Yardage & Cutting Specifications

Queen Size

Quilt Size: 94" x 94"
Star Size: 64" between seamlines
Requires: 4 Y, 4 Z

Yardage

Cream Background 4⅛ yards
4 borders 4¾" x 73¾" (mitered)
384 D
280 L
4 N
4 O
4 P

Red Prints 6 fat quarters
40 A
384 D
64 E
4 I
280 L

Dark Blue Print 1 fat quarter
16 A
16 B
16 C

Light Blue Print 1 fat quarter
16 B
16 C
4 I
4 J
4 K

Dark Green Print 1 fat quarter
16 A
16 B
16 C

Light Green Print 1 fat quarter
16 B
16 C
4 J
4 K

Medium Blue #1 (Big Star) 3⅝ yards
4 borders 10" x 95¼" (mitered)
16 F
4 G
8 Gr (reversed)
4 H

Medium Blue #2 (Big Star) ⅝ yard
8 F
2 G
4 Gr (reversed)
2 H *continued at right*

Wall Size

Quilt Size: 32½" x 32½"
Star Size: 18¾" between seamlines
Requires: 4 Unit 1, 4 Unit 2

Yardage

Cream Background 1⅜ yards
4 borders 4⅞" x 28¾" (mitered)
4 borders 1¾" x 33¾" (mitered)
136 L
4 M
4 P
4 Q

Red Prints 2 fat quarters
8 A
4 I
136 L

Light Blue Print 1 fat quarter
4 I
4 J
4 K

Light Green Print 1 fat quarter
4 J
4 K

Backing 1¼ yards
1 panel 40½" x 40½"

Binding ½ yard
10 strips 2" x 18"

Batting
40½" x 40½"

Queen Size Continued

Medium Blue #3 (Big Star) ⅝ yard
8 F
2 G
4 Gr (reversed)
2 H

Backing 9 yards
3 panels 34½" x 102"

Binding ¾ yard
18 strips 2" x 27"

Batting
102" x 102"

Optional Templates

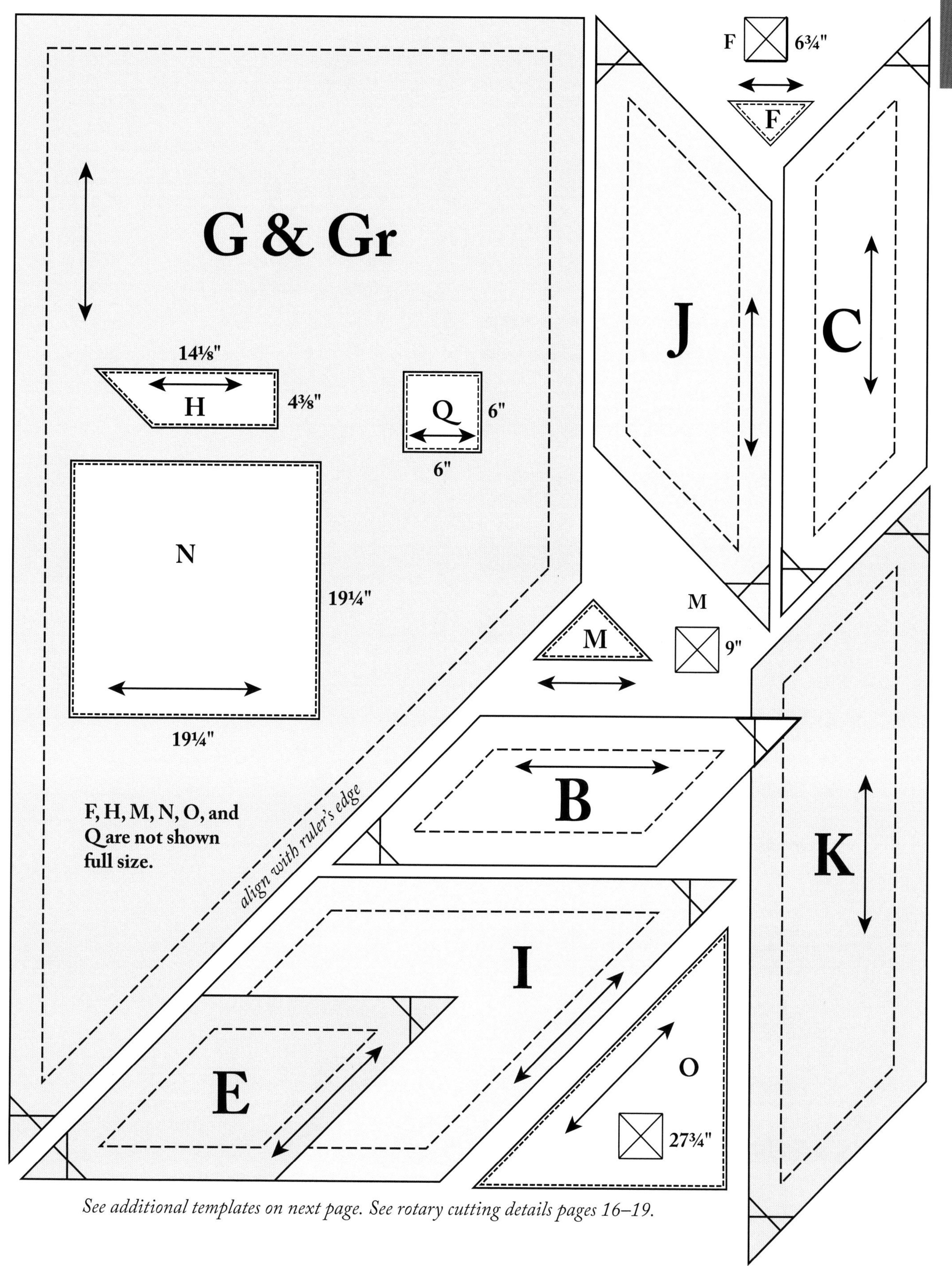

See additional templates on next page. See rotary cutting details pages 16–19.

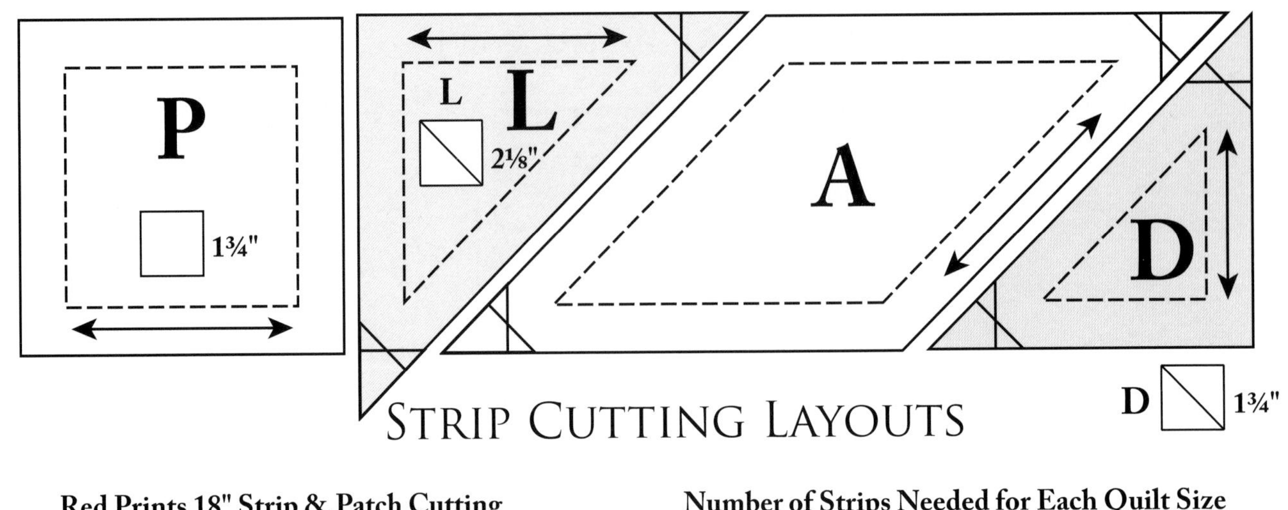

Strip Cutting Layouts

Red Prints 18" Strip & Patch Cutting

Strip	Number of Strips Needed for Each Quilt Size
2¼"	1 Queen/1 Wall
2⅛" (2⅛")	18 Queen/9 Wall
1¾"	7 Queen/2 Wall
1¾" (1¾")	22 Queen
1⅜"	8 Queen

See the Special Rotary Cutting Details on pages 18–19.

Do not cut just one type of strip or patch letter from a red fat quarter. Instead, cut a variety of patch letters from each red fat quarter.

Dk. Blue 18" Strip & Patch Cutting

Strip	Patches	Number of Strips
1¾"	A A A A A A	3 Queen
1⅛"	C C C C	4 Queen
1⅛"	B B B B B B	3 Queen

Lt. Blue 18" Strip & Patch Cutting

Strip	Patches	Number of Strips
2¼"	I I I I	1 Queen/1 Wall
1⅜"	K K K	2 Queen/2 Wall
1⅜"	J J J J	1 Queen/1 Wall
1⅛"	C C C C	4 Queen
1⅛"	B B B B B B	3 Queen

Dk. Green 18" Strip & Patch Cutting		Number of Strips Needed for Each Quilt Size
 1¾"	A A A A A A	3 Queen
1⅛"	C C C C	4 Queen
1⅛"	B B B B B B	3 Queen

Lt. Green 18" Strip & Patch Cutting

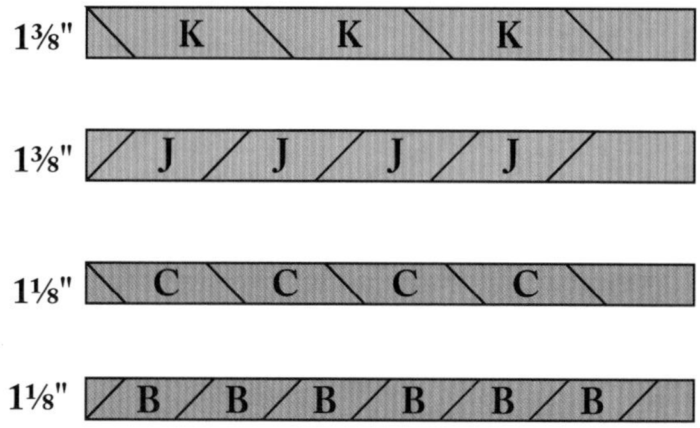 1⅜"	K K K	2 Queen/2 Wall
1⅜"	J J J J	1 Queen/1 Wall
1⅛"	C C C C	4 Queen
1⅛"	B B B B B B	3 Queen

Cream 18" Strip & Patch Cutting

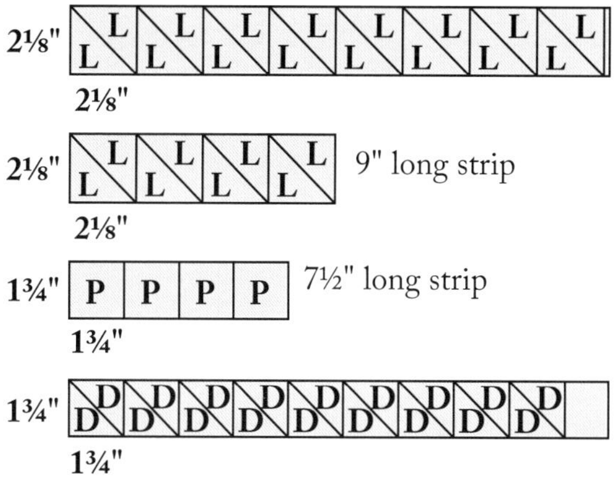

2⅛"	L L L L L L L L L L L L L L L L (2⅛")	18 Queen
2⅛"	L L L L L L L L (2⅛") 9" long strip	17 Wall
1¾"	P P P P (1¾") 7½" long strip	1 Queen/1 Wall
1¾"	D D D D D D D D D D D D D D D D D D D D (1¾")	22 Queen

Cream Yardage Cutting Layout for Queen Size

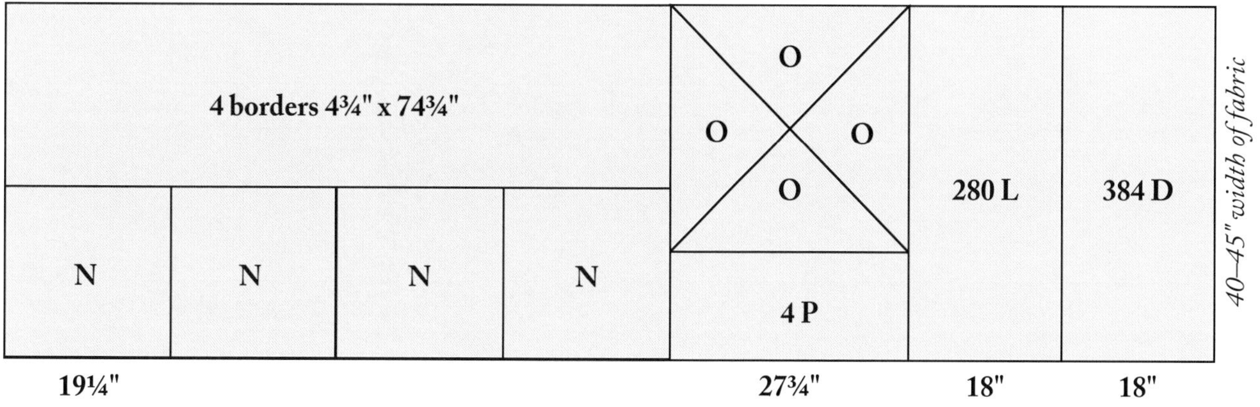

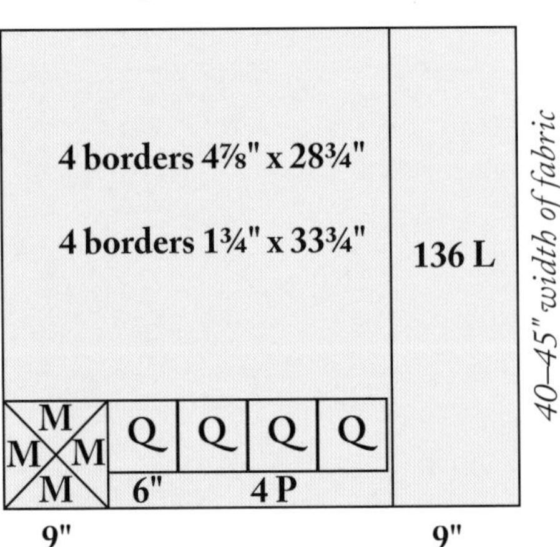

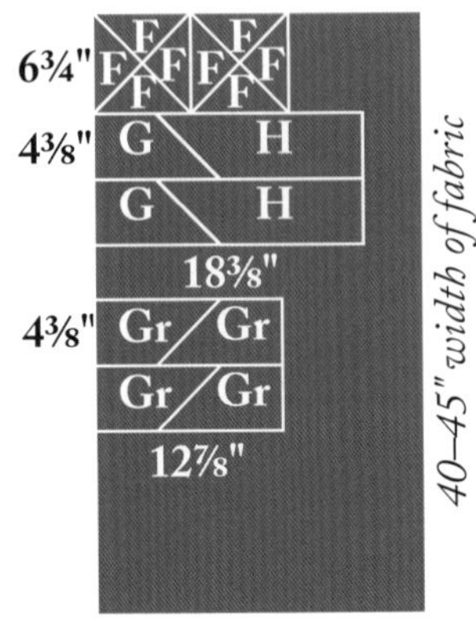

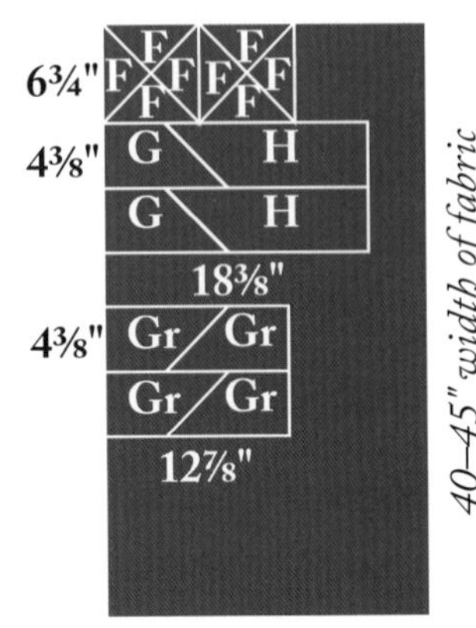

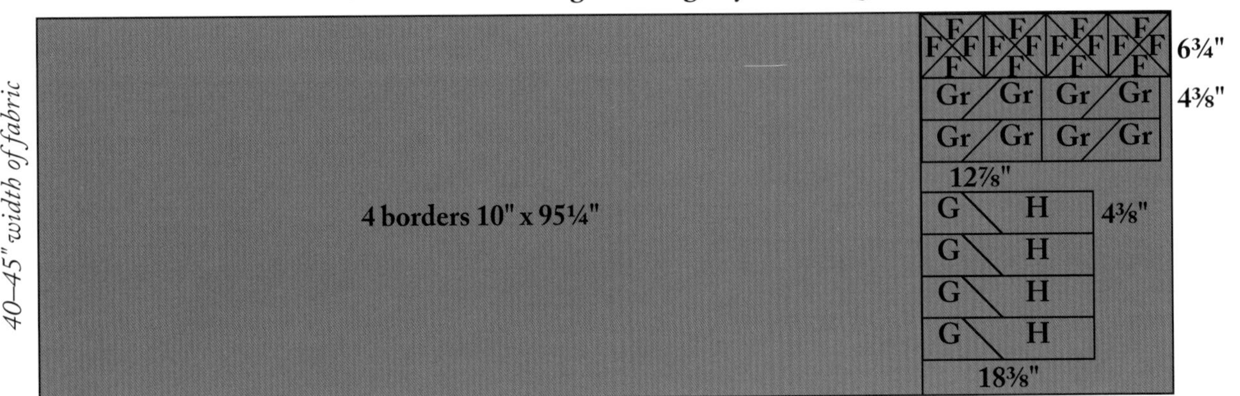

Special Rotary Cutting Details

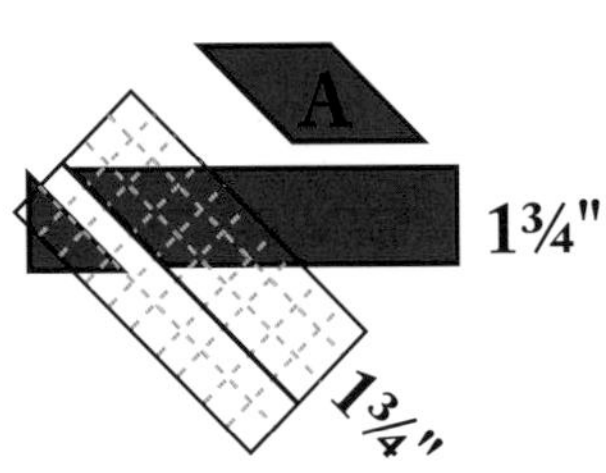

A: Cut a strip 1¾" wide. Cut off the end of the strip at a 45-degree angle as shown. Align the 1¾" ruling of a rotary cutting ruler with the angled end of the strip. Cut along the ruler's edge to complete an A diamond. Check your diamond against the A template in the book. Cut A diamonds down the length of the strip.

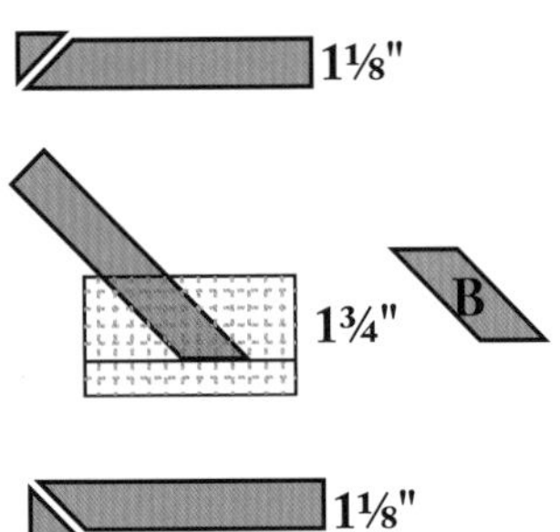

B: Cut a strip 1⅛" wide. Cut off the end of the strip at a 45-degree angle as shown. Align the 1¾" ruling of a rotary cutting ruler with the angled end of the strip. Cut along the ruler's edge to complete a B parallelogram. Check your patch against the B template in the book. Cut B's down the length of the strip.

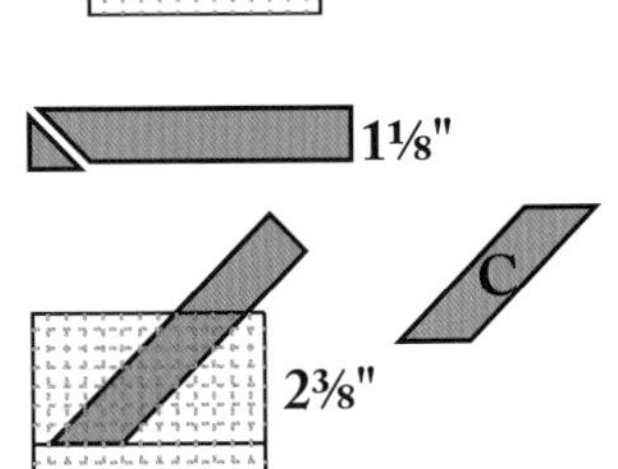

C: Cut a strip 1⅛" wide. Cut off the end of the strip at a 45-degree angle as shown. Align the 2⅜" ruling of a rotary cutting ruler with the angled end of the strip. Cut along the ruler's edge to complete a C parallelogram. Check your patch against the C template in the book. Cut C's down the length of the strip.

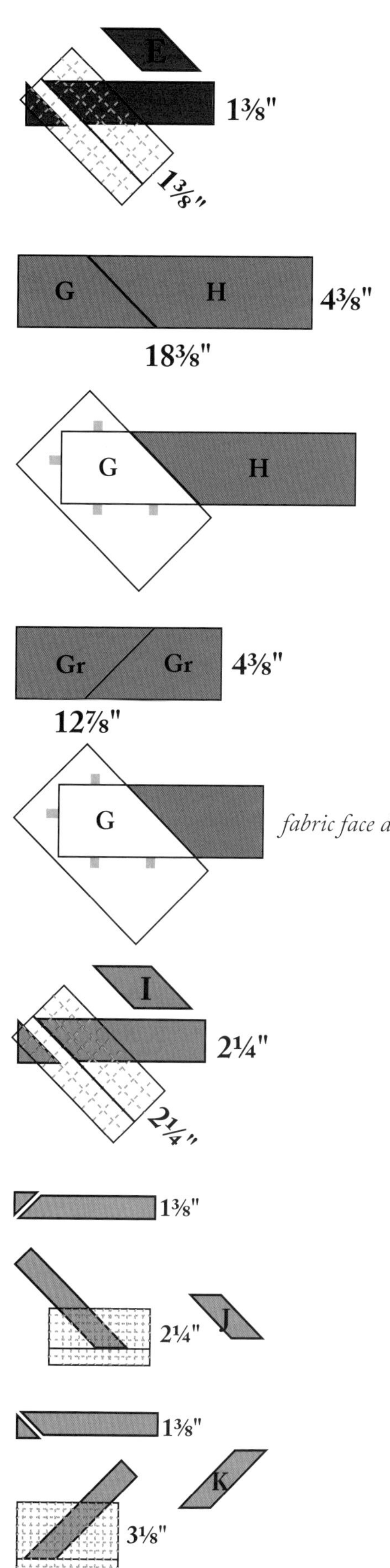

E: Cut a strip 1⅜" wide. Cut off the end of the strip at a 45-degree angle as shown. Align the 1⅜" ruling of a rotary cutting ruler with the angled end of the strip. Cut along the ruler's edge to complete an E diamond. Check your diamond against the E template in the book. Cut E diamonds down the length of the strip.

G & H: Cut a rectangle 4⅜" x 18⅜". Trace or download the template for G. Download is available at http://www.judymartin.com/templates.cfm. Be sure not to scale printing to a size other than 100%. Check template against the one in the book. Cut out and tape the template to a rotary cutting ruler so that the angled side is on the ruler's edge, as shown at left. Align top, left, and bottom of template with fabric rectangle as shown. Cut along the ruler's edge to complete G. The remainder of the rectangle is H.

Gr: Cut a rectangle 4⅜" x 12⅞". Place it face down on the cutting mat. Align top, left, and bottom of G template with fabric rectangle as shown. Cut along the ruler's edge to complete Gr. The remainder of the rectangle is another Gr.

I: Cut a strip 2¼" wide. Cut off the end of the strip at a 45-degree angle as shown. Align the 2¼" ruling of a rotary cutting ruler with the angled end of the strip. Cut along the ruler's edge to complete an I diamond. Check your diamond against the I template in the book. Cut I diamonds down the length of the strip.

J: Cut a strip 1⅜" wide. Cut off the end of the strip at a 45-degree angle as shown. Align the 2¼" ruling of a rotary cutting ruler with the angled end of the strip. Cut along the ruler's edge to complete a J parallelogram. Check your patch against the J template in the book. Cut J's down the length of the strip.

K: Cut a strip 1⅜" wide. Cut off the end of the strip at a 45-degree angle as shown. Align the 3⅛" ruling of a rotary cutting ruler with the angled end of the strip. Cut along the ruler's edge to complete a K parallelogram. Check your patch against the K template in the book. Cut K's down the length of the strip.

Queen Block & Unit Construction

Note the pressing arrows in Unit 1, Unit 3, Unit 7, and Block Y, below. Pressing is the same for Units 1 and 2; Units 3–6; and Blocks Y and Z. Make 4 each of Units 1 and 2 as shown below and described on page 22 for the wall quilt.

Similarly make 16 each of Units 3, 4, 5, and 6 as shown below.

Note the set-in seams, indicated by green dots. Use Units 1, 3, and 4 to make Block Y as shown; make 4 Y's. Use Units 2, 5, and 6 to make Block Z as shown; make 4 Z's, 2 with medium blue #2 and 2 with medium blue #3 in the background.

Make 232 Border Unit 7's, as shown below, pressing the seam allowances open.

Unit 1
Make 4 queen

Unit 2
Make 4 queen

Units 1 & 2 Piecing

Unit 3
Make 16 queen

Unit 4
Make 16 queen

Unit 5
Make 16 queen

Unit 6
Make 16 queen

Units 3–6 Piecing

Border Unit 7
Make 232 queen

Block Y
Make 4 queen with medium blue #1 in background

Block Z
Make 4 queen (2 with medium blue #2 and 2 with medium blue #3)

Queen Quilt Assembly

Note the set-in seams indicated by green dots. Arrange 4 Y blocks alternated with 4 Z blocks, noting that the Z's made using medium blue #3 are placed opposite each other. Sew an N to a Y and a Z with set-in seams. Stitch the seam joining Y to Z last. Press the seam clockwise. This makes a quarter star. Repeat to make 4 quarter stars. Sew an O between a Z and a Y, using set-in seams. Stitch the Z to the Y last. This completes a half star. Make another half star. Sew the last 2 O's between the Z and Y of the 2 halves. Sew the seam across the center of the star last. Press this seam open.

Pin and attach cream borders using set-in seams. Stitch the miters at the corners.

Join 29 Border Unit 7's; add 29 more turned differently, as shown. Make 3 more pieced borders like this. Pin and stitch 2 pieced borders to opposite sides of the quilt. Sew a P square to each end of the remaining 2 pieced borders. Pin and stitch these to the top and bottom of the quilt.

Pin and stitch plain outer borders to each side, starting and stopping ¼" from the raw edge. Miter the corners with set-in seams. This completes the quilt top.

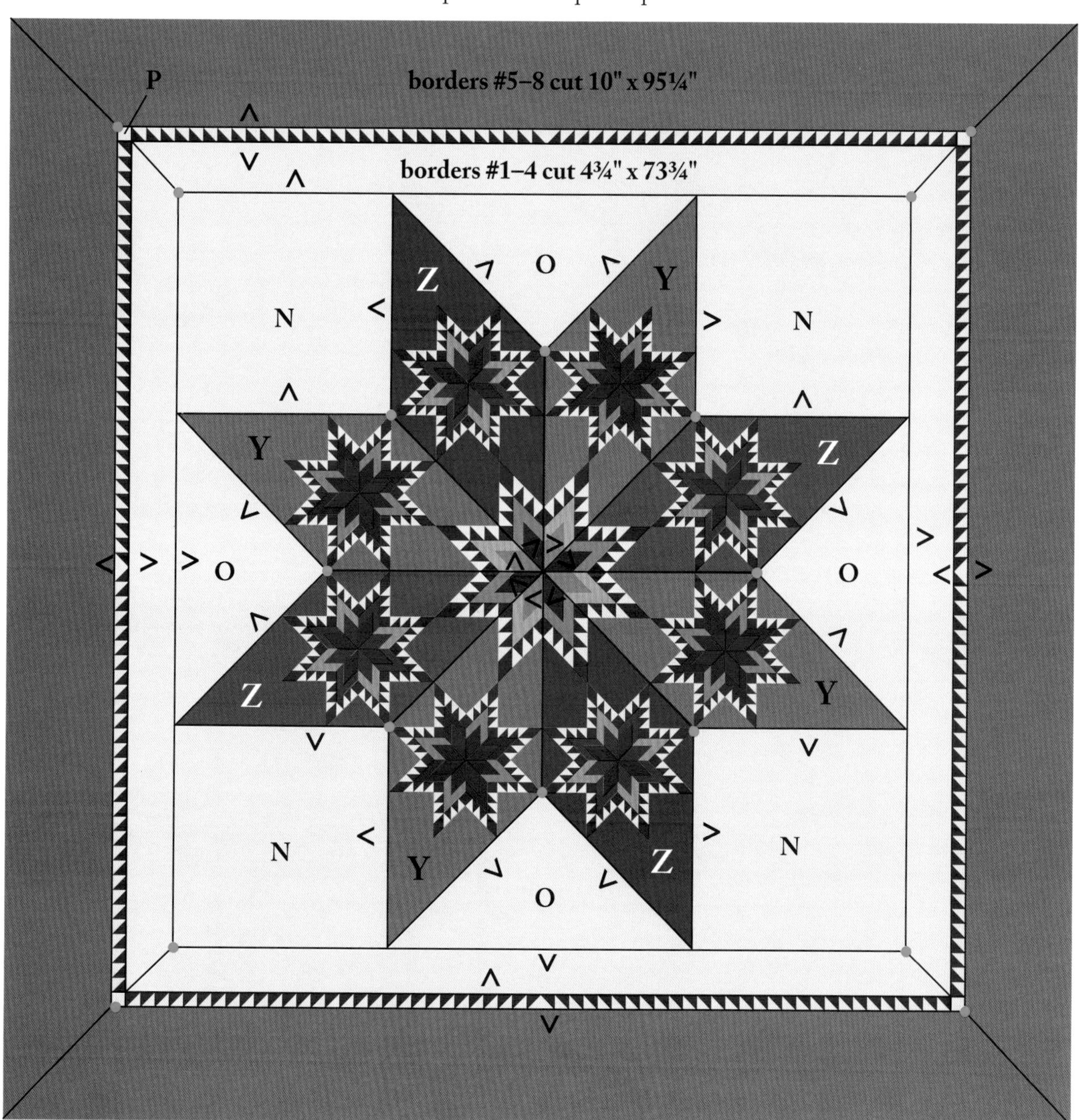

Queen Quilt Diagram

Wall Quilt Unit Construction

See the unit diagrams below. Note that the pressing indicated in the Unit 1 diagram also applies to Unit 2. For either unit, start by joining red and cream L's in pairs to make 4 squares per unit. Press seams open. Arrange these squares and other patches as shown for a unit. Sew J to I; press seam allowances toward I. Add K, pressing seam allowances toward K.

For the bottom of the unit, join 2 L-L squares, pressing seam allowances to the left. Add a red L to the right end; press seam allowances to the right. Add a cream L to the left end, pressing seam allowances toward the left. Sew this segment to the bottom of the unit. Press seam allowances away from the L's.

For the left end of the unit, join two L-L squares, pressing seam allowances toward the red. Add a red L to the cream end, pressing seam allowances toward the red. Add a cream L to the opposite end of the segment, pressing the seam allowances toward the red. Add a red A to the cream end of the segment, pressing seam allowances toward the A. Stitch this segment to the rest to complete the Unit 1 or Unit 2.

Make 4 each of Unit 1 and Unit 2. Also make 88 of Unit 7, pressing seams open.

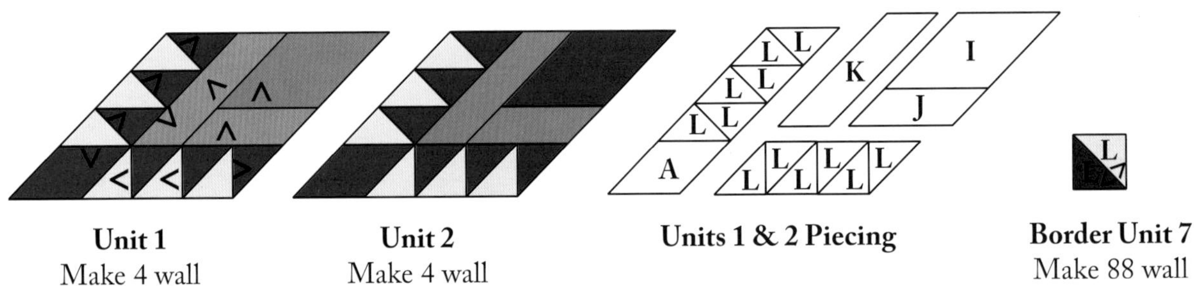

Unit 1
Make 4 wall

Unit 2
Make 4 wall

Units 1 & 2 Piecing

Border Unit 7
Make 88 wall

Wall Quilt Assembly

Note that the pink dots indicate set-in seams. Using a set-in seam, sew a Q to a Unit 1 and a Unit 2, as shown at right. Sew the seam joining Unit 1 to Unit 2 last. Repeat to make 4 star quarters. Sew an M between 2 star quarters, using a set-in seam. Sew the seam joining Unit 2 to Unit 1 last. This completes the half block. Repeat. The seams between Units 1 and 2 should be pressed clockwise in each case. Sew an M on either side, between halves. Join halves to complete block, pressing the final seam open.

Pin and attach wide borders using set-in seams. Stitch the miters at the corners. Join 11 Border Unit 7's; add 11 more turned differently, as shown. Make 3 more pieced borders like this. Pin and stitch 2 pieced borders to opposite sides of the quilt. Sew a P square to each end of the remaining 2 pieced borders. Pin and stitch these to the top and bottom of the quilt. Pin and stitch plain outer borders to each side with a Y-seam, starting and stopping ¼" from the raw edge. Miter the corners with a set-in seam.

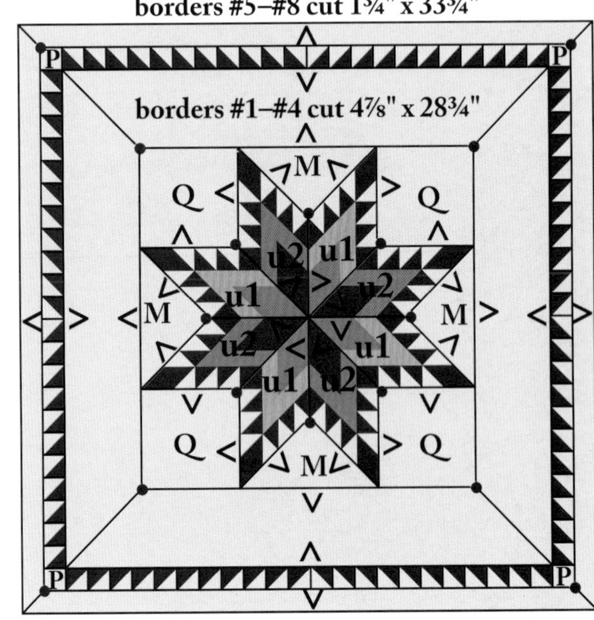

Wall Quilt Diagram

Quilting

Quilt in the ditch around all patches except between red and cream feathers. Quilt a simple feather motif in the medium blue star points. Quilt a large motif in the cream background triangles, and quilt 2 of these motifs in background squares, as shown in the photo below.

Quilt a cable in the inner border and feathers in the wide blue outer border.

Other Coloring Ideas

The example immediately below features the same blue and green as in my quilt, but with black feathers and green for the large star. Below that is a version with a dark background and light gray large star. Immediately below this column is a beach-inspired color scheme. Finally, below that is a State Fair Star in russets and greens with charcoal feathers.

Friends Forever

This quilt is cut from simple shapes and sewn quickly and easily. The staggered arrangement makes this a project that requires the full participation of your brain, however. You'll need to keep track of patches for use later and be careful with block and patch placement as you sew.

Friends Forever was designed and pieced by Judy Martin and quilted by Lana Corcoran. It was named after an Old 97's song.

It is a perfect choice for a signature or friendship quilt, with its light star centers. If you like, plan a setting party, and let your friends help you decide on the placement for the variously colored blocks. Friends Forever is also a candidate for a setting party when blocks are finished or a reveal party when everyone's quilt is complete and ready to show off.

Yardage & Cutting Specifications

Throw Size

Quilt Size: 56" x 72"
Star Block Size: 8" between seamlines
Requires: 22 Y, 23 Z

Yardage
Light Prints 11 fat quarters
22 A
176 B
in 22 sets of 1 A and 8 B
108 D

Bright Prints 16 fat quarters
88 C
88 D
88 E
in 22 sets of 4 C, 4 D, and 4 E
60 A
66 more E

Backing 4¾ yards
2 panels 32½" x 80½"

Binding ½ yard
19 strips 2" x 18"

Batting
64" x 80"

Queen/King Size

Quilt Size: 108" x 104"
Star Block Size: 8" between seamlines
Requires: 82 Y, 83 Z

Yardage
Light Prints 41 fat quarters
82 A
656 B
in 82 sets of 1 A and 8 B
192 D

Bright Prints 43 fat quarters
328 C
328 D
328 E
in 82 sets of 4 C, 4 D, and 4 E
102 A
120 more E

Backing 9⅞ yards
3 panels 39¼" x 112"

Binding ¾ yard
20 strips 2" x 27"

Batting
116" x 112"

Fruit Salad Recipe

Makes 12 Side Servings

This makes a lovely summer salad for an autograph party/potluck. Substitute your favorite seasonal fruit, if you like. We use apples instead of strawberries in winter.

For a fruity dessert, use 15 oz. vanilla pudding (4 snack cups) in place of the yogurt and top with whipped cream. Sugar-free pudding and lite nondairy topping make this a diet-conscious treat.

Ingredients

1 pint fresh strawberries
2 bananas
½ fresh pineapple
1 orange
½ of a 15 oz. angel food cake
12 oz. vanilla yogurt

Method

Wash and dry the strawberries; cut them in bite-size pieces. Peel and slice the bananas. Core and cut the pineapple into chunks. Peel and section the orange; cut sections in half. Cut or tear cake into 1" cubes. (You can freeze the remaining cake for use next time you make the salad.)

In a large bowl, stir the yogurt into the fruit and cake. Serve promptly.

Optional Templates

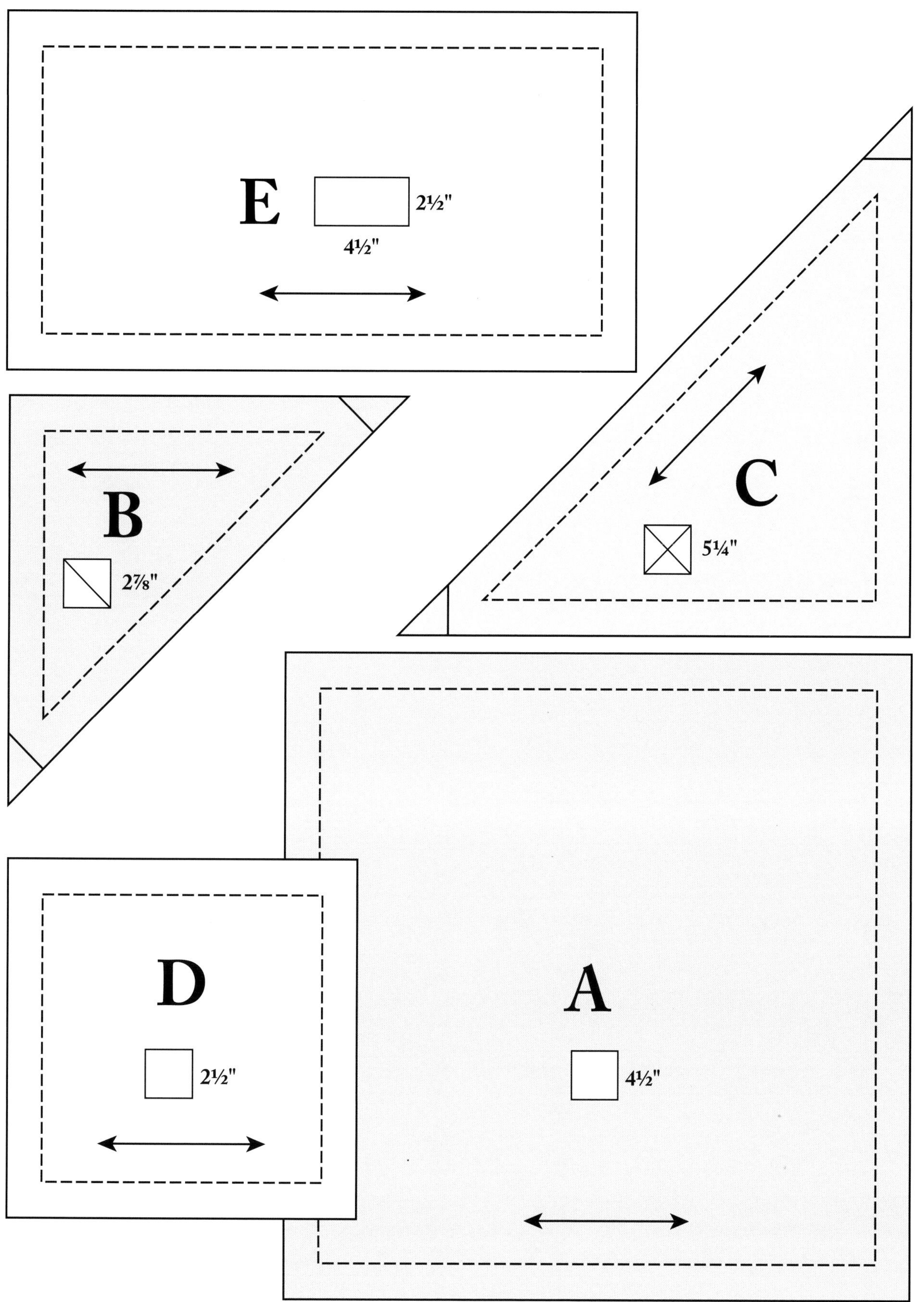

Strip Cutting Layouts

Light Prints 18" Strip & Patch Cutting

Number of Strips Needed for Each Quilt Size

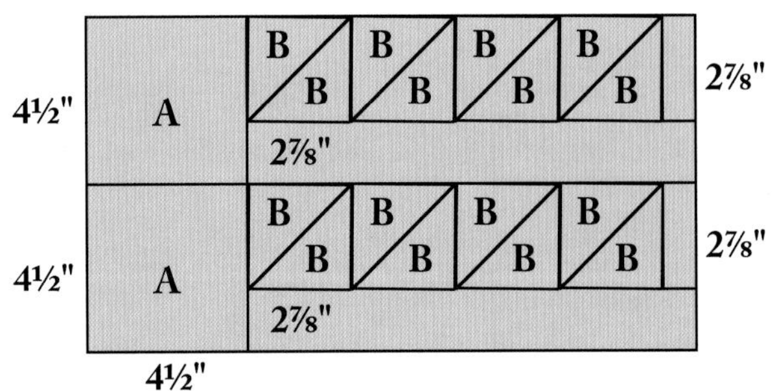

11 Throw/41 Queen-King

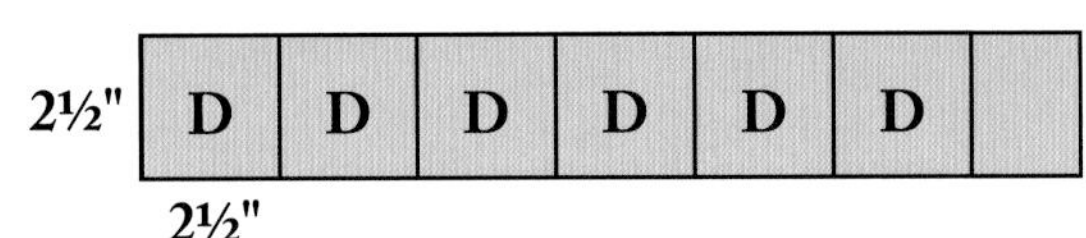

18 Throw/32 Queen-King

Bright Prints 18" Strip & Patch Cutting

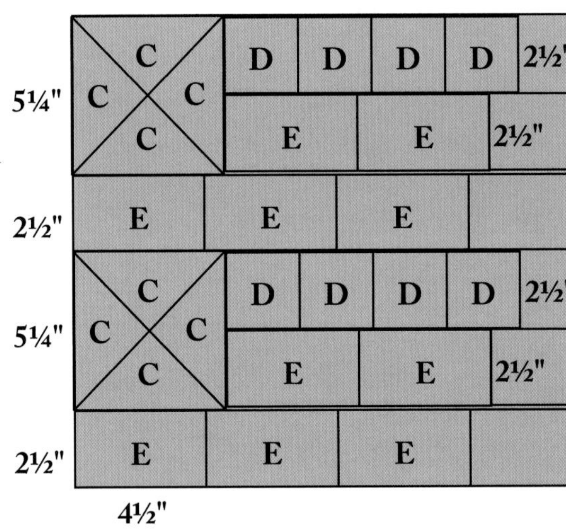

11 Throw/41 Queen-King

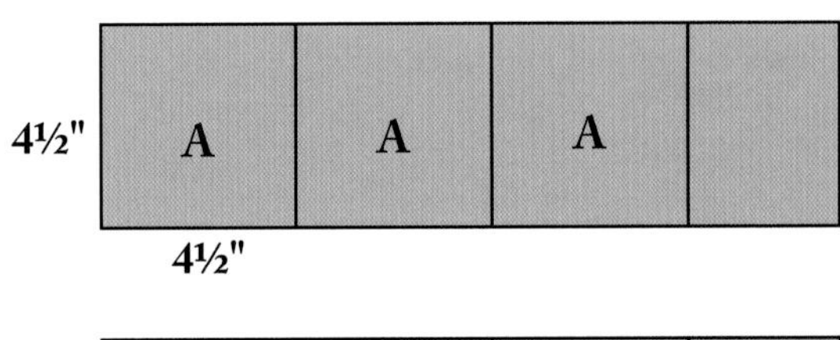

20 Throw/34 Queen-King

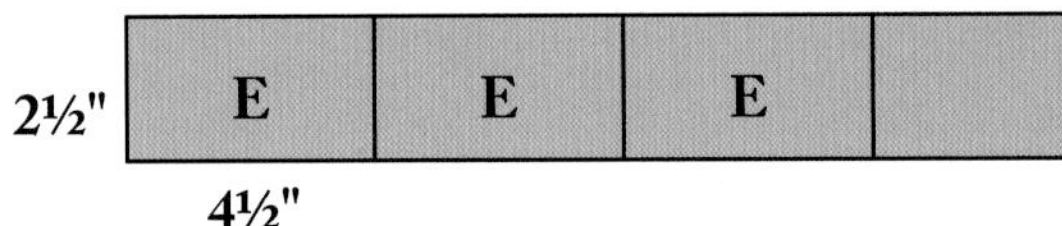

15 Throw/13 Queen-King

Note that Light Prints and Bright Prints are in a variety of hues, with each bright having a corresponding lighter colored tint. Furthermore, 2 sets of 4 C, 4 D, and 4 E in bright are cut from the same fabric. The corresponding light fabric is cut in 2 sets of 1 A and 8 B. Additional A and E patches in bright are needed for the borders; additional D patches in light are needed for the border, as well.

Block Construction

Stitch a light B to a bright C. Press seam allowance toward the B. Stitch another B to the C, again pressing the seam toward the B. Repeat to make four of these for the block. Sew one of these segments to the side of a light A square. Press seams toward A. Repeat on the opposite side. Sew a bright D to each end of the two remaining B-C-B segments. Press seams toward the D squares. Pin and stitch these to the top and bottom to finish the block. Press the seams toward the A. Make the listed number of Y's, pinning to each block the stack of four E rectangles that matches the C's and D's in the block.

Do not make the Z blocks until after you lay out all of the Y blocks in position for the quilt. The layout of the Y's will determine which fabrics belong in each Z block.

When the time comes to stitch the Z's, start by joining the 2 horizontal E's. Press the seam allowance toward the bottom E. Add 2 vertical E's, one to each side. Press seam allowances toward the block center.

Note: Do not make the Z blocks until after laying out all the Y blocks in position in the quilt. The four E patches must match the fabrics of the four Y blocks that touch the Z. Pin the stack of 4 matching E rectangles to the Y block to keep track of them before laying out the blocks.

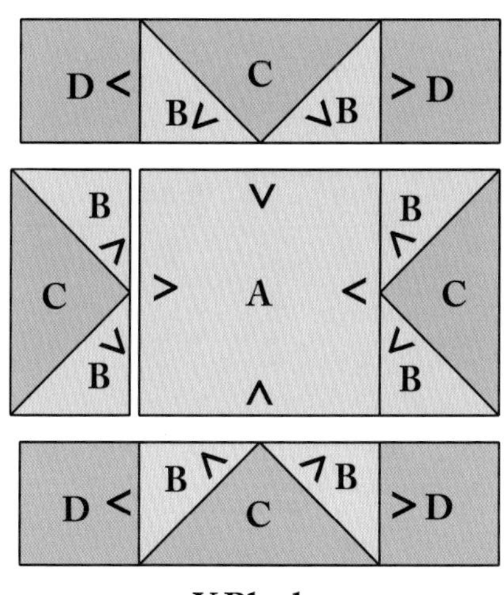

Y Block
Make 22 Throw
Make 82 King

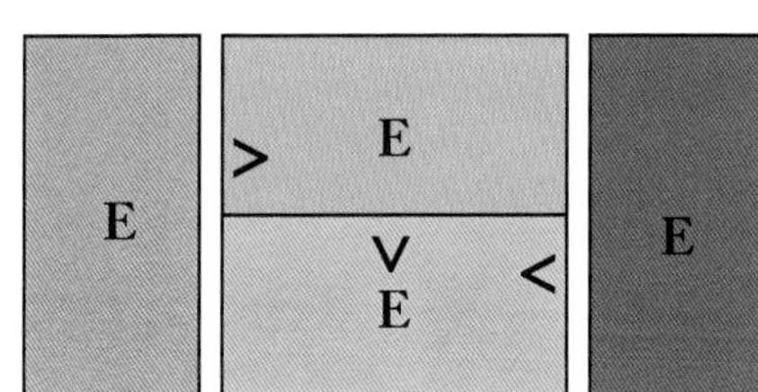

Z Block
Make 23 Throw
Make 83 King

Throw Quilt Assembly

Referring to the diagram below, lay out Y blocks in 5 vertical columns, leaving space between the blocks in a column to add Z blocks later. The first column has 4 Y blocks. The next column is staggered and has 5 Y's. Continue laying out columns of 4, 5, and 4 Y blocks, as shown below.

You should have pinned 4 matching E patches to each block. Unpin these and arrange one each on top, bottom, and two sides of the matching Y block. Around the edges of the quilt, add contrasting E rectangles to fill the Z block layouts. Also add 2 E's at the top and 2 more E's at the bottom of each column of 4 Y star blocks. Lay out leftover E's around the perimeter to fill in around the E's surrounding each Y block. Lay out 108 light D's for a border and 60 bright A's for the outer border.

Pick up and stitch together Z blocks, one at a time, replacing them in the layout after stitching. Also join E-E pairs for column ends.

Pin and stitch Y and Z blocks alternately to make columns. Add E-E to the top and bottom of odd-numbered columns. Press all seams toward Z's. Join columns in order. Press seam allowances to the right.

Join the 14 E's along each side. Pin and stitch to quilt. Join the 11 E's for top and bottom. Stitch to quilt. Press seams away from the quilt center.

Join 30 D's for a side border. Attach. Press away from center. Repeat for opposite side. Join 24 D's each for top and bottom; attach and press away from center. Join 16 A's for each side border; attach and press away from center. Join 14 A's for top and bottom borders. Sew to quilt. Press seams away from the quilt center. This completes the top.

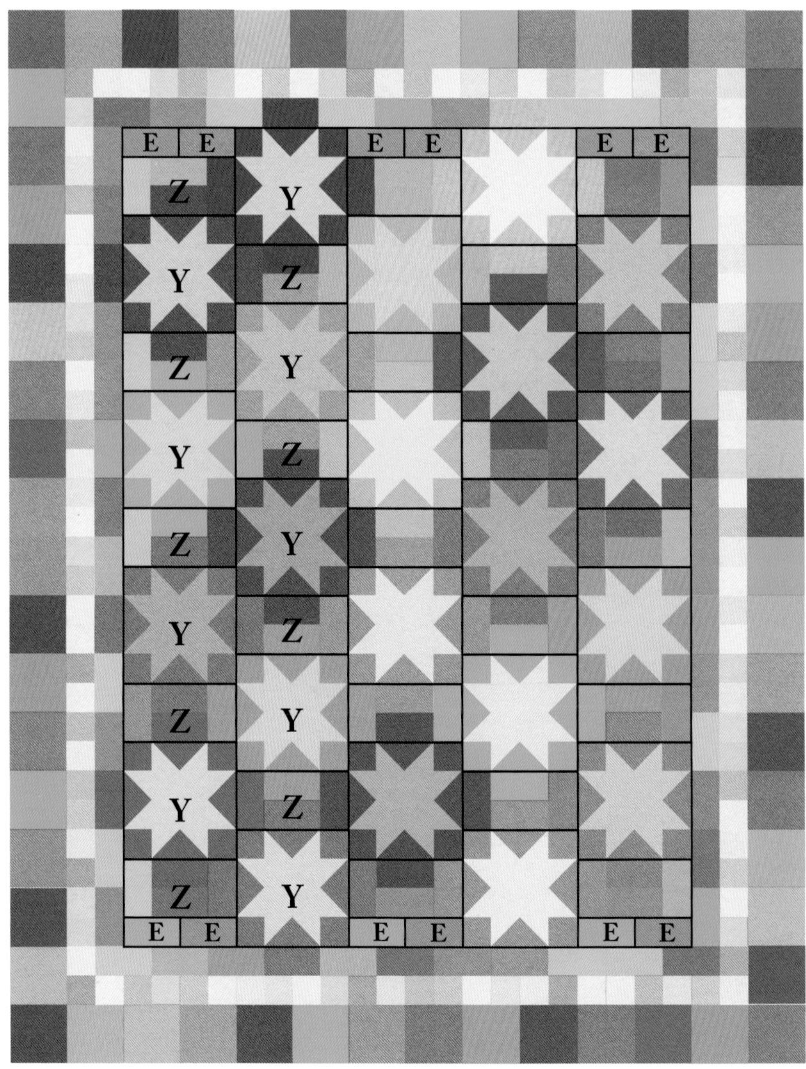

Throw Quilt Diagram

Queen/King Quilt Assembly

Referring to the diagram below, lay out Y blocks in 11 horizontal rows, leaving space between the blocks in a row to add Z blocks later. The first row has 7 Y blocks. The next row is staggered and has 8 Y's. Continue laying out rows until you have 6 rows of 7 Y blocks alternated with 5 rows of 8 Y's, as shown below.

You should have pinned 4 matching E patches to each block. Unpin these and arrange one each on top, bottom, and two sides of the matching Y block. Around the edges of the quilt, add contrasting E rectangles to fill the Z block layouts. Also add 2 E's at each end of each row of 7 Y blocks. Lay out leftover E's around the perimeter to fill in around the initial E's surrounding each Y block. Lay out 192 light D's for a border and 102 bright A's for the outer border.

Pick up and stitch together Z blocks, one at a time, replacing them in the layout after stitching. Also join E-E pairs for row ends.

Pin and stitch Y and Z blocks alternately to make rows. Add E-E to the ends of odd-numbered rows. Press all seams toward Z's. Join rows in order. Press seam allowances toward the bottom.

Join the 23 E's for top and bottom. Pin and stitch to quilt. Join the 23 E's for each side. Stitch to quilt. Press seams away from the quilt center.

Join 46 D's for a side border. Attach. Press away from center. Repeat for opposite side. Join 50 D's each for top and bottom; attach and press away from center. Join 24 A's for each side border; attach and press away from center. Join 27 A's for top and bottom borders. Sew to quilt. Press seams away from the quilt center. This completes the top.

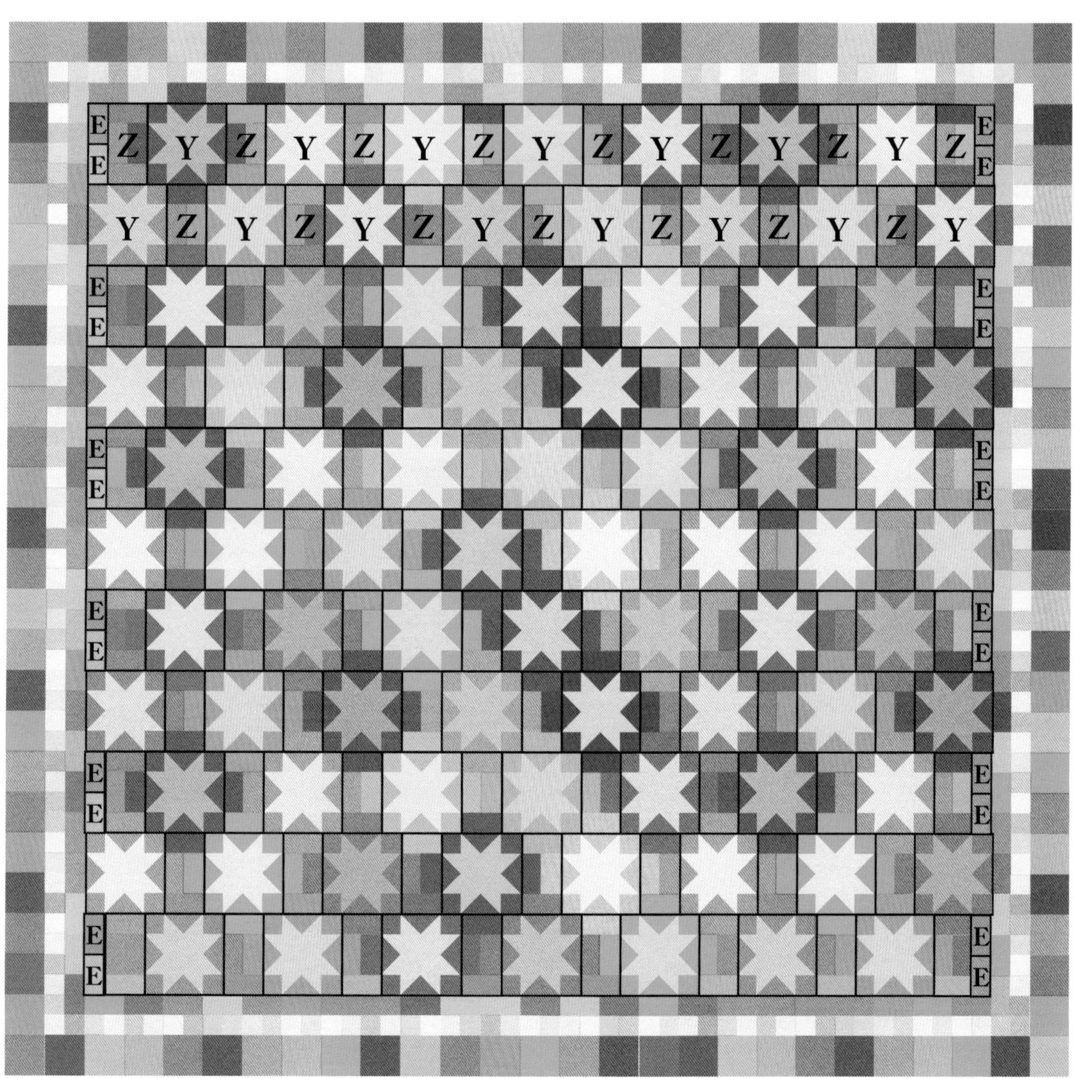

Queen/King Quilt Diagram

Quilting

Quilt in the ditch around the stars and around the perimeter of the bright C-D-E ring around each star. Quilt ¼" in from the edges of each star. Quilt a small motif in the center square of each star. Quilt freehand feathers in the bright rings of C, D, and E patches around each star. Also quilt freehand feathers in the combined E, D, and A patch borders.

Other Coloring Ideas

Friends Forever works best in multi-colors. Clockwise from the upper left are versions in ice cream colors, cool colors, earth tones, and sizzling hot colors.

Chinese Chicken Salad Recipe

Makes 8–10 Servings

This makes a lovely light supper or a side dish to accompany Asian Pork Balls or take-out Chinese food. The vegetables are not really Chinese, but the dressing has an Asian flair.

Ingredients

12 oz. cooked chicken, diced
1 head iceberg lettuce, chopped
3 scallions, chopped
½ cup red cabbage, chopped
1 carrot, grated
1 celery stalk, sliced
1 package (2 oz.) sliced almonds
2 oz. chow mein noodles

Dressing Ingredients:
3 tablespoons sugar
3 tablespoons vinegar
1½ teaspoons salt
½ teaspoon pepper
1 pinch ground ginger
1 tablespoon soy sauce
2 tablespoons peanut oil

Method

Toss the salad ingredients, except the chow mein noodles, in a large bowl.

In a small saucepan, mix the dressing ingredients. Cook on low heat until sugar dissolves.

Just before serving, toss the dressing with the salad. Add chow mein noodles and toss again. If you plan on leftovers, reserve some salad without dressing and noodles and add them later.

Porketta Recipe

Makes 10 Servings

This is an Italian-style pork roast. Serve it as an entrée with pasta or potatoes, or serve it on sandwich buns. Leftovers are especially good in Lasagna *(recipe on page 36).*

Ingredients

2½ lb. pork loin roast
1 teaspoon salt
1 tablespoon ground black pepper
½ teaspoon paprika
1½ tablespoons fennel seed
1 teaspoon dried rosemary
1 teaspoon dried basil
6 cloves fresh garlic, minced
3–4 tablespoons olive oil, enough to make a paste of the rub ingredients

Method

Preheat the oven to 325 degrees.

Slice the pork loin along its long edge and open the loin as if it were a book. Make a rub of the remaining ingredients. Massage the rub into all surfaces of the loin, inside and out, and then "close the book." Place the pork loin in a roasting pan, cover it, and put it in the oven for approximately 2 hours. (Figure 35–45 minutes per pound.) Cook to an internal temperature of 170 degrees. The pork should simply break off when pulled with a fork. Serve in slices, or pull the meat off in shreds using 2 forks and serve on buns with melted provolone to make pulled pork sandwiches with an Italian accent.

Steve's Spaghetti Sauce Recipe

Makes 12 Servings

This is my husband, Steve's, recipe, and a staple around our house. We always say, "Daddy makes the best spaghetti," which is the name of one of Kate's favorite childhood books. We also use this recipe in the making of our Lasagna. (See the recipe on the next page.)

Ingredients

3 Italian sausages
1 lb. ground beef
1 medium onion, finely chopped
6 cloves garlic, minced
3 cans (15 oz. each) tomato sauce
1 can (14½ oz.) diced tomatoes
2 cans (6 oz. each) tomato paste
1 tomato paste can of water
½ cup red wine
1 tablespoon dried oregano
1 tablespoon dried thyme
½ teaspoon dried rosemary, crushed
2 teaspoons dried basil
1 tablespoon sugar
2 tablespoons Romano cheese (grated)

Method

Grill the sausages on a gas or charcoal grill or fry them in a skillet on the range. Cut the cooked sausage into bite-sized disks. In a large stock pot, brown the ground beef with the onion and garlic. Drain off the fat. Add the remaining ingredients, including the sausage. Simmer for an hour, stirring occasionally. Serve over your favorite pasta.

Judy's Spaghetti Sauce Recipe

Makes 6–8 Servings

This is the recipe I used before I got married and had children who objected to mushrooms and peppers. This is a thick sauce flavored with vegetables and simmered for hours.

Ingredients

1½ lbs. ground beef
1 medium onion, chopped
3 cloves garlic, minced
2 cans (8 oz. each) tomato sauce
1 can (14½ oz.) diced tomatoes
1 can (6 oz.) tomato paste
2 tomato paste cans of water
½ cup red wine
1 carrot, peeled and grated
1 stalk celery, chopped
1 cup fresh mushrooms, thickly sliced
¼ green pepper, chopped
1 tablespoon dried oregano
½ teaspoon dried thyme
½ teaspoon dried rosemary, crushed
½ teaspoon dried basil
½ teaspoon dried parsley
½ teaspoon salt
½ teaspoon ground black pepper

Method

In a large stock pot, brown the ground beef with the onion and garlic. Drain off the fat. Wash and chop the vegetables (grate the carrot). Add the vegetables and the remaining ingredients. Simmer for two hours or more, stirring occasionally. Serve over your favorite pasta.

Lasagna Recipe

Makes 12 Servings

This is a lasagna in the Northern Italian style, with a cream sauce rather than ricotta. Make it with Steve or Judy's Spaghetti Sauce or with either sauce without the meat and add leftover Porketta.

Ingredients

1½ lbs. leftover Porketta, cut up (page 34)
or ½ lb. ground beef + ½ lb. Italian sausage
½–⅔ recipe of Steve's Spaghetti Sauce (page 35)
or 1 recipe of Judy's Spaghetti Sauce (page 35)
Note: You can reduce or eliminate the meat in the sauce if you are making lasagna with Porketta.
8 oz. lasagna, cooked or no-boil
4 oz. Romano cheese, grated (or Parmesan)
4 oz. Fontina cheese, grated (or Gouda)

White Sauce Ingredients:
3 tablespoons butter
4 tablespoons flour
1 can (10½ oz.) chicken broth, condensed
½ chicken broth can of water
½ chicken broth can of white wine
⅛ teaspoon nutmeg
½ teaspoon ground black pepper
1 cup heavy cream

Method

First, cook the lasagna according to package directions if you are not using the no-boil variety. Cook the additional ground beef and Italian sausage if you are using it. Preheat the oven to 450 degrees.

Next, make the white sauce: In a medium saucepan, melt the butter. Whisk in the flour, cooking and stirring over medium-low heat until the mixture is smooth. Stir in the chicken broth, water, and wine. Cook and stir constantly until the sauce thickens and is smooth. Add the nutmeg, pepper, and cream. Simmer gently for five minutes.

We make lasagna in a 10" x 14" x 2" rectangular pan. You might have to alter the number of layers if your pan is substantially different.

Start with a thin layer of spaghetti sauce in the bottom of the pan. Add a layer of pasta, followed by more spaghetti sauce. Dot this with half the Porketta or cooked meats. Drizzle with half of the white sauce. Repeat, with pasta, sauce, meat, and the remaining half of the white sauce.

Mix the grated cheeses together and sprinkle liberally over the top.

Bake for 35 minutes on the center oven rack. Let stand for at least 10 minutes before serving. Lasagna will not be firmly set until the next day. (For neat squares, bake the lasagna a day ahead and refrigerate overnight. Cut into squares and microwave individually to reheat.)

Thanksgiving

This is an original design pieced by Judy Martin and quilted by Lana Corcoran. Simple leaf blocks made from batiks and contemporary prints are arranged in circles evocative of swirling fall wind currents. A scattering of leaves forms an organic border to frame the quilt handsomely.

Thanksgiving takes some time to make the many leaf blocks in the queen and twin sizes but the cutting and sewing are basic, especially if you opt to leave off the stems. The table runner is a quick and easy project. The staggering of leaves makes the quilt look more complex while actually simplifying the sewing of joints.

Thanksgiving, with its light center rectangle, is suitable for a signature quilt. It is also a good choice for a raffle quilt, with its many simple blocks. Split and share fat quarters in fall colors for scrap variety.

Yardage & Cutting Specifications

Queen Size

Quilt Size: 99" x 99"
Block Y Size: 16½" between seamlines
Leaf Size: 4½" between seamlines
Requires: 208 X*, 16 Y, 40 Z

Yardage
Fall Colored Prints 17 fat quarters
208 B
208 C
416 Cr (reversed)
208 stems cut ¾" x 3" (optional)

Light Background Prints 37 fat quarters
2 borders cut 7¼" x 71"
2 borders cut 7¼" x 84½"
2 borders cut 2" x 96½"
2 borders cut 2" x 99½"
217 A (425 A if no stems)
1248 B (832 B if no stems)
176 D
64 E
16 F
24 G

Backing 9½ yards
3 panels 36½" x 107½"

Binding ¾ yard
19 strips 2" x 27"

Batting
107" x 107"

Twin Size

Quilt Size: 76½" x 94½"
Block Y Size: 16½" between seamlines
Leaf Size: 4½" between seamlines
Requires: 164 X*, 12 Y, 32 Z

Yardage
Fall Colored Prints 13 fat quarters
164 B
164 C
328 Cr (reversed)
164 stems cut ¾" x 3" (optional)

Light Background Prints 28 fat quarters
2 borders cut 5" x 71"
2 borders cut 5" x 62"
2 borders cut 2" x 77"
2 borders cut 2" x 92"
170 A (334 A if no stems)
984 B (656 B if no stems)
140 D
48 E
12 F
17 G

Backing 7½ yards
3 panels 35" x 85"

Binding ¾ yard
16 strips 2" x 27"

Batting
85" x 103"

**Note that X block totals include those used in Y and Z blocks.*

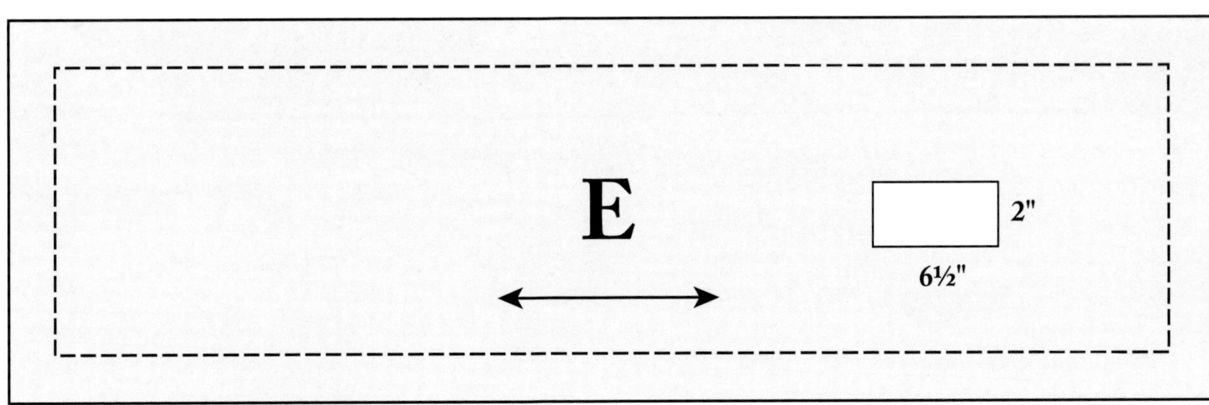

Yardage Continued

Table Runner

Quilt Size: 19½" x 55½"
Block Y Size: 16½" between seamlines
Leaf Size: 4½" between seamlines
Requires: 24 X*, 3 Y

Yardage
Fall Colored Prints 3 fat quarters
24 B
24 C
48 Cr (reversed)
24 stems cut ¾" x 3" (optional)

Light Background Prints 5 fat quarters
2 borders cut 2" x 53"
2 borders cut 2" x 20"
24 A (48 A if no stems)
144 B (96 B if no stems)
18 D
12 E
3 F
2 G

Backing 1⅞ yards
1 panel 27½" x 63½"

Binding ½ yard
12 strips 2" x 18"

Batting
27½" x 63½"

See rotary cutting details on pages 40–41.

Optional Templates

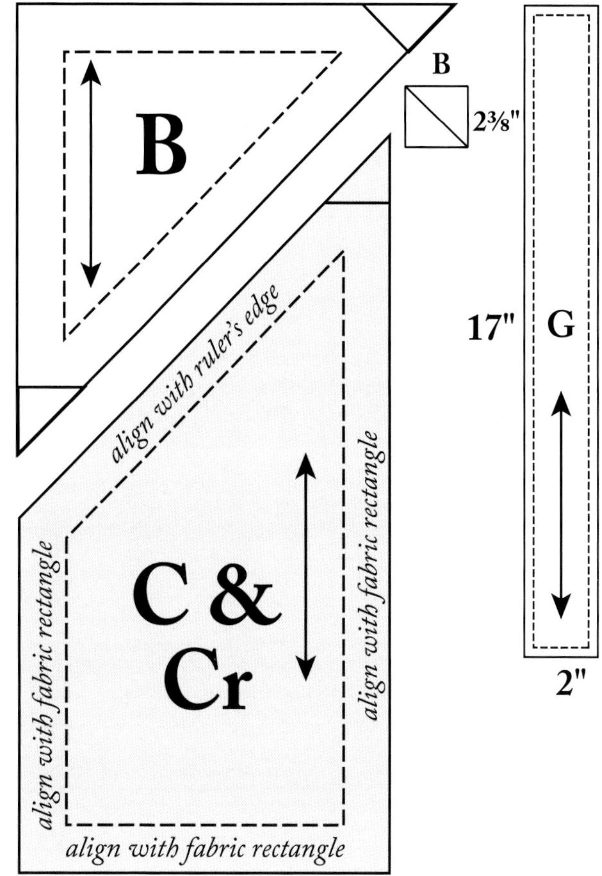

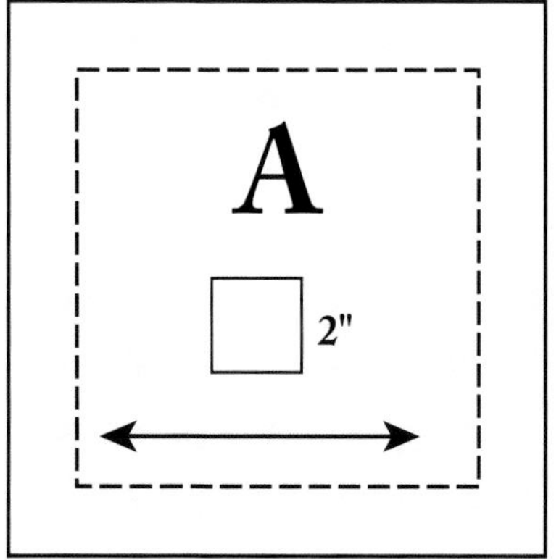

F & G are not shown full size.

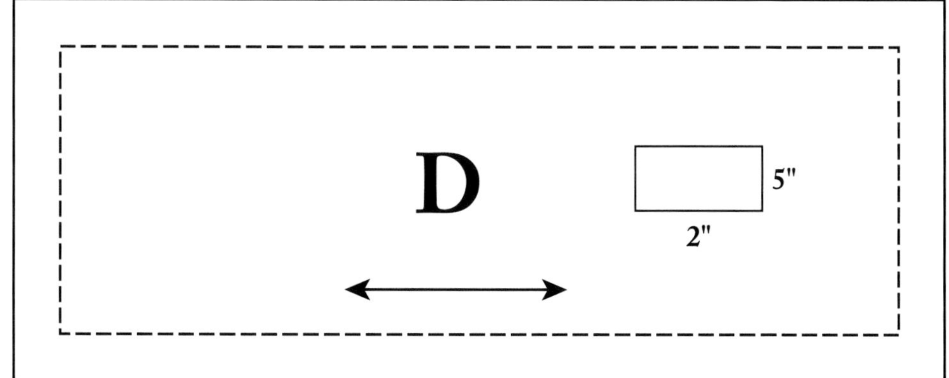

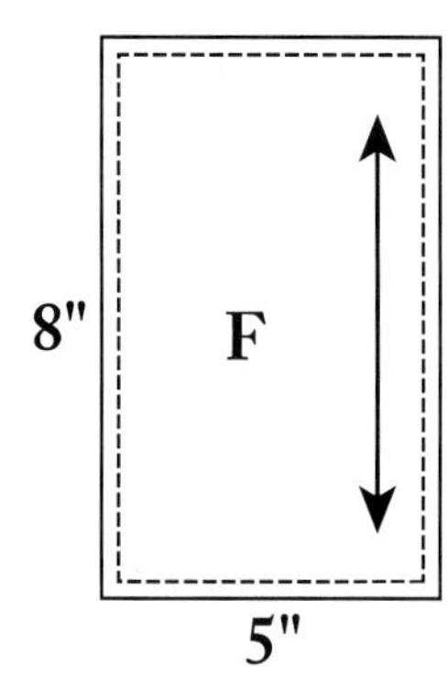

Strip Cutting Layouts

It is not necessary to cut all of the patches before you start sewing. In fact, I recommend sewing a single sample block before proceeding with the rest of the cutting. This will allow you to adjust your seam allowances until the block is perfect.

If you like, do as I do: Cut enough to make a few blocks at a time, alternating cutting with sewing.

Do not cut all of the strips of a single type or patch letter from one fabric. Instead, cut a variety of strips and patch letters from each fat quarter. Choose either the listing for stems or no stems. See the next page for details for cutting C and Cr.

Fall Print 18" Strip & Patch Cutting

Number of Strips Needed for Each Quilt Size

2⅜"
B B B B B B B
B B B B B B B
2⅜"

15 Queen/12 Twin/2 Table Runner

42 Queen/33 Twin/5 Table Runner

See the cuttting details for C/Cr on the next page.

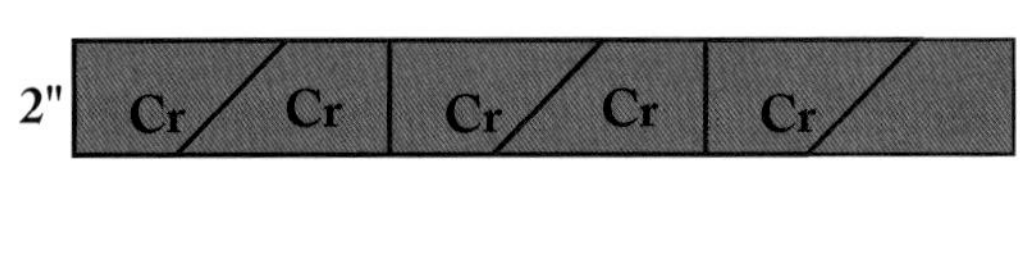

84 Queen/66 Twin/10 Table Runner

Optional Stem: 42 Queen/33 Twin/5 Table Runner

Light Print 18" Strip & Patch Cutting

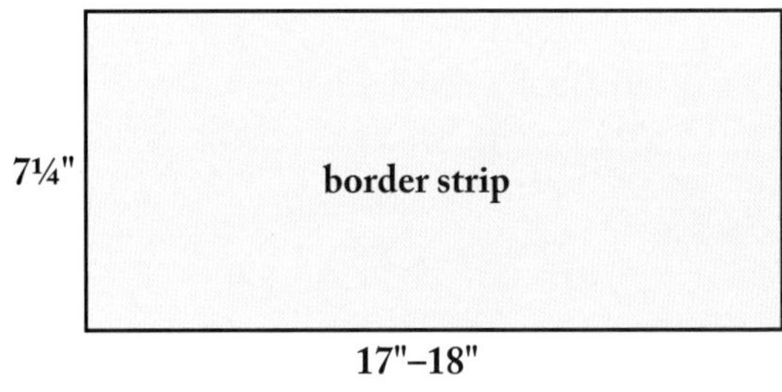

20 Queen

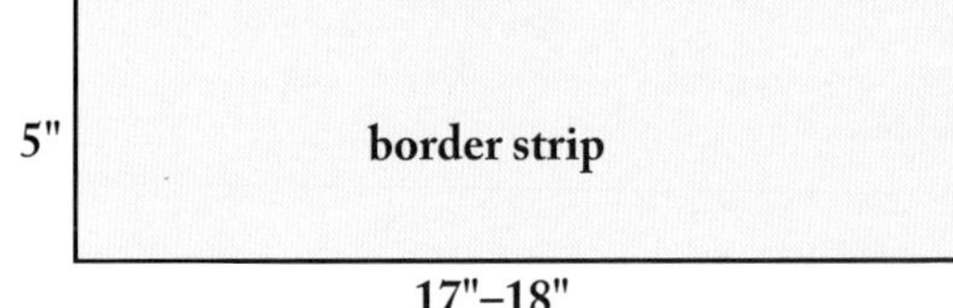

18 Twin

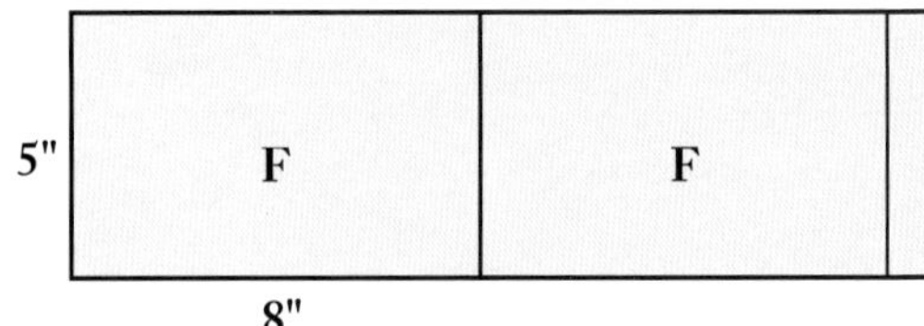

8 Queen/6 Twin/2 Table Runner

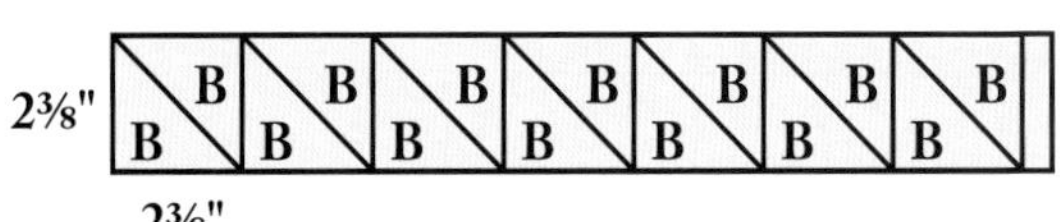

90 Queen/71 Twin/11 Table Runner (if stems)
60 Queen/47 Twin/7 Table Runner (if no stems)

Light Print 18" Strip Cutting, continued	Number of Strips Needed for Each Quilt Size
2" border strip, 17"–18"	25 Queen/22 Twin/10 Table Runner
2" G, 17"	24 Queen/17 Twin/2 Table Runner
2" E, E (6½"), A, A (2")	32 Queen/24 Twin/6 Table Runner
2" D, D, D (5"), A (2")	59 Queen/47 Twin/6 Table Runner
2" A, A, A, A, A, A, A, A (2")	12 Queen/10 Twin/1 Table Runner (if stems) 38 Queen/30 Twin/4 Table Runner (if no stems)

Special Rotary Cutting Details

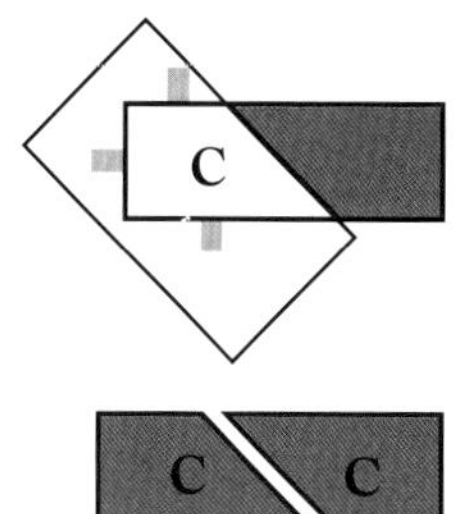

C: Trace or download the C & Cr template. Download is available at http://www.judymartin.com/templates.cfm. Be sure not to scale printing to a size other than 100%. Check template against the one in the book. Cut out and tape the template to a rotary cutting ruler so that the angled side is on the ruler's edge, as shown at left. Cut fabric into 2" x 5¾" rectangles. Align template over the end of the fabric rectangle as shown. Cut along the ruler's edge to make 2 C patches.

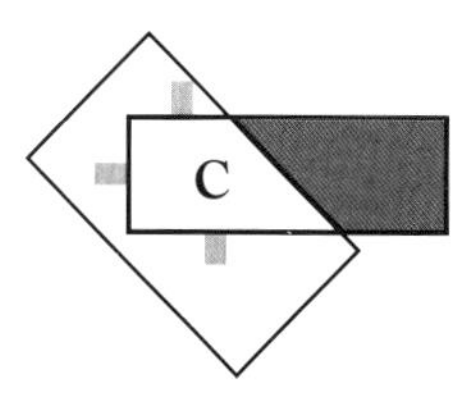

fabric face down

Cr: Cut fabric into 2" x 5¾" rectangles. Place fabric rectangle face down on cutting mat. Align the C template over the end of the fabric rectangle as shown. Cut along the ruler's edge to make 2 Cr patches.

Note that if you have my Shapemaker 45 tool (S45), you can cut the C and Cr without a template. Cut a 2" x 5¾" rectangle in two using the 3⅞" ruling of the S45, keeping the tool's long edge aligned with the long side of the rectangle. Check your patch against the C template in the book.

Block & Unit Construction

See the block and unit diagrams below. If you would like a simpler block, make the X block without the stem, substituting a single A square for the two B triangles. Note that the table runner does not require any Unit 2's or Z blocks.

Start by making a sample X block. Measure to see if it comes out 5" from raw edge to raw edge. If not, adjust seam allowances and make another sample. Try to blend the colors of the scraps within a leaf. First sew a light B triangle to each of the dark B, C, and Cr patches. Press seam allowances toward the dark. Attach an A to the dark B as shown, pressing toward the A. Stitch together the B, C, and Cr segments, pressing seams toward the top and left of the block. If desired, make the stem unit as described below. Add the light B-B or A to the Cr as shown. Press seam toward Cr. Add this segment to the block, pressing toward block's top.

Being careful to turn the leaf as shown, sew a light D rectangle to some of the X blocks to make Unit 1's in the quantities listed below. Press seams toward D. Turning the leaves as shown, make Unit 2's, pressing seams toward D's. Reserve the Unit 2's for the border.

Following the diagram below, make Y blocks in the listed quantities. Y requires six Unit 1's, 2 X blocks, an F and 4 E patches. Follow the arrows to press seam allowances. Press blocks.

Use remaining Units 1 and 2 to make Z border blocks for the twin- and queen-size quilts.

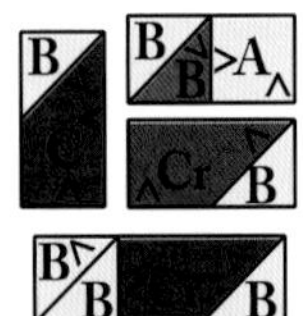

Block X
Make 208 queen*
Make 164 twin*
Make 24 runner*

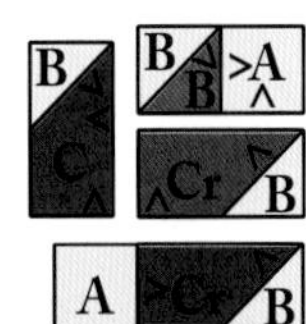

Optional Block X without Stem
Make instead of Block X at left if an easier block is desired

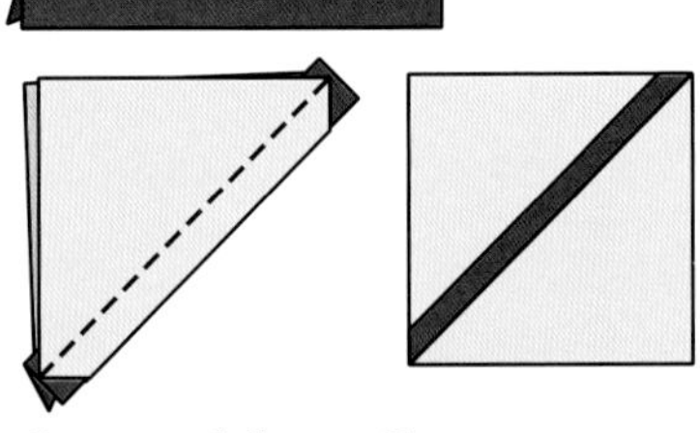

Optional Stem Construction
Cut stem ¾" x 3". Fold in half lengthwise with right sides out. Press. Insert between two B triangles with raw edges of B's and stem aligned. Stitch. Trim excess.

**X block totals include those used in Units 1 and 2, Blocks Y and Z.*

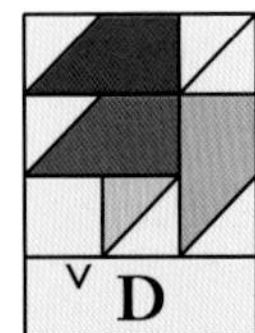

Unit 1
Use some X blocks to make Unit 1:
136 queen
104 twin
18 runner

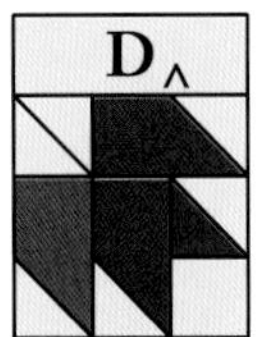

Unit 2
Use some X blocks to make Unit 2:
40 queen
36 twin

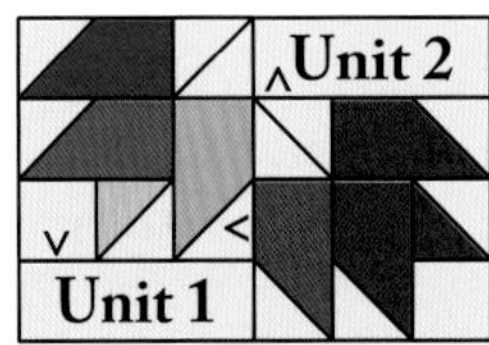

Border Block Z
Use some of the Unit 1's and Unit 2's to make Z blocks as follows:
Make 40 queen
Make 32 twin

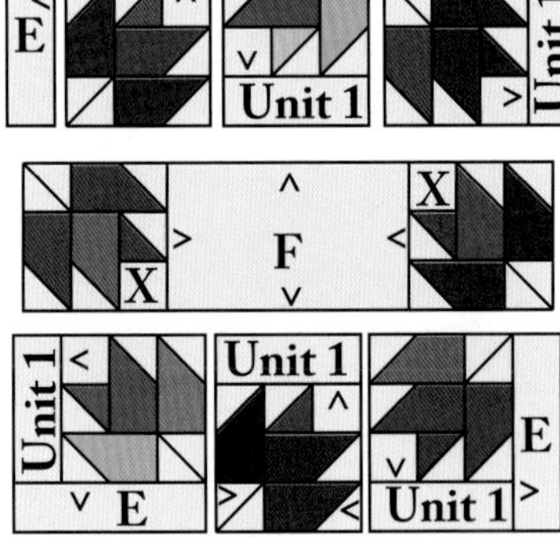

Block Y
Use some of the X blocks and Unit 1's to make Y blocks as follows:
Make 16 queen
Make 12 twin
Make 3 table runner

Note that blocks and units of each type are made in various colors.

Queen Quilt Assembly

Sew 3 G sash rectangles alternately with 4 Y blocks. Press seam allowances toward the G sashes. Make 4 rows of 4 blocks.

Sew 4 sashes alternately with 3 light A squares. Press seam allowances toward the sashes. Sew 4 block rows alternately with 3 sash rows. Press seams toward the sashes.

Make borders of the listed lengths by joining 18"-long strips end to end. Pin and stitch the shorter wide plain borders to the sides of the quilt. Pin and stitch the longer wide plain borders to the top and bottom.

Join 10 Z border blocks for each pieced border, turning them as shown below. Attach the top pieced border at the upper left corner of the quilt with a partial seam, indicated in pink. Pin and stitch the left pieced border, followed by the bottom pieced border and the right pieced border. Pin and stitch to complete the partial seam of the top pieced border.

Pin and stitch plain side borders followed by plain top and bottom borders to complete the top.

Queen Quilt Diagram

Twin Quilt Assembly

Sew 2 G's alternately with 3 Y's. Press seams toward the G sashes. Make 4 rows of 3 blocks.

Sew 3 sashes alternately with 2 light A squares. Press seam allowances toward the sashes. Sew 4 block rows alternately with 3 sash rows. Press seams toward the sashes.

Make borders of the listed lengths by joining 18"-long strips end to end. Pin and stitch the longer wide plain borders to the sides of the quilt. Pin and stitch the shorter wide plain borders to the top and bottom. Join 7 Z and 1 Unit 2, turning them as shown for the top border. Repeat for the bottom border. Join 9 Z and 1 Unit 2, turning them as shown for the left border Repeat for the right side. Attach the top pieced border at the upper left corner of the quilt with a partial seam as indicated in pink. Pin and stitch the left pieced border, followed by the bottom pieced border and the right pieced border. Complete the partial seam of the top pieced border.

Pin and stitch the plain side borders followed by the top and bottom ones to complete the quilt top.

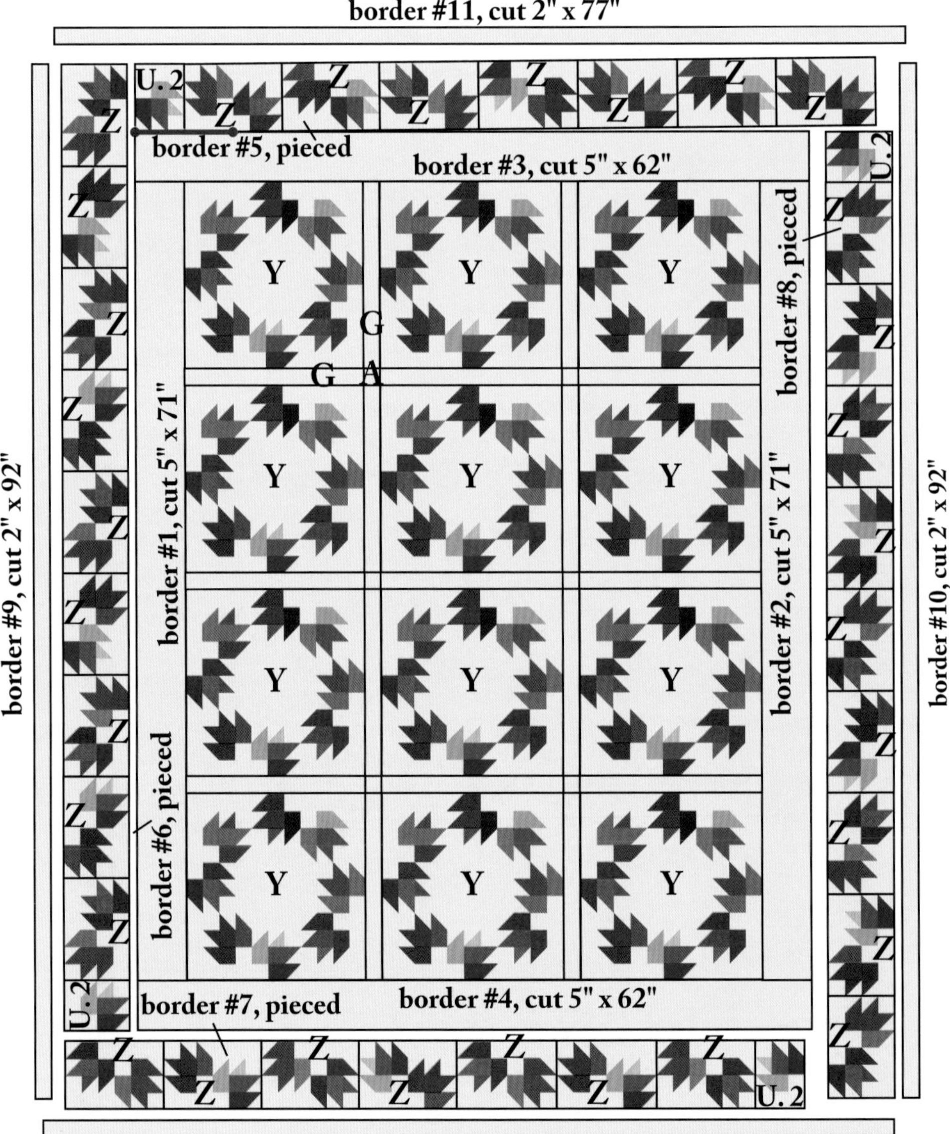

Twin Quilt Diagram

Table Runner Assembly

Sew 2 G's alternately with 3 Y's. Press seam allowances toward the G sashes. Make 53" borders by joining 18"-long strips end to end. Pin and stitch long borders to the quilt. Pin and stitch short borders. Press seam allowances away from quilt center. This completes the top.

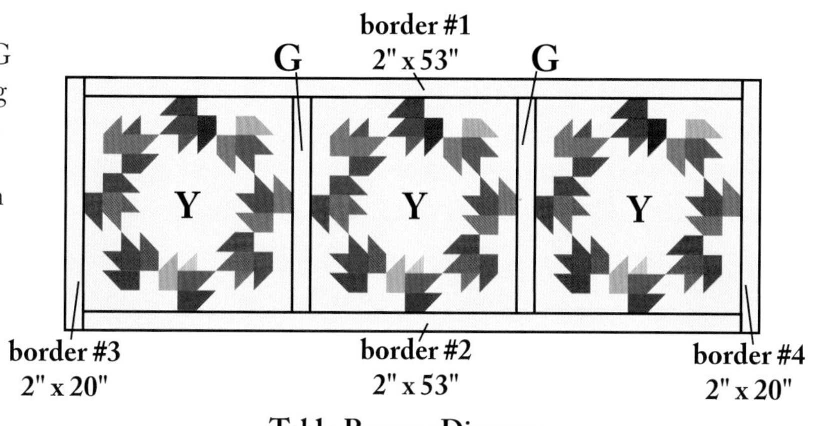

Table Runner Diagram

Quilting

Leaf patches are quilted in the ditch alongside the seamlines. A leaf motif is quilted in the wide plain border. A related circle of leaves is quilted in the center of each leafy ring. Between rings, quilt a related motif. Stripes 1½" wide are quilted in the outer border and in D and E patches outside the leaves in the border. The stripes run perpendicular to the edges of the quilt.

Other Coloring Ideas

You can make pink or blue leaves if you want a surreal look. However, most of you will want your fall leaves in their natural colors, so I have not altered the leaves in the drawings below. Instead, I show different background colors from which to choose: ivory, black, pumpkin, or green. You may want to adjust the mix of colors in the leaves for contrast. For example, leave out the gold leaves in the pumpkin example or leave out the lighter green leaves in the version with the green background.

Morning Glory

This quilt was designed by my son, Will Bennett, and I couldn't wait to make it. I used Asian print scraps and fat quarters. I love the way the light ring around the stars appears to weave over and under the surrounding diamonds.

The cutting involves uncommon shapes, and the sewing is complicated by set-in seams, so this is not a quick-and-easy project. Still, it is worth the effort.

This is a great quilt for a class. An experienced teacher could demonstrate the intricacies of the pattern. Morning Glory is also suitable for a fat quarter split or strip exchange for the various colored diamonds.

Yardage & Cutting Specifications

Throw Size

Quilt Size: 59" x 74¾"
Block Size: 15¹¹⁄₁₆" between seamlines
Requires: 12 Z

Yardage
Ivory Prints 8 fat quarters
48 B
48 C
96 D
48 Fr (reversed)

Taupe Prints 5 fat quarters
96 E
48 F

Orange Prints 5 fat quarters
96 A

Aqua Prints 5 fat quarters
96 A

Teal Prints 1⅞ yards plus 1 or more fat qtrs.
2 borders 6½" x 63¼"
2 borders 6½" x 59½"
48 A

Backing 5 yards
2 panels 34" x 82¾"

Binding ½ yard
20 strips 2" x 18"

Batting
67" x 82¾"

King Size

Quilt Size: 115¾" x 100⅛"
Block Size: 15¹¹⁄₁₆" between seamlines
Requires: 42 Z

Yardage
Ivory Prints 27 fat quarters
168 B
168 C
336 D
168 Fr (reversed)

Taupe Prints 18 fat quarters
336 E
168 F

Orange Prints 17 fat quarters
336 A

Aqua Prints 17 fat quarters
336 A

Teal Prints 3¼ yards plus 1 or more fat qtrs.
2 borders 3½" x 100⅝"
2 borders 3½" x 110¼"
168 A

Backing 11 yards
3 panels 36½" x 124"

Binding ¾ yard
20 strips 2" x 27"

Batting
108" x 124"

Spinach Salad Recipe

Makes 8–12 Side Servings

This is my all-time favorite salad. Substitute sliced almonds for the pecans, if desired. Fresh strawberries also substitute nicely for the craisins. A salad-and-dessert potluck makes a fine luncheon.

Ingredients

1 bag (9 oz.) baby spinach
½ cup cherry-infused craisins (dried cranberries)
3½–4 oz. fresh goat cheese (chevre)
½ cup pecans, chopped
½ cup Brianna's Poppy Seed Dressing or your favorite bottled dressing

Method

Wash and dry the spinach. Crumble the goat cheese with a fork. Toss the spinach, craisins, goat cheese, and pecans in a large salad bowl. Add salad dressing and toss to coat the spinach. If you prefer, serve the salad naked with a bottle of dressing on the side.

Optional Templates

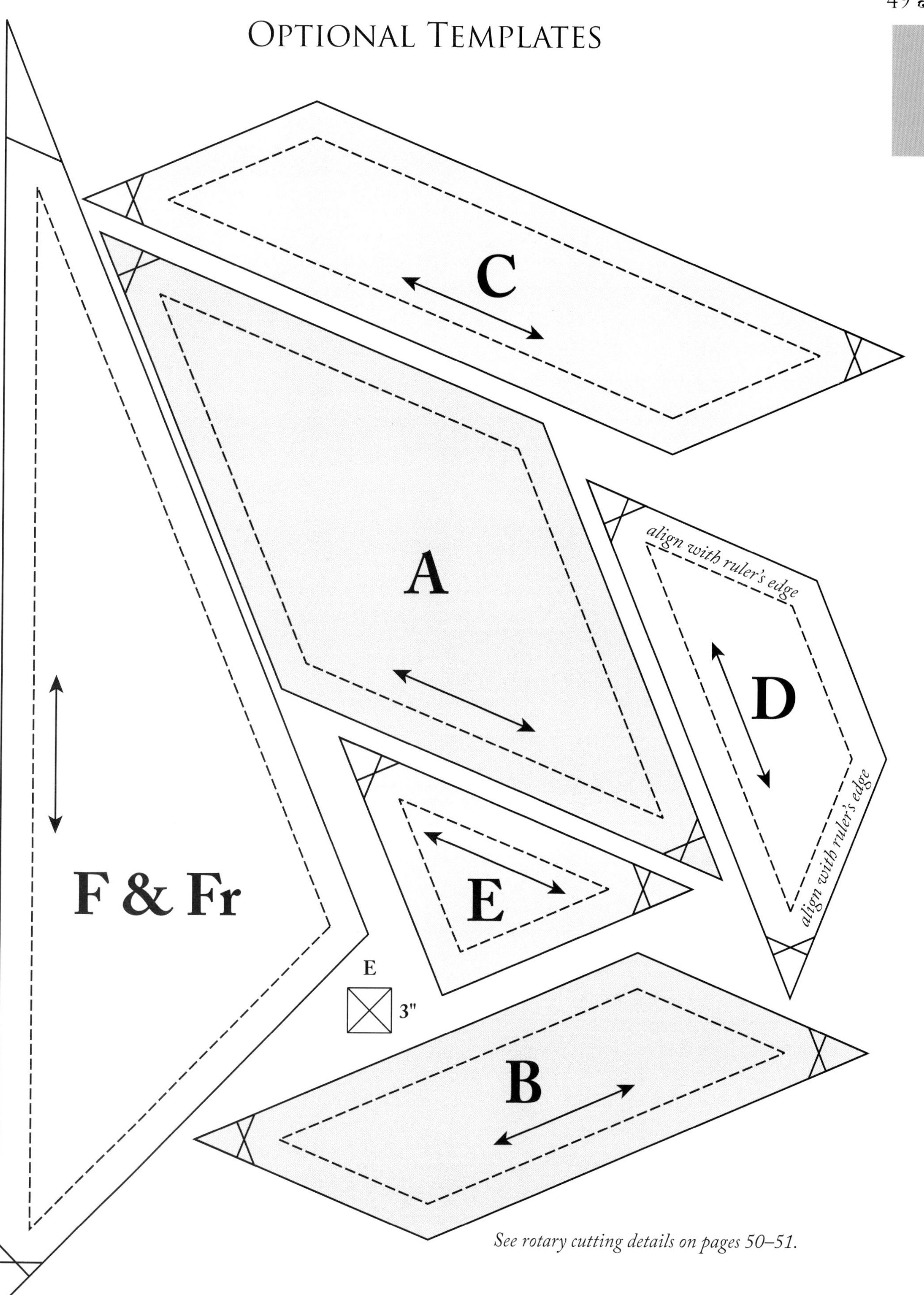

See rotary cutting details on pages 50–51.

Strip Cutting Layouts

It is not necessary to cut all of the patches before you start sewing. In fact, I recommend sewing a single sample block before proceeding with the rest of the cutting. This will allow you to adjust your seam allowances until the block is perfect.

If you like, do as I do: Cut enough to make a few blocks at a time, alternating cutting with sewing.

Do not cut all of the strips of a single type from one ivory or taupe fat quarter. Instead, cut a variety of patch letters from each fat quarter.

Ivory 18" Strip & Patch Cutting

Number of Strips Needed for Each Quilt Size

2⅞"

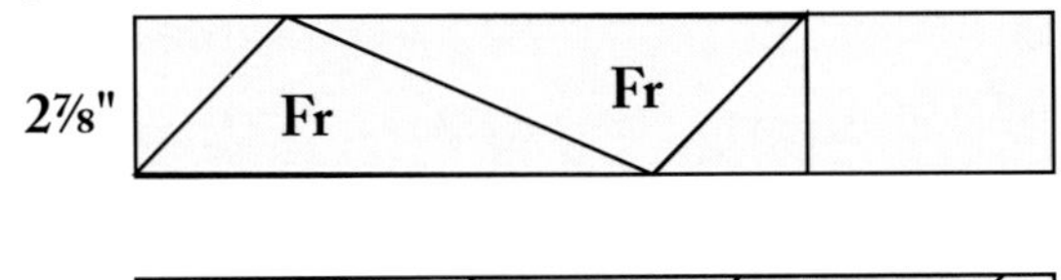

24 Throw/84 King

See the Special Rotary Cutting Details on the next page.

1⅜" C C C

16 Throw/56 King

1⅜"

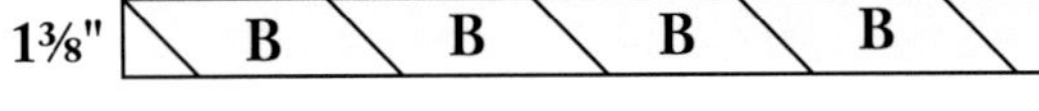

12 Throw/42 King

1⅜" D D D D D

20 Throw/68 King

Note that if you have my Shapemaker 45 tool (S45), you can cut the D without a template. Cut off one end of a 1⅜"-wide strip at a 45-degree angle. Cut D's using the 4¼" ruling of the S45, keeping the tool's long edge aligned with the long edge of the strip. Check your patch against the D template in the book.

Taupe 18" Strip & Patch Cutting

3"

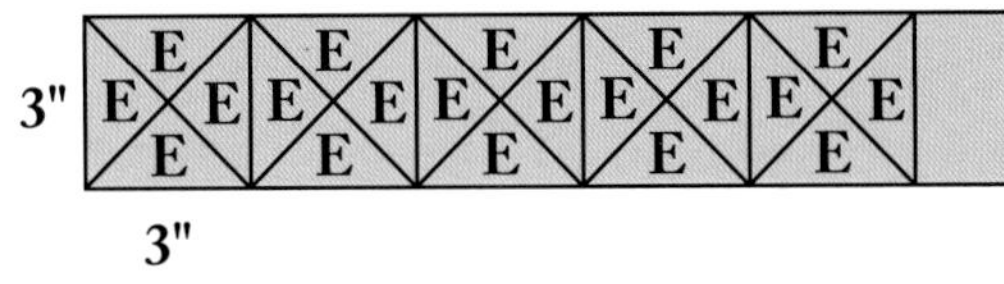

3"

5 Throw/17 King

2⅞" F F

24 Throw/84 King

Orange 18" Strip & Patch Cutting

2⅝"

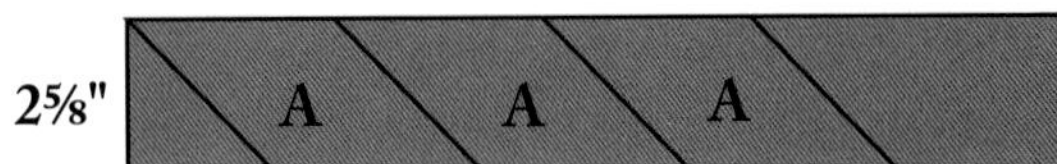

32 Throw/112 King

Aqua 18" Strip & Patch Cutting

2⅝"

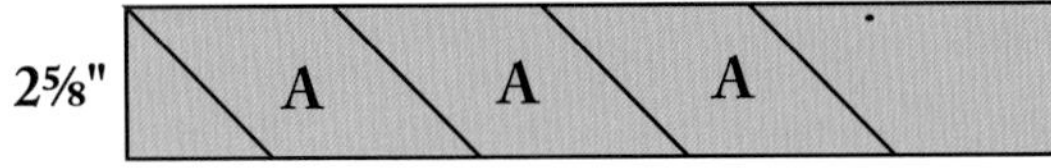

32 Throw/112 King

Teal 18" Strip & Patch Cutting

2⅝"

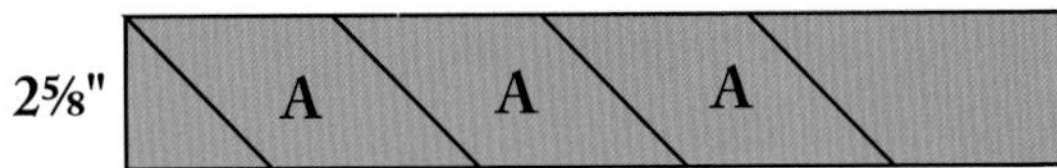

16 Throw/56 King

Cut lengthwise borders first from teal fabric. Cut remaining teal yardage into 18" lengths from which to cut A's.

Special Rotary Cutting Details

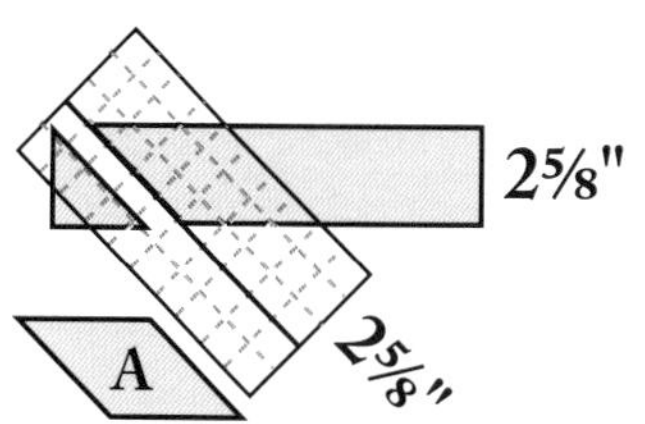

A: Cut a strip 2⅝" wide. Cut off the end of the strip at a 45-degree angle as shown. Align the 2⅝" ruling of a rotary cutting ruler with the angled end of the strip. Cut along the ruler's edge to complete an A diamond. Check your diamond against the A template in the book. Cut A diamonds down the length of the strip.

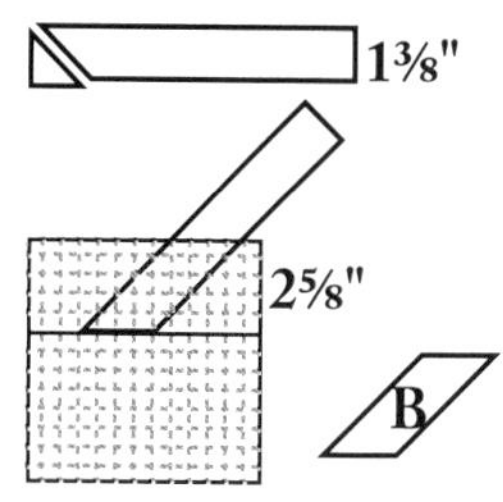

B: Cut a strip 1⅜" wide. Cut off the end of the strip at a 45-degree angle as shown. Align the 2⅝" ruling of a rotary cutting ruler with the angled end of the strip. Cut along the ruler's edge to complete a B parallelogram. Check your B patch against the template in the book. Cut B's down the length of the strip.

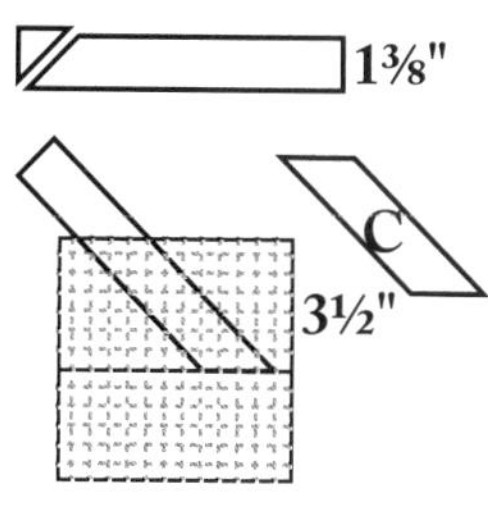

C: Cut a strip 1⅜" wide. Cut off the end of the strip at a 45-degree angle as shown. Align the 3½" ruling of a rotary cutting ruler with the angled end of the strip. Cut along the ruler's edge to complete a C parallelogram. Check your C patch against the template in the book. Cut C's down the length of the strip.

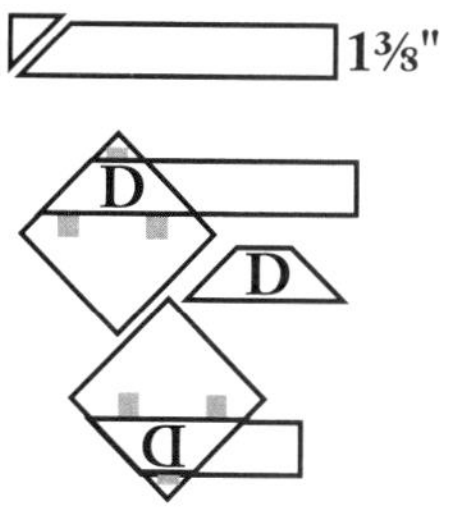

D: Cut a strip 1⅜" wide. Cut off the end of the strip at a 45-degree angle as shown. Trace or download the template for D. Download is available at http://www.judymartin.com/templates.cfm. Be sure not to scale printing to a size other than 100%. Check template against the one in the book. Cut out and tape the template to a rotary cutting ruler so that the 2 angled sides are on the ruler's edges, as shown at left. Align the top, left, and bottom of template with fabric strip as shown. Cut along the ruler's edge to complete D. Check your D patch against the template in the book. Turn the template around to cut the next D. Cut D's down the length of the strip.

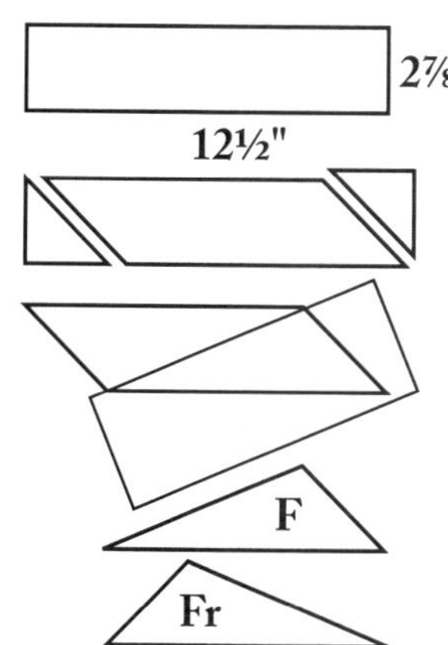

F: Cut a rectangle 2⅞" x 12½". Cut off both ends of the rectangle at a 45-degree angle as shown to make a parallelogram. Align the edge of a rotary cutting ruler with two corners of the fabric parallelogram as shown. Cut along the ruler's edge to complete 2 F patches. Check your F patch against the template in the book.

Fr: Cut a rectangle 2⅞" x 12½". Place the rectangle face down on the cutting mat. Cut off both ends of the rectangle at a 45-degree angle as shown for F to make a parallelogram. Align the edge of a rotary cutting ruler with two corners of the fabric parallelogram as shown. Cut along the ruler's edge to complete 2 Fr patches.

Block Construction

See the Z block diagram below. Pink dots indicate set-in or Y-seams, where you must stitch only to the end of the seamline, ¼" in from raw edge. Start by sewing 2 D's to an orange A as shown. Press seams of the first D toward A; press seams of the second D away from A. Add 2 E triangles, noting the set-in seam. Press seams toward E's. Add an aqua A diamond. Press seams toward the aqua A. Stitch another aqua A to a teal A, turning them as shown. Press seams toward the aqua A. Add this segment to the A-E-D-A-D-E segment. Press seam allowances toward the A-A segment.

Sew an A diamond to a B as shown. Press seams toward A. Add C. Press seam allowances toward C. Sew this to the previous segment with set-in seams. Press seam allowances away from the A-B-C segment. Add a taupe F and an ivory Fr with set-in seams. Press F-Fr seams toward the taupe. Press the long seams away from the block center. This completes a quarter block.

Make four quarter blocks. Join them in pairs to make half blocks, pressing seams counter-clockwise. Join halves to complete the Z block, again pressing seams counter-clockwise.

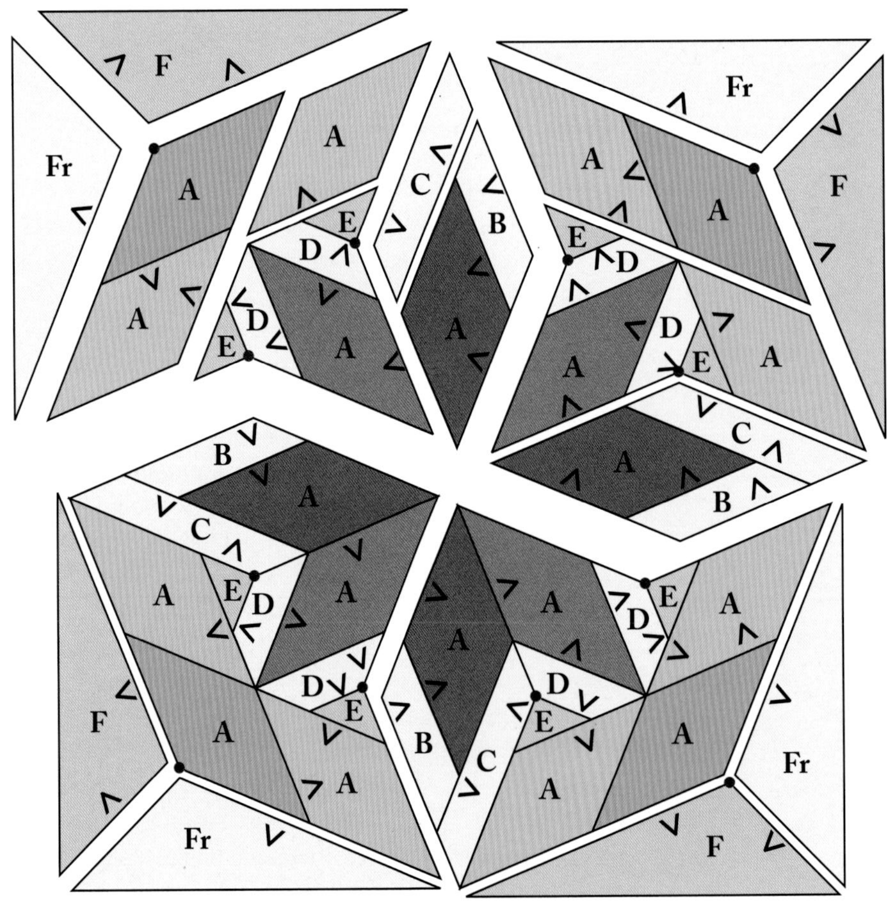

Block Z
Make 12 throw
Make 42 king

Throw Quilt Assembly

See the throw quilt diagram below. Make 12 Z blocks. Press them. Join 3 Z's to make a row. Make 4 rows, pressing odd-numbered rows to the right and even-numbered rows to the left. Join rows to complete the quilt center.

Pin and stitch the longer borders to the sides of the quilt. Press seam allowances away from the quilt center. Pin and stitch the shorter borders to the top and bottom of the quilt. Press seam allowances away from the quilt center.

Throw Quilt Diagram

King Quilt Assembly

See the king quilt diagram below. Make 42 Z blocks. Press them. Join 7 Z's to make a row. Make 6 rows, pressing odd-numbered rows to the right and even-numbered rows to the left. Join rows to complete the quilt center.

Pin and stitch the longer borders to the top and bottom of the quilt. Press seam allowances away from the quilt center. Pin and stitch the shorter borders to the sides of the quilt. Press seam allowances away from the quilt center.

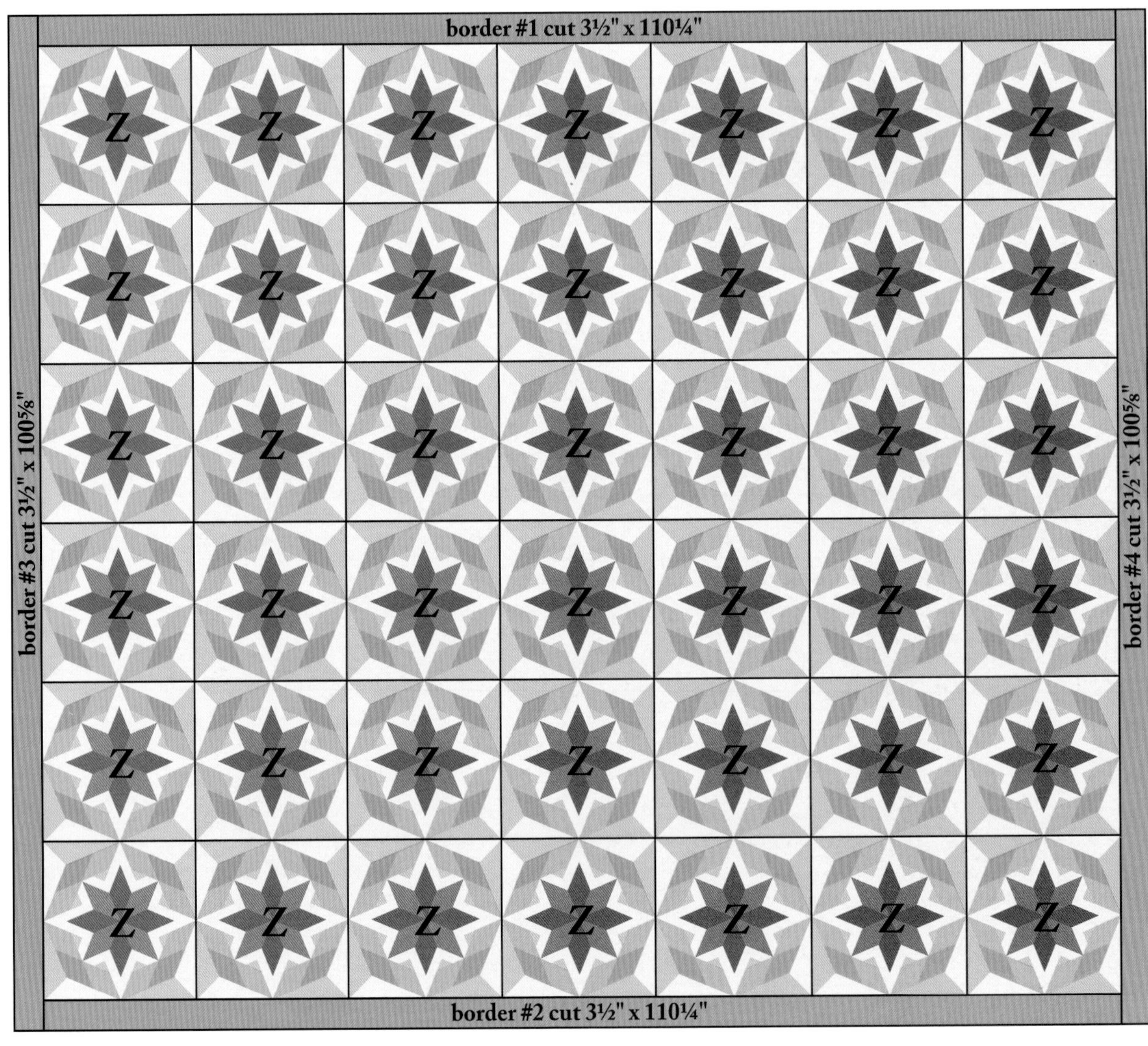

King Quilt Diagram

Quilting

See the photo below. Quilt in the ditch around all patches. Quilt a pumpkin seed in each orange diamond. Quilt a feather motif in the F-Fr pairs. Quilt a simple straight line motif in the teal and aqua diamonds. Quilt freehand feathers in the borders to finish the quilt with a flourish.

Other Coloring Ideas

Morning Glory looks very different when the lights, darks, and accents highlight different elements. Study the examples below for inspiration as you plan your own Morning Glory.

Sun Valley Log Cabin

Sun Valley Log Cabin combines Log Cabin blocks with a Sunburst medallion. Smaller blue diamonds mark the transition from Sunburst to Log Cabin. Trapezoids cut using paper templates taped to your rotary ruler square off the quilt center. This may sound fussy, but there are only eight of each type, so it goes quickly. These trapezoids help you align neighboring patches and actually simplify the quilt making.

This quilt was designed and pieced by Judy Martin and quilted by Debbi Treusch.

A setting party is the obvious social event to tie to this project. You might also split fat quarters to swap.

Yardage & Cutting Specifications

Queen Size

Quilt Size: 99¼" x 99¼"
Block Sizes: 7" & 21" between seamlines
Requires: 112 Y*, 4 Z

Yardage
Light Prints 20 fat quarters
112 A through F
32 H
4 J through W
4 Jr through Wr (reversed)
168 X

Pink Prints 15 fat quarters
112 A
37 D through G
240 H

Dark Blue Prints 14 fat quarters
56 B through C
38 D through G
24 H
168 I
176 X
16 Y

Light Blue Prints ¼ yard/scraps
16 H

Dark Brown Prints 14 fat quarters
56 B through C
37 D through G
216 H

Backing 9½ yards
3 panels 36½" x 107¼"

Binding ¾ yard
19 strips 2" x 27"

Batting
108" x 108"

Wall Size

Quilt Size: 56" x 56"
Block Sizes: 7" & 21" between seamlines
Requires: 32 Y*, 4 Z

Yardage
Light Prints 8 fat quarters
32 A through F
32 H
4 J through W
4 Jr through Wr (reversed)

Pink Prints 4 fat quarters
32 A
10 D through G
56 H

Dark Blue Prints 5 fat quarters
16 B through C
11 D through G
24 H
168 I

Light Blue Prints ¼ yard/scraps
16 H

Dark Brown Prints 4 fat quarters
16 B through C
11 D through G
40 H

Backing 3¾ yards
2 panels 32½" x 64"

Binding ½ yard
17 strips 2" x 18"

Batting
64" x 64"

**Note that Y total includes those used in Z blocks.*

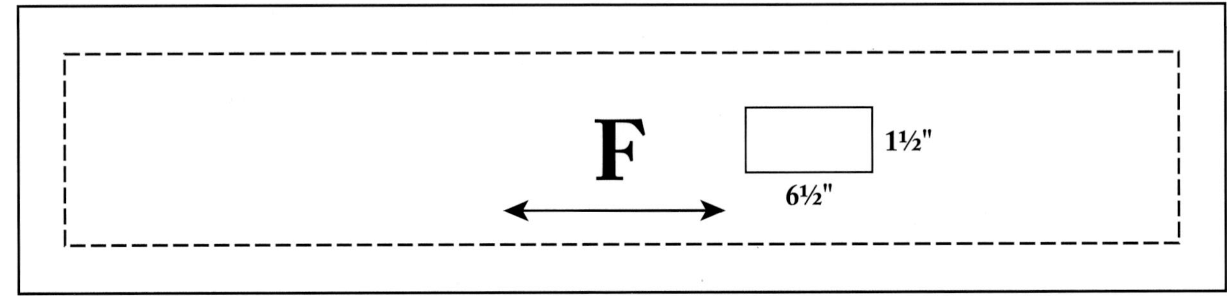

Optional Templates

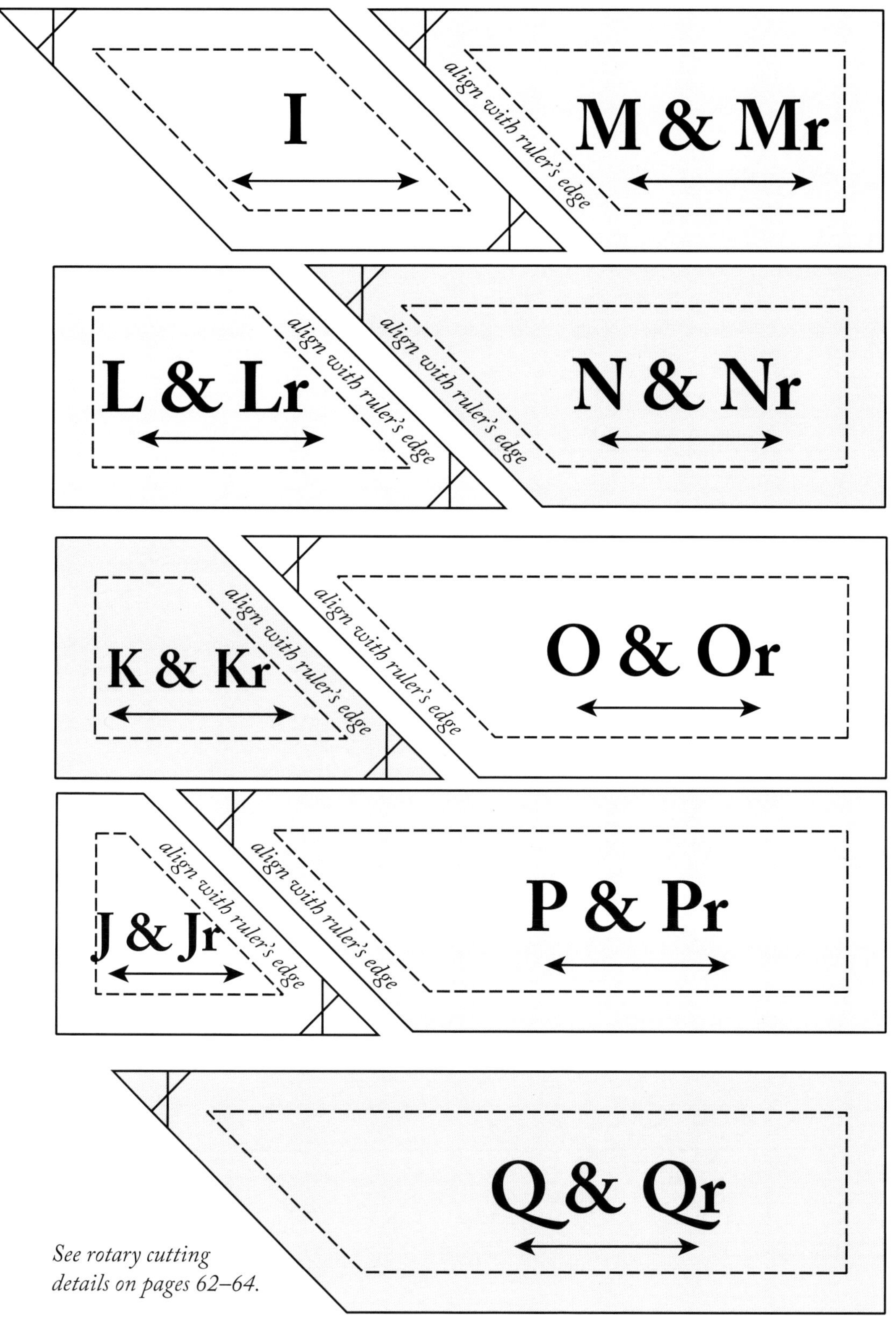

See rotary cutting details on pages 62–64.

U & Ur

T & Tr

S & Sr

See rotary cutting details on pages 62–64.

R & Rr

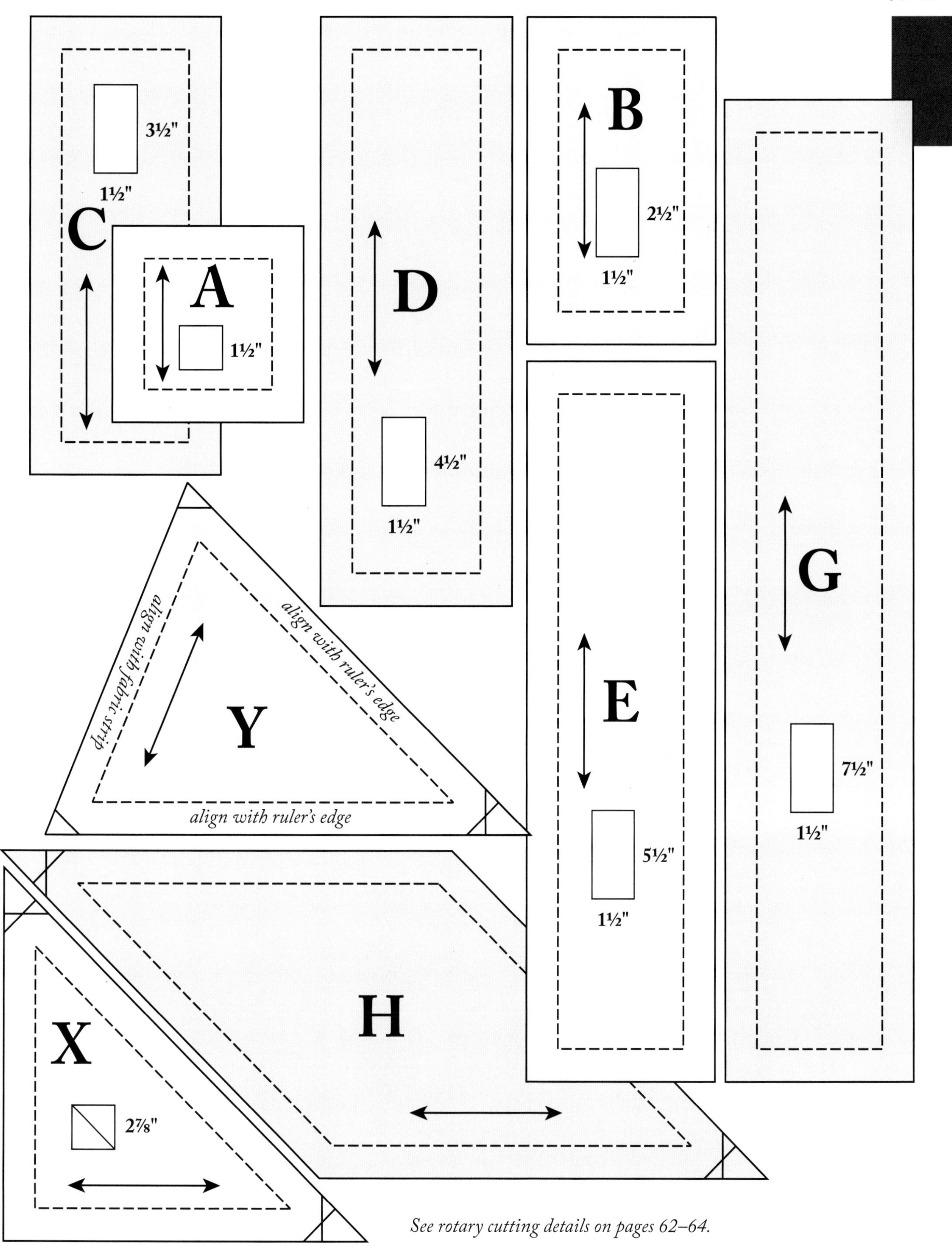

See rotary cutting details on pages 62–64.

Strip Cutting Layouts

Do not cut all of the strips of a single type or patch letter from one fat quarter. Instead, cut a variety of strips and patch letters from each of the fat quarters.

Light Prints 18" Strip & Patch Cutting

Number of Strips Needed for Each Quilt Size

2⅞"

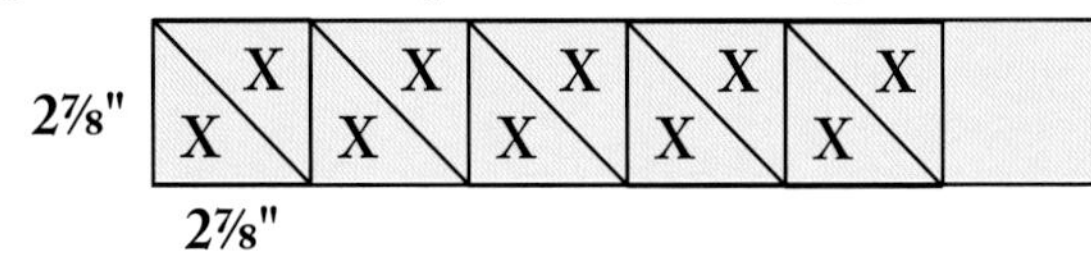

17 Queen

See the Special Rotary Cutting Details on page 64.

2½"

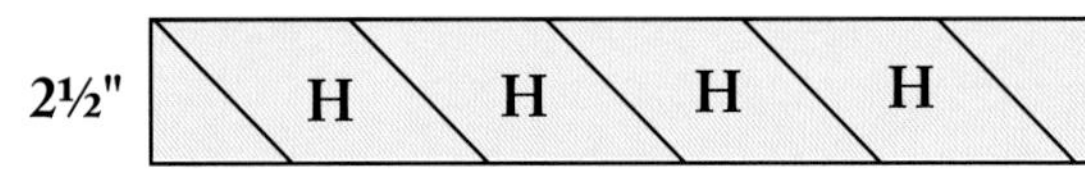

8 Queen/8 Wall

1½"

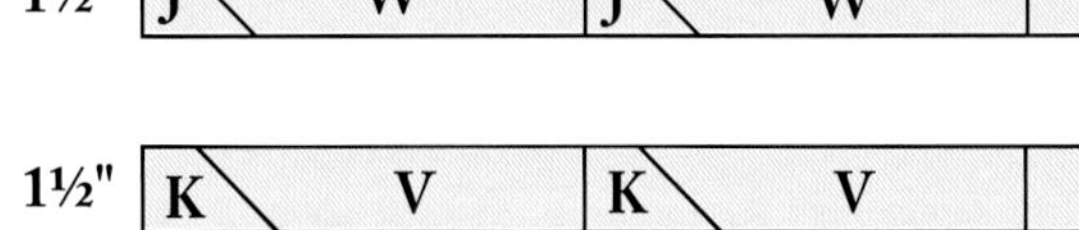

2 & 2 reversed Queen/2 & 2 reversed Wall

1½"

2 & 2 reversed Queen/2 & 2 reversed Wall

1½"

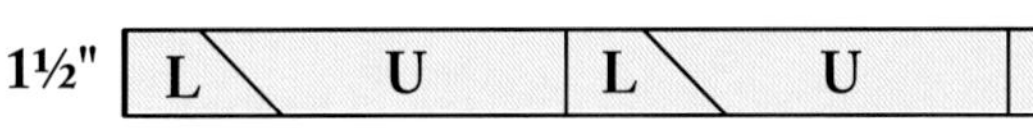

2 & 2 reversed Queen/2 & 2 reversed Wall

1½"

2 & 2 reversed Queen/2 & 2 reversed Wall

1½"

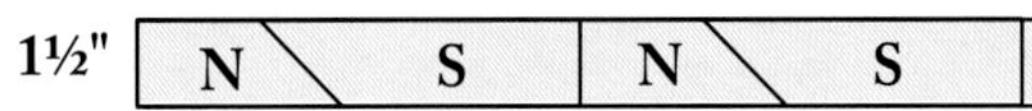

2 & 2 reversed Queen/2 & 2 reversed Wall

1½"

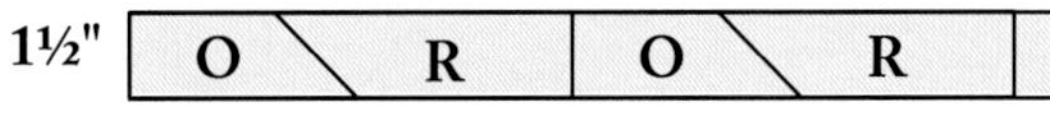

2 & 2 reversed Queen/2 & 2 reversed Wall

1½"

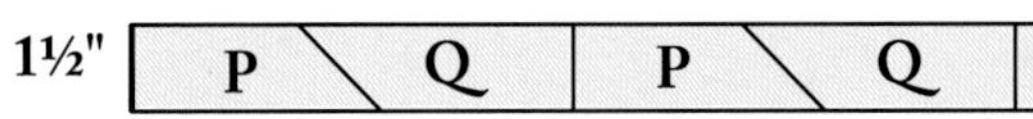

2 & 2 reversed Queen/2 & 2 reversed Wall

1½"

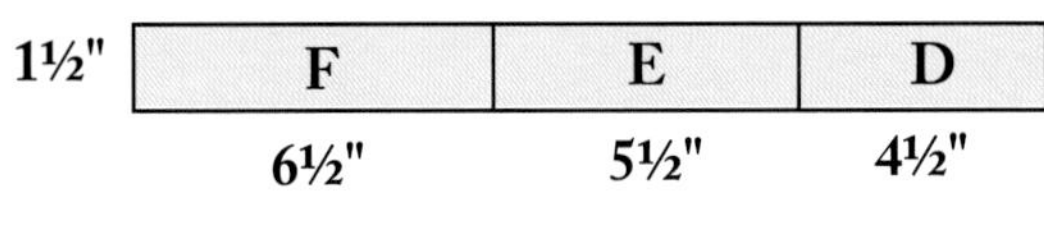

112 Queen/32 Wall

1½"

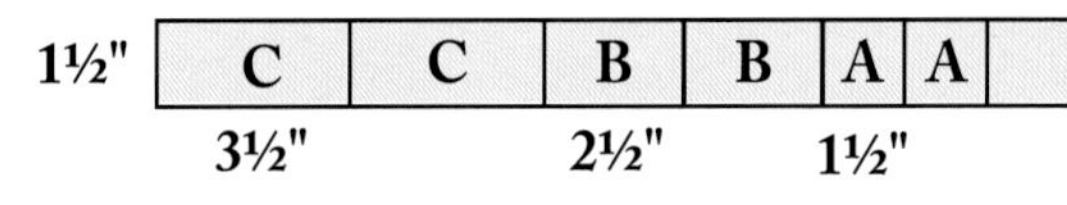

56 Queen/16 Wall

Pink Prints 18" Strip & Patch Cutting

2½"

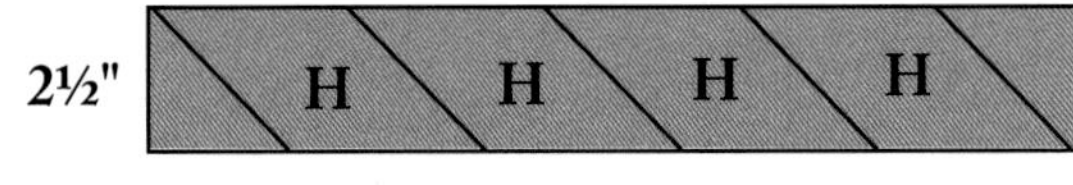

60 Queen/14 Wall

Note that all A's are pink. In order to contrast with the A's, no B's and C's are pink.

1½"

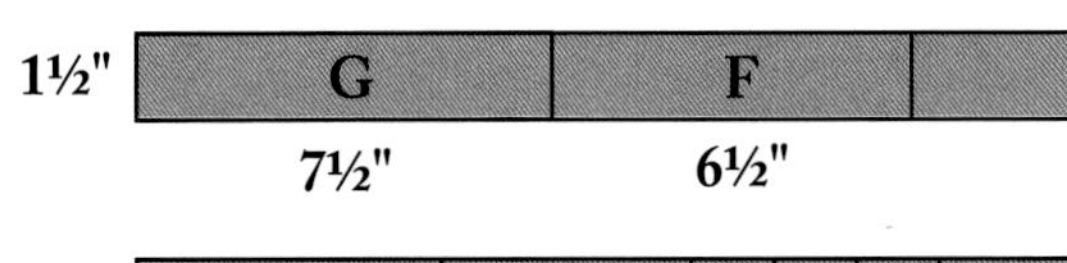

37 Queen/10 Wall

1½"

38 Queen/11 Wall

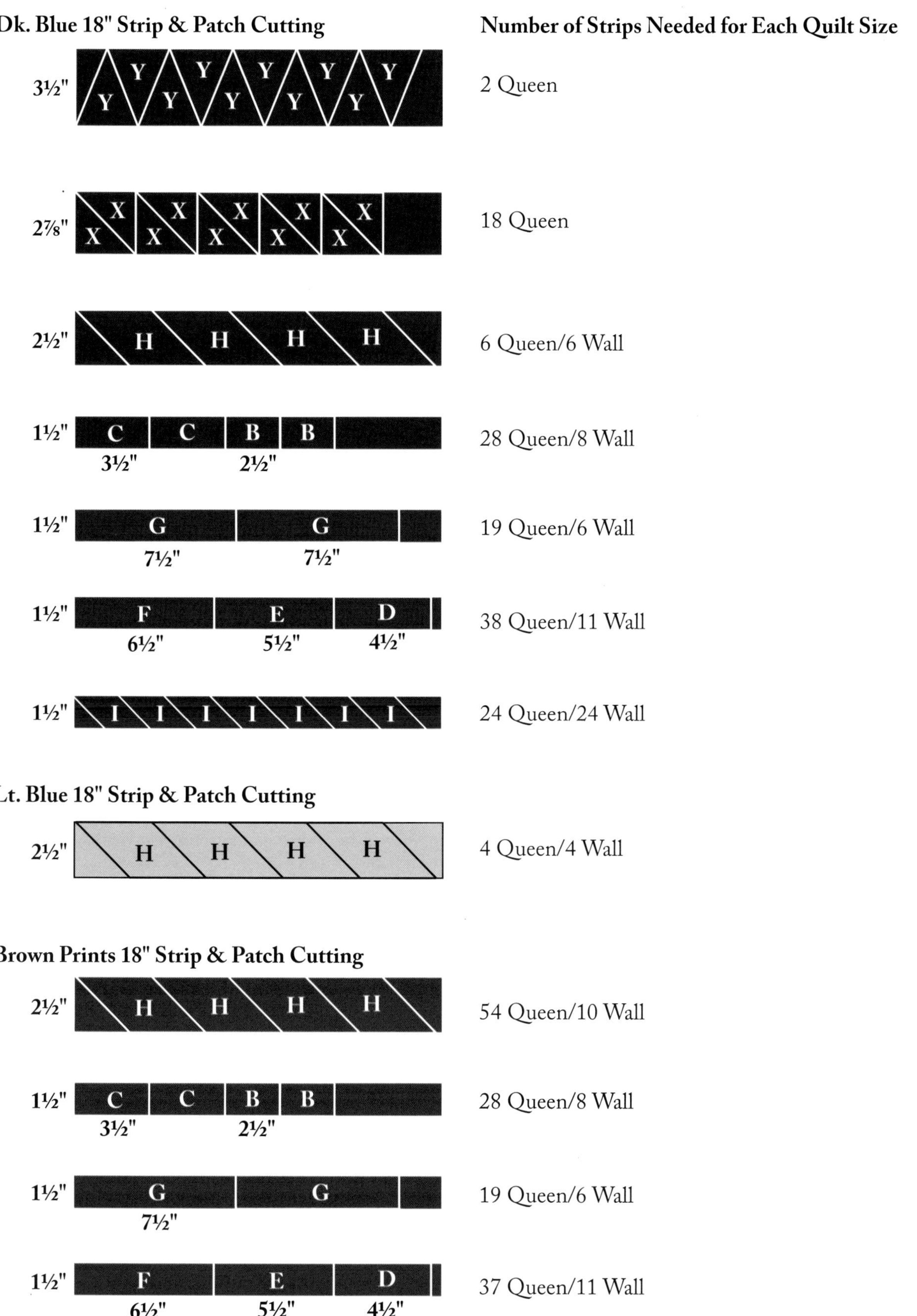
Dk. Blue 18" Strip & Patch Cutting
Number of Strips Needed for Each Quilt Size
3½"
Y Y Y Y Y Y Y Y Y Y
2 Queen
2⅞"
X X X X X X X X X X
18 Queen
2½"
H H H H
6 Queen/6 Wall
1½"
C C B B
3½" 2½"
28 Queen/8 Wall
1½"
G G
7½" 7½"
19 Queen/6 Wall
1½"
F E D
6½" 5½" 4½"
38 Queen/11 Wall
1½"
I I I I I I I
24 Queen/24 Wall
Lt. Blue 18" Strip & Patch Cutting
2½"
H H H H
4 Queen/4 Wall
Brown Prints 18" Strip & Patch Cutting
2½"
H H H H
54 Queen/10 Wall
1½"
C C B B
3½" 2½"
28 Queen/8 Wall
1½"
G G
7½"
19 Queen/6 Wall
1½"
F E D
6½" 5½" 4½"
37 Queen/11 Wall

Special Rotary Cutting Details

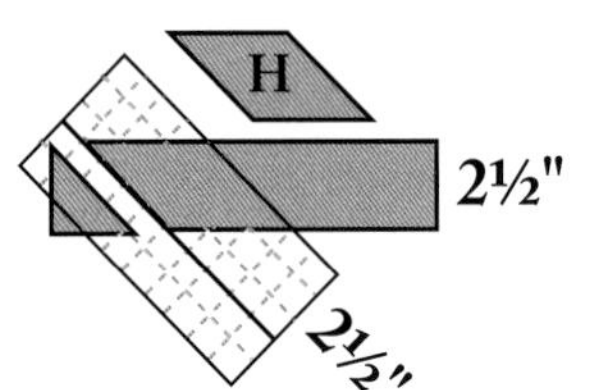

H: Cut a strip 2½" wide. Cut off the end of the strip at a 45-degree angle as shown. Align the 2½" ruling of a rotary cutting ruler with the angled end of the strip. Cut along the ruler's edge to complete an H diamond. Check your diamond against the H template in the book. Cut H diamonds down the length of the strip.

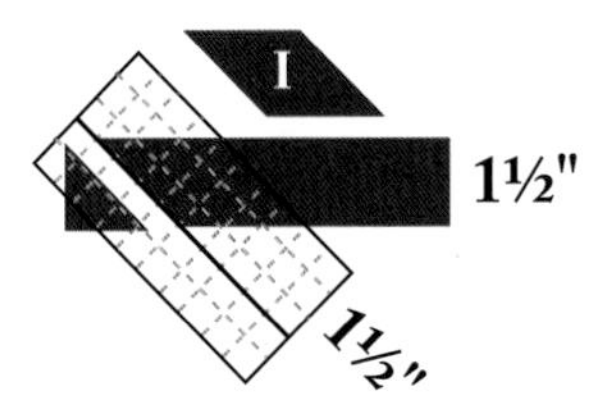

I: Cut a strip 1½" wide. Cut off the end of the strip at a 45-degree angle as shown. Align the 1½" ruling of a rotary cutting ruler with the angled end of the strip. Cut along the ruler's edge to complete an I diamond. Check your diamond against the I template in the book. Cut I diamonds down the length of the strip.

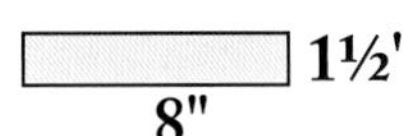

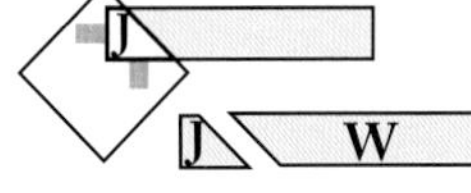

J & W: Cut a rectangle 1½" x 8". Trace or download the templates for J–P. Download is available at http://www.judymartin.com/templates.cfm. Be sure not to scale printing to a size other than 100%. Check templates against the ones in the book. Cut out and tape the J template to a rotary cutting ruler so that the angled side is on the ruler's edge, as shown at left. Align top, left, and bottom of template with fabric rectangle as shown. Cut along the ruler's edge to complete J. The remainder of the rectangle is W. Check your patches against the templates in the book. Cut a total of 4 J and 4 W.

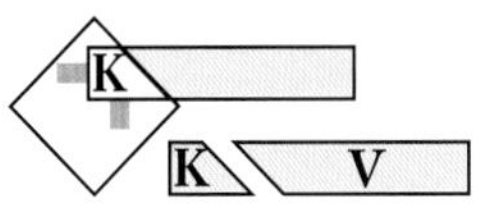

K–V: Cut K through V from 1½" x 8" rectangles in the following pairs (shown on page 62): K-V, L-U, M-T, N-S, O-R, and P-Q. Cut these in a fashion similar to the way you cut J-W. After cutting K through P using their templates, Q through V will be the rectangles' leftovers. Check your patches against the templates in the book. Cut 4 of each patch letter.

Jr–Wr: Also cut 4 each of Jr through Wr. Cut these reversed patches using J through P templates, but with the fabric rectangles face down on the cutting mat.

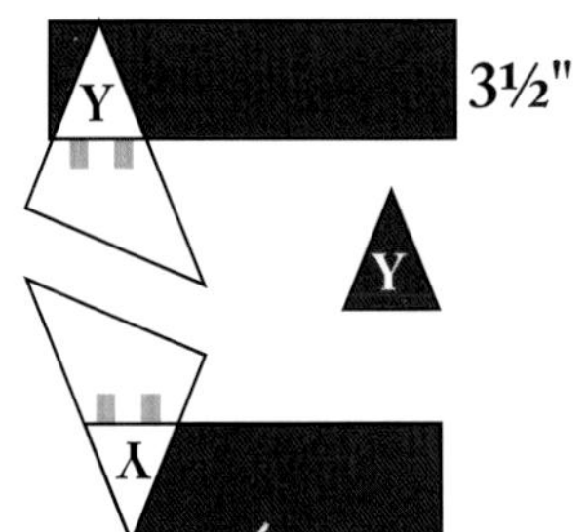

Y: Cut a strip 3½" wide. Trace or download the template for Y. Download is available at http://www.judymartin.com/templates.cfm. Be sure not to scale printing to a size other than 100%. Check template against the one in the book. Cut out and tape the template to a triangular rotary cutting ruler that matches the 45-degree angle of the Y. The 2 long sides should be on the ruler's edge, as shown at left. Align the bottom of the template with the fabric as shown. Cut along the ruler's edge to complete a Y patch. Check your Y patch against the template in the book. Turn the template on the strip, as shown, and cut another Y. It is helpful to use a revolving mat so it is not awkward to cut the patches. Cut Y's down the length of the strip.

Block Construction

See Y below. The left diagram identifies the patches; the right one shows the piecing order. Make a test Y block, taking scant ¼" seam allowances. Start in the block center, joining pink and light A's (both #1). Always press seams away from the center (pink A). Add a light B, followed by a dark B (#2 and #3), continuing in numerical order through #12, the dark G log. If your test block does not measure precicsely 7½" from raw edge to raw edge, adjust your seam allowances slightly and make another test block. When your seam allowance is right, make the number of Y blocks listed for your quilt size.

See Z below. Sew a dark blue I diamond to the angled end of each patch J–W and reverses Jr–Wr. Sew a second I to J, L, N, P, R, T, and V patches and their reverses. Stitch J to K, L to M, N to O, P to Q, R to S, T to U, and V to W. Similarly, join reversed segments. Arrange these segments, along with H diamonds, according to the Z diagram below. Add the appropriate number (from 0 to 6) and color of H diamonds to each segment. Join J–W segments. Also join Jr–Wr segments.

Sew the Y to the W and Wr segments with a set-in seam, stopping ¼" in from the raw edge. Stitch the angled seam to complete Z.

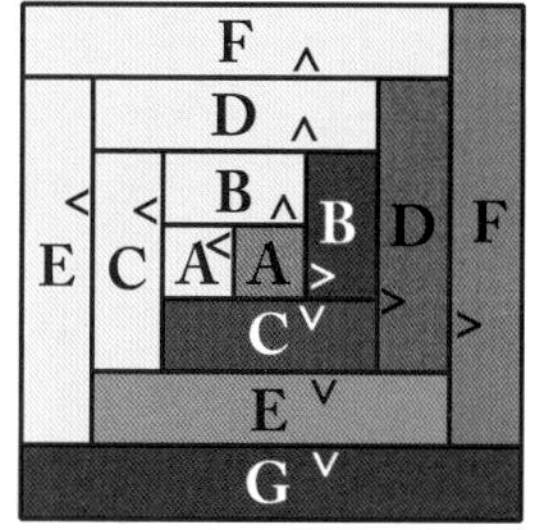

Block Y Patches
Make 112 queen*
Make 32 wall*

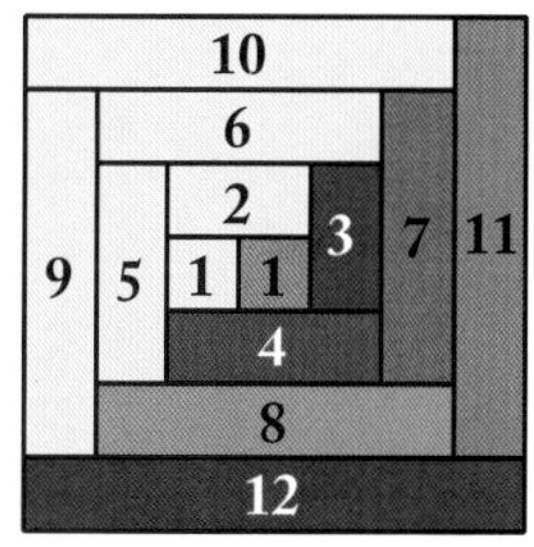

Block Y
Piecing Sequence

Note that Y block totals include those used in Z blocks.

Block Z
Make 4 queen
Make 4 wall

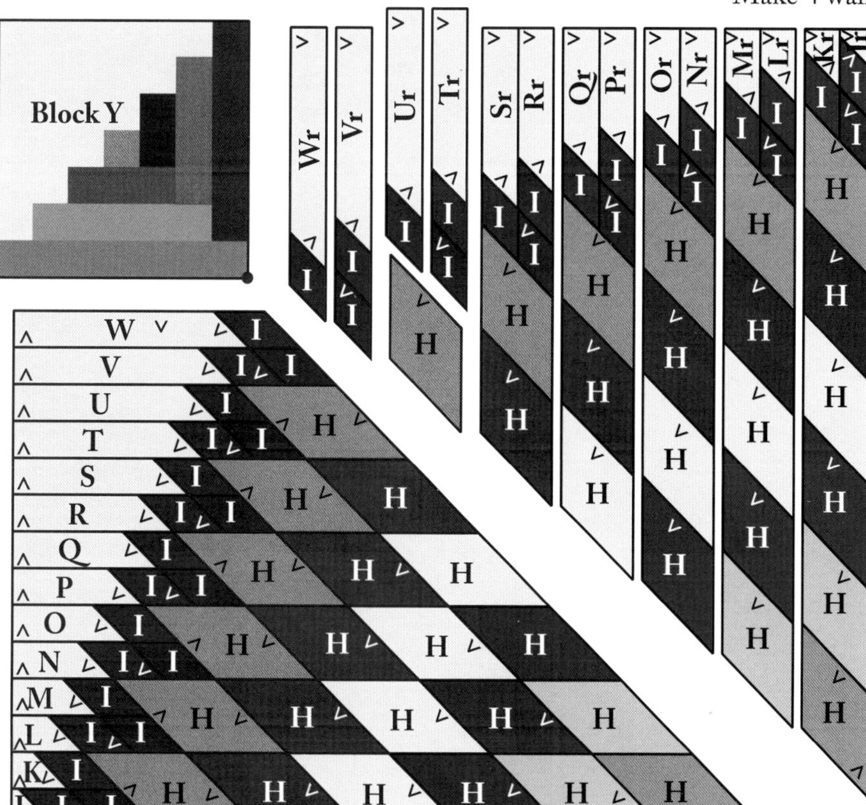

Queen Quilt Assembly

See the queen quilt diagram below. Join 2 Z blocks; press seams to the right. Repeat. Sew the 2 segments together, opposing seam allowances at the center.

Arrange Y blocks as shown below or on page 69. If you prefer, devise your own arrangement. Sew 3 columns of 6 blocks for each side of the quilt. Pin and stitch to the quilt. Sew 3 rows of 12 blocks each for the top of the quilt; attach. Repeat for the bottom of the quilt.

See the border units and border corners on the next page. Make them as described. Join 3 Border Unit 1's followed by 3 Border Unit 2's to make a border as shown below. Press seam allowances away from the center. Make 4 borders. Pin and stitch borders to the top and bottom of the quilt. Press seams away from the quilt center. Add 2 border corners to each remaining border, turning them as shown. Press seam allowances away from the corners. Pin and stitch to the quilt. Press the seam allowances away from the quilt center to complete the quilt top.

Queen Quilt Diagram

Wall Quilt Assembly

See the wall quilt diagram below. Join 2 Z blocks; press seams to the right. Repeat. Sew the 2 segments together, opposing seam allowances at the center.

Arrange Y blocks as shown or in your own arrangement. Sew together 6 blocks for the sides and 8 blocks for the top and bottom. Pin and stitch sides, then top and bottom, to complete quilt top.

Wall Quilt Diagram

Queen Border Unit Construction

See Border Corner diagram below. Join a brown and a pink H; add a blue X to the pink end. Press seams toward the brown end. Sew 2 blue Y triangles to the same end of a pink H. Press the first seam toward and the second seam away from H. Join the two segments, pressing seams away from the brown H. Make second half as shown below, pressing seams toward brown H. Join halves.

See the Border Unit 1 and 2 diagrams below. Join a light X, brown H, pink H, and blue X end to end as shown. Press seams toward light end of Unit 1 and blue end of Unit 2. Make 7 segments alike; join to make Border Unit 1 or Border Unit 2. Press seams to the left in Border Unit 1 and to the right in Border Unit 2. Note that the same patches are turned differently to make the two units.

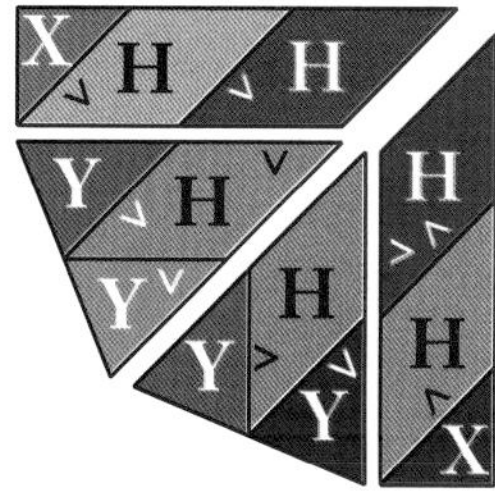

Border Corner
Make 4 Queen

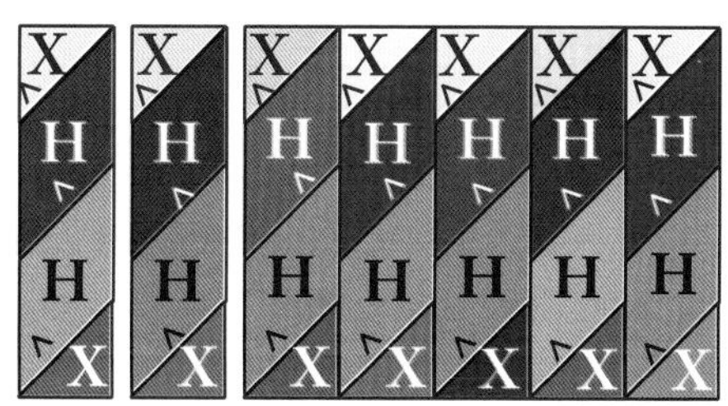

Border Unit 1
Make 12 Queen

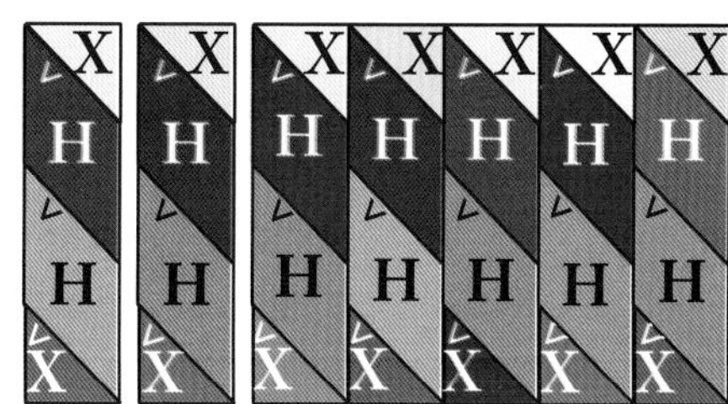

Border Unit 2
Make 12 Queen

Quilting

See the photo below. Dark logs are quilted in the ditch, as are H diamonds. Feathers are quilted freehand in the light blue ring of H diamonds extending into the dark blue; in the pink ring of H diamonds extending into the brown; and in the dark blue ring of I diamonds. Freehand feathers also grace the J–W and Jr–Wr areas and the swaths of light logs.

Other Setting Variations

Sun Valley Log Cabin lends itself to all the Log Cabin setting variations. Below are four queen-size setting options shown without borders in order to allow you to better see the block details.

Sugar Cookie Recipe

Makes 4 Dozen Cookies

These simple cookies are great for an ice cream social, a cookie exchange, or a potluck dinner.

Ingredients

1 cup (2 sticks) butter, cold and cut up
2⅓ cups granulated sugar
½ teaspoon salt
1½ teaspoons vanilla
2 eggs
3⅓ cups flour
1½ teaspoons baking soda
additional sugar in which to roll dough balls

Method

Preheat the oven to 400°. Cut cold butter into ¼-tablespoon cubes. By hand or with a mixer, cream together the butter, sugar, salt, and vanilla.

When the mixture is uniform, mix in (low speed) the eggs, flour, and baking soda. Beat (medium low speed) until well mixed. Expect the dough to be somewhat stiff.

Pinch off dough and form into 48 balls 1¼" in diameter. Cover the bottom of a plate or small cake pan with granulated sugar. Roll each ball in the sugar to coat all sides. You may leave the dough covered in the refrigerator for a few days.

Place 9 dough balls widely spaced on an ungreased, insulated cookie sheet. If you have refrigerated the dough, let the balls warm up outside the refrigerator for ten minutes or so before baking.

On the center oven rack, bake one tray at a time for 9 minutes. The top should be cracked and faintly golden. Remove the cookie sheet to a cooling rack.

Cool 15 minutes. With a spatula, remove cookies onto a wire cooling rack to cool further. Serve just slightly warm or completely cooled.

Strawberry Shortcake Recipe

Makes 9-12 Servings

Who can resist shortcake when berries are in season? Mash or purée some of the berries in the blender so the juice will soak into the shortcake. Sprinkle the berries with sugar if desired.

Ingredients

2⅔ cups flour
1 tablespoon baking powder
1 teaspoon salt
2 tablespoons sugar
½ cup (1 stick) butter
1⅓ cups milk
3 pts. strawberries, washed, hulled, and sliced
3 tablespoons granulated sugar (optional)
½ pt. heavy cream
2 tablespoons powdered sugar (optional)

Method

Freeze butter for 45 minutes. Preheat the oven to 450°. Grease an 8"–9" square pan.

Stir together the first four (dry) ingredients. Grate in the butter, tossing it with the flour mixture as you grate. After the butter is all grated, toss it with a fork until the butter is evenly distributed. Stir in the milk, mixing the dough just until there are no dry spots.

Spread the dough in the greased pan. Bake on the center oven rack for 20 minutes. The top should be golden. Cool slightly. Cut into 9–12 pieces. Split each piece and place cut side up on a plate.

Sprinkle the berries with sugar, if you like. Whip the cream with the powdered sugar. Top the shortcake with berries and whipped cream.

Rolling Hills Log Cabin

This curvaceous Log Cabin is pieced entirely out of squares and rectangles with simple straight seams. Rolling Hills Log Cabin is an easy quilt to cut and sew. An accurate scant ¼" seam allowance and patience for the many pieces are helpful. The deep curves are accomplished with Drunkard's Path-inspired blocks in two block colorings used in equal numbers.

Rolling Hills Log Cabin is an original quilt designed by Judy Martin, pieced by Doris Hareland, and quilted by Jenise Antony.

Rolling Hills Log Cabin is ideal for a strip swap or a setting party.

Yardage & Cutting Specifications

Twin Size

Quilt Size: 73" x 96"
Block Size: 11½" between seamlines
Requires: 24 Y, 24 Z

Yardage
Bright Prints 21 fat quarters
2 borders cut 2½" x 92½"
2 borders cut 2½" x 73½"
24 A
96 B
48 C
96 D
96 E
96 F
120 G
96 H
48 I
48 J
72 K
48 L

Light Prints 18 fat quarters
24 A
96 B
48 C
96 D
96 E
96 F
120 G
96 H
48 I
48 J
72 K
48 L

Backing 7¼ yards
3 panels 35½" x 81"

Binding ¾ yard
16 strips 2" x 27"

Batting
81" x 104"

Queen Size

Quilt Size: 96" x 96"
Block Size: 11½" between seamlines
Requires: 32 Y, 32 Z

Yardage
Bright Prints 27 fat quarters
2 borders cut 2½" x 96½"
2 borders cut 2½" x 92½"
32 A
128 B
64 C
128 D
128 E
128 F
160 G
128 H
64 I
64 J
96 K
64 L

Light Prints 24 fat quarters
32 A
128 B
64 C
128 D
128 E
128 F
160 G
128 H
64 I
64 J
96 K
64 L

Backing 9¼ yards
3 panels 35½" x 104"

Binding ¾ yard
18 strips 2" x 27"

Batting
104" x 104"

Yardage continued

Table Runner

Quilt Size: 15½" x 50"
Block Size: 11½" between seamlines
Requires: 2 Y, 2 Z

Yardage
Bright Prints 3 or more fat quarters
2 borders cut 2½" x 46½"
2 borders cut 2½" x 16"
2 A
8 B
4 C
8 D
8 E
8 F
10 G
8 H
4 I
4 J
6 K
4 L

Light Prints 2 or more fat quarters
2 A
8 B
4 C
8 D
8 E
8 F
10 G
8 H
4 I
4 J
6 K
4 L

Backing 1¾ yards
1 panel 23½" x 58"

Binding ½ yard
10 strips 2" x 18"

Batting
23½" x 58"

Optional Templates

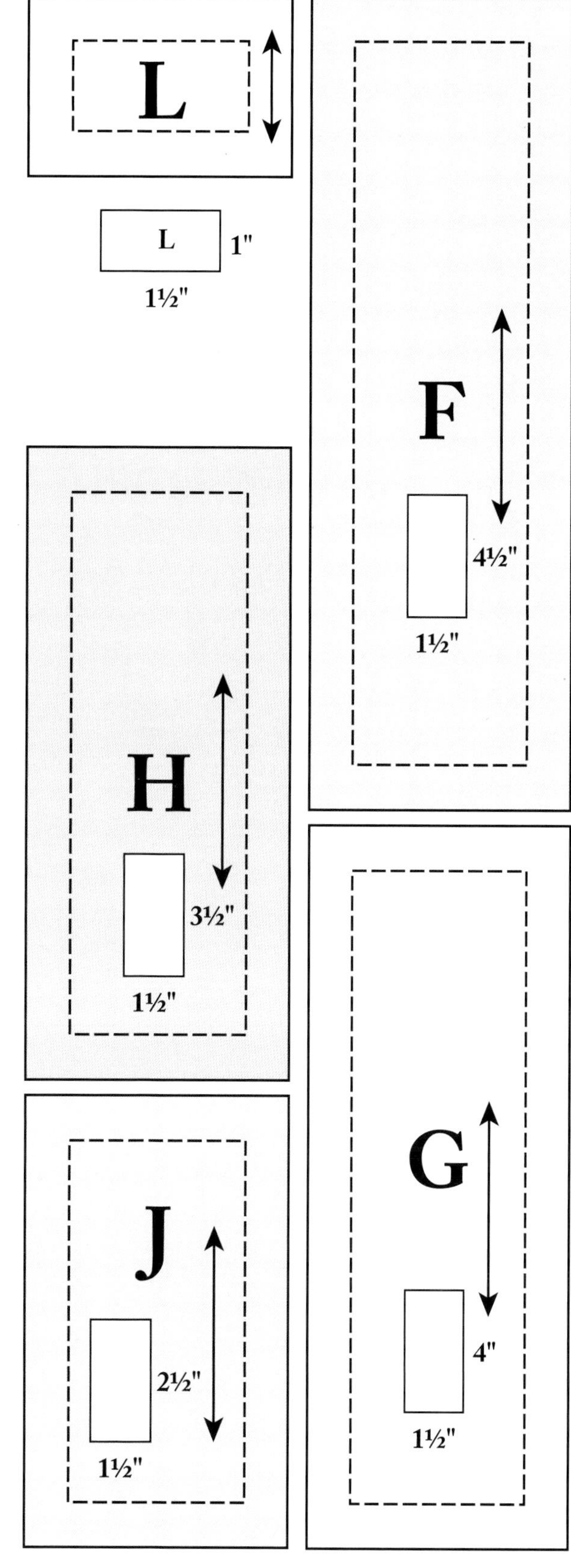

Optional Templates

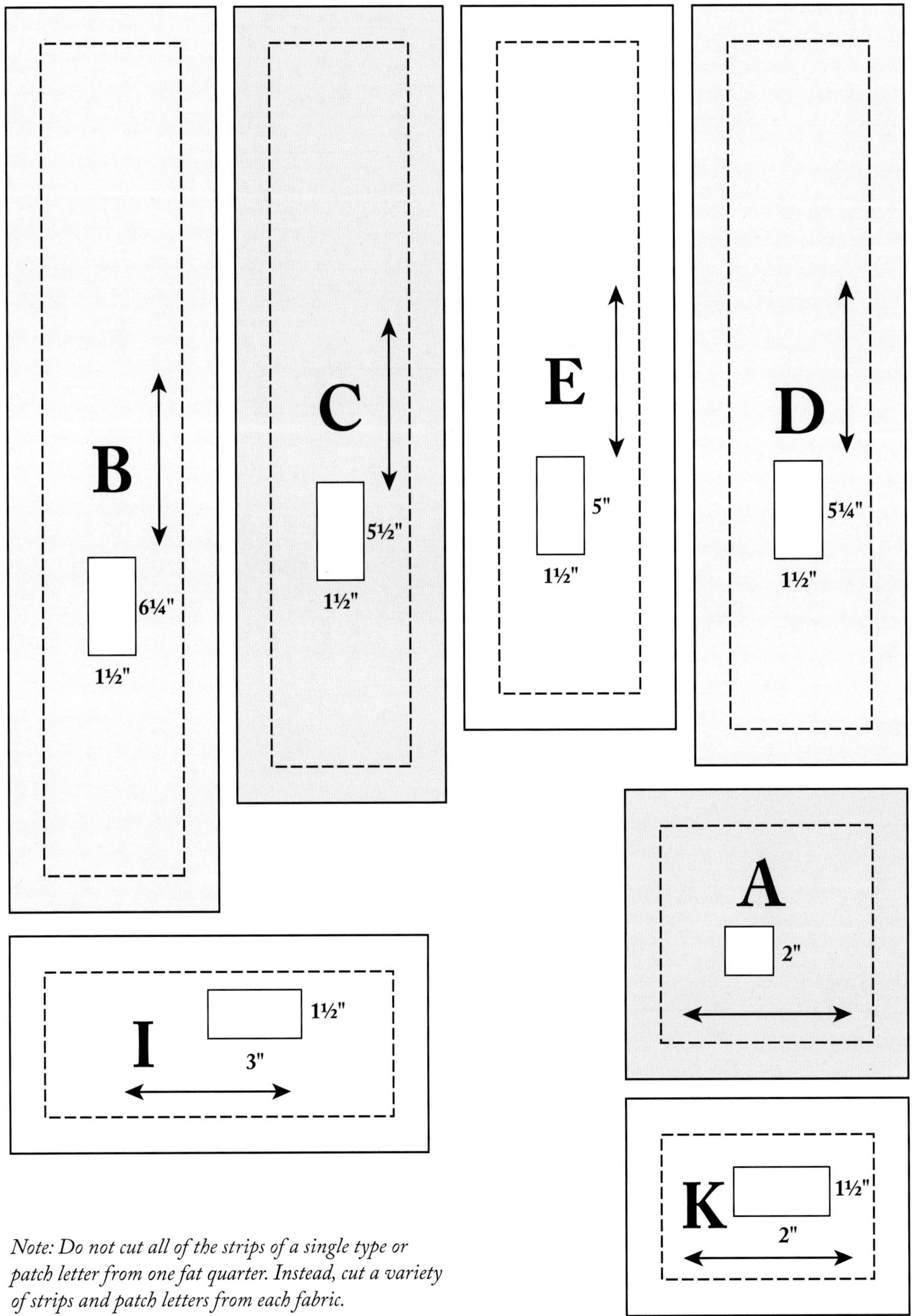

Note: Do not cut all of the strips of a single type or patch letter from one fat quarter. Instead, cut a variety of strips and patch letters from each fabric.

Strip Cutting Layouts

Bright Print 18" Strip & Patch Cutting

Number of Strips Needed for Each Quilt Size

Strip width	Patches	Number of Strips Needed for Each Quilt Size
2½"	border strip, 18"	22 Twin/24 Queen/8 Table Runner
2"	A A A A A A A A (2")	3 Twin/4 Queen/1 Table Runner
1½"	B 6¼", D 5¼", E 5"	96 Twin/128 Queen/8 Table Runner
1½"	F 4½", H 3½", H 3½", K 2", K 2"	48 Twin/64 Queen/4 Table Runner
1½"	F 4½", J 2½", C 5½", I 3", L 1"	48 Twin/64 Queen/4 Table Runner
1½"	G 4", G 4", G 4", G 4"	30 Twin/40 Queen/3 Table Runner

Light Print 18" Strip & Patch Cutting

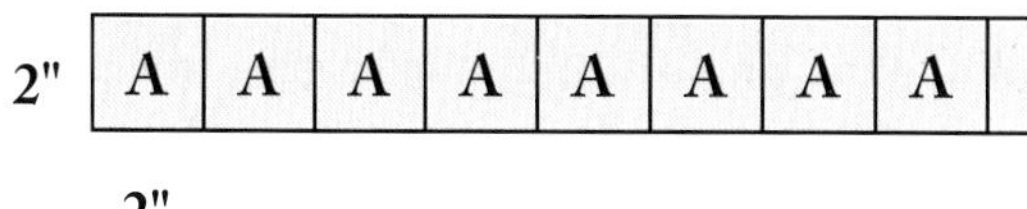

Strip width	Patches	Number of Strips Needed for Each Quilt Size
2"	A A A A A A A A (2")	3 Twin/4 Queen/1 Table Runner
1½"	B 6¼", D 5¼", E 5"	96 Twin/128 Queen/8 Table Runner
1½"	F 4½", H 3½", H 3½", K 2", K 2"	48 Twin/64 Queen/4 Table Runner
1½"	F 4½", J 2½", C 5½", I 3", L 1"	48 Twin/64 Queen/4 Table Runner
1½"	G 4", G 4", G 4", G 4"	30 Twin/40 Queen/3 Table Runner

Block Construction

Refer to the two diagrams below. The left diagram shows the Y block coloring as well as patch letters for both Y and Z blocks. The right diagram shows the coloring for Z as well as the piecing sequence for both the Y and Z blocks. In the right diagram, first stitch together logs having the same number, such as log #5 to #5 or #6 to #6. Then stitch in numerical order: 1, 2, 3, and so on.

When joining two logs of the same number, press seam allowances toward the light log in the Y block and toward the dark log in the Z block. After adding a log or a log pair to the block, press seam allowances away from the block center. The arrows in the diagrams below show which way to press each seam.

Make a sample block first. If a log or log pair extends beyond the block, your seam allowance is too deep. If a log or log pair does not extend to the block's edges, your seam allowance is too shallow. The adjustment is probably slight, just a thread or two. Make a tape guide for your sewing machine reflecting the adjustment you need, and make another sample block.

After getting your seam allowance right, make the number of blocks of each type listed for your quilt size.

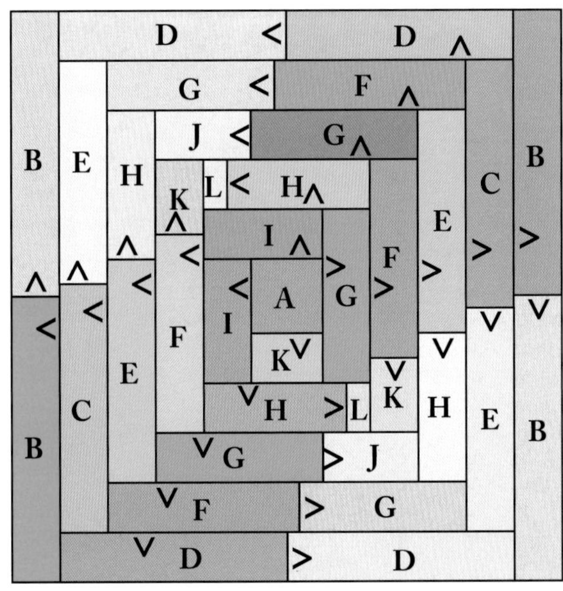

Block Y Coloring and Y & Z Patches
Make 24 Y twin
Make 32 Y queen
Make 2 Y table runner

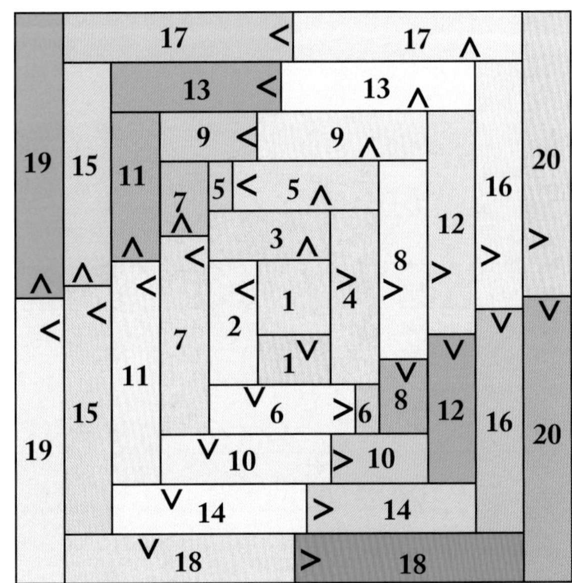

Block Z Coloring and Y & Z Piecing Sequence
Make 24 Z twin
Make 32 Z queen
Make 2 Z table runner

Twin Quilt Assembly

Arrange the blocks as shown below, in one of the sets shown on page 80, or in a set of your own devising. Stand back and squint at the arrangement to catch any mistakes.

In the upper left corner of each block, pin a label listing row and block numbers. Then you may pick up blocks in order in preparation for sewing them together. If you remember to keep the label in the upper left corner, all blocks will remain turned according to your planned layout.

Sew six blocks in a row. Press seam allowances to the right in odd numbered rows and to the left in even numbered rows. Make eight rows. Join rows, pressing seam allowances toward the bottom of the quilt top.

Join border strips to make borders in the lengths listed. Pin and stitch longer borders to sides of the quilt. Press seams away from quilt center. Pin and stitch shorter borders to top and bottom of the quilt. Press seams away from quilt center.

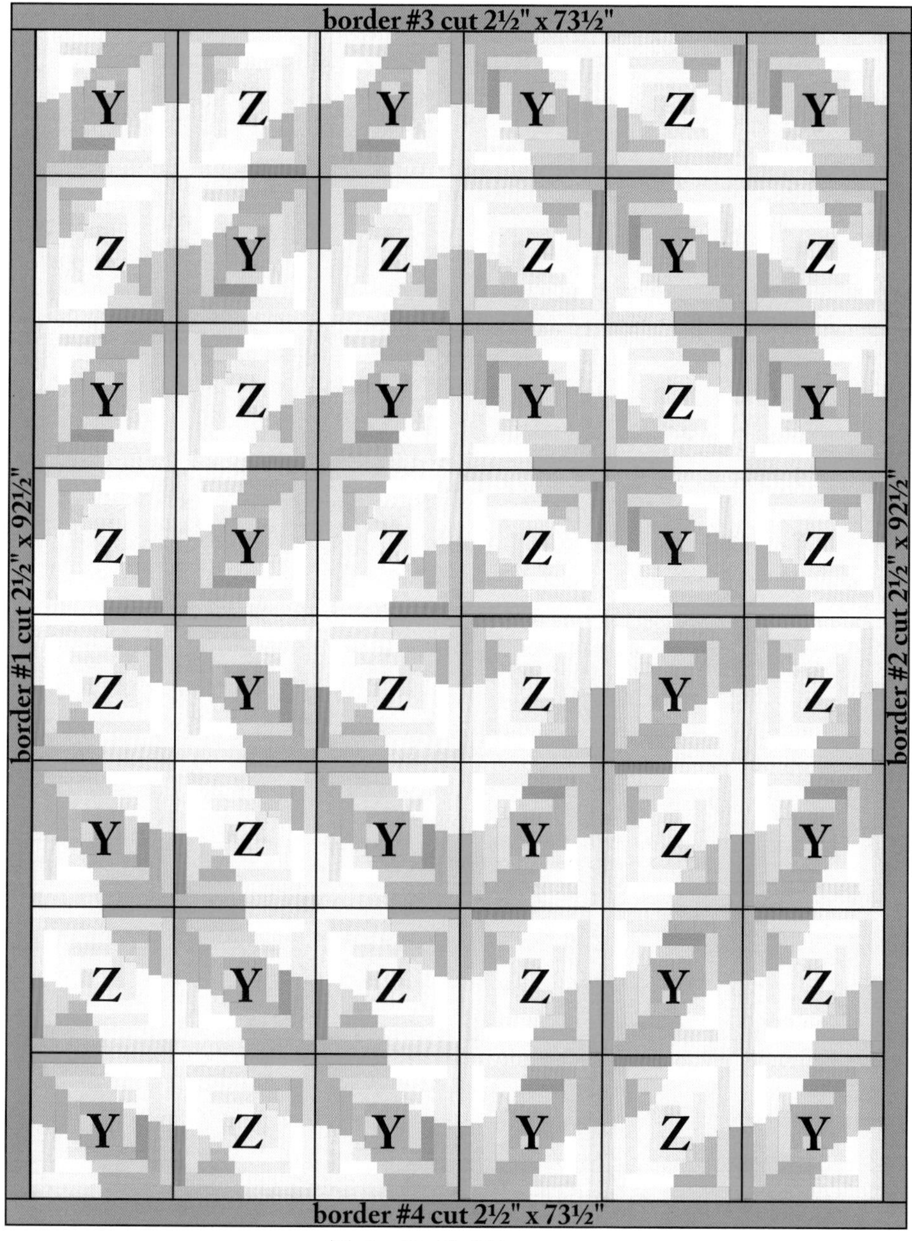

Twin Quilt Diagram

Queen Quilt Assembly

Arrange the blocks as shown below, in one of the sets shown on page 80, or in a set of your own devising. If you use one of the sets from page 80, you will need to add one column of blocks to the left end and another to the right end of the quilt. Stand back and squint at the arrangement to catch any mistakes.

In the upper left corner of each block, pin a label listing row and block numbers. Then you may pick up blocks in order in preparation for sewing them together. If you remember to keep the label in the upper left corner, all blocks will remain turned according to your planned layout.

Sew eight blocks in a row. Press seams to the right in odd numbered rows and to the left in even numbered rows. Make eight rows. Join rows, pressing seams toward the bottom of the quilt top.

Join border strips to make borders in the listed lengths. Pin and stitch shorter borders to sides of the quilt. Press seams away from quilt center. Pin and stitch longer borders to the top and bottom of the quilt. Press seams away from quilt center.

border #3 cut 2½" x 96½"

border #1 cut 2½" x 92½"

border #2 cut 2½" x 92½"

Z	Y	Z	Y	Y	Z	Y	Z
Y	Z	Y	Z	Z	Y	Z	Y
Z	Y	Z	Y	Y	Z	Y	Z
Y	Z	Y	Z	Z	Y	Z	Y
Y	Z	Y	Z	Z	Y	Z	Y
Z	Y	Z	Y	Y	Z	Y	Z
Y	Z	Y	Z	Z	Y	Z	Y
Z	Y	Z	Y	Y	Z	Y	Z

border #4 cut 2½" x 96½"

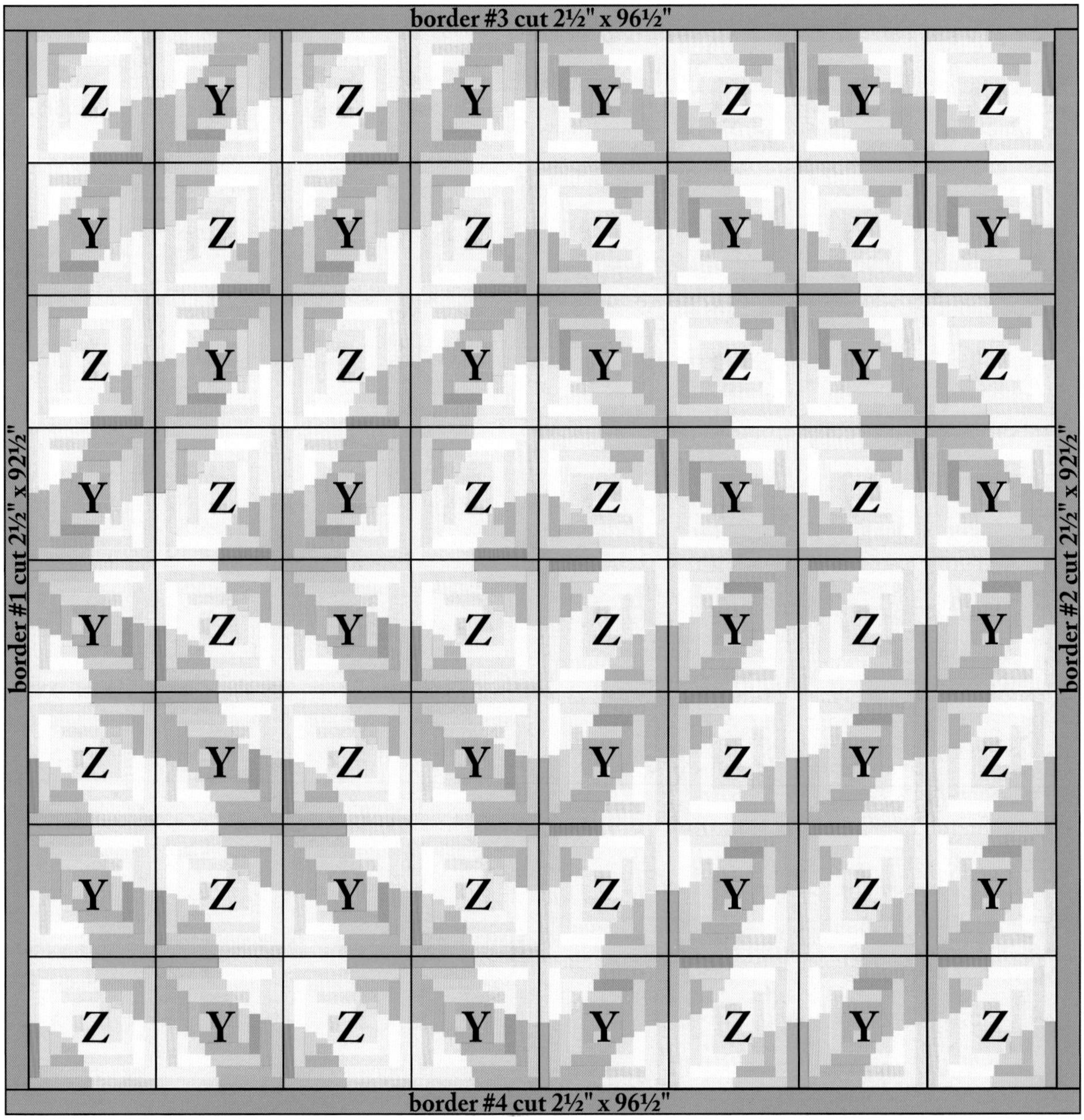

Queen Quilt Diagram

Table Runner Assembly

Arrange the blocks as shown at right. Stand back and squint at the arrangement to catch any mistakes in the layout.

In the upper left corner of each block, pin a label listing block numbers. Then you may pick up blocks in order in preparation for sewing them together. If you remember to keep the label in the upper left corner, all blocks will remain turned according to your planned layout. Sew the four blocks in a row. Press seam allowances to the right.

Join 18"-long strips end to end to make 46½"-long borders. Pin and stitch these longer borders to the top and bottom of the quilt. Press seam allowances away from the quilt center. Pin and stitch shorter borders to the sides of the quilt. Press seam allowances away from the quilt center.

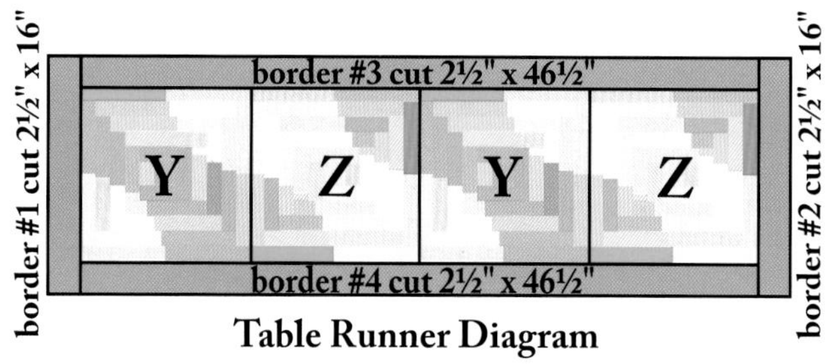

Table Runner Diagram

Quilting

Quilt freehand feathers in the blocks, ignoring block boundaries, but paying attention to light areas and dark areas. Quilt a small, one-sided feather in the outer border.

Other Setting Ideas

Rolling Hills Log Cabin looks strikingly different when the blocks are turned according to various setting plans. Six ideas for setting this quilt are shown below.

Boston Beauty

Boston Beauty has unusual shapes and a large number of patches, but the sewing is straightforward, and the results are worth the work involved.

This quilt is an original design by Judy Martin that was pieced by Tami Hemmer and quilted by Lee Plisch of Cornerstone Quilts.

The quilt was inspired by a New York Beauty quilt, from which I derived the name, as well as the general feel of the quilt.

Boston Beauty is a good possibility for a class. A teacher could demonstrate the patch cutting idiosyncrasies. Boston Beauty is also suitable for a strip swap.

Yardage & Cutting Specifications

Queen Size

Quilt Size: 98⅛" x 98⅛"
Block Size: 12" between seamlines
Requires: 36 X, 144 Y, 4 Z

Yardage
Ivory Print Background 8 yards
2 borders 2¾" x 77¼"
2 borders 2¾" x 72¾"
108 B
72 D
72 Dr (reversed)
144 E
72 G
312 H
4 I

Tan Print 4 yards
2 borders 3½" x 98⅝"
2 borders 3½" x 92⅝"
152 A
432 F

Dark Prints 17 fat quarters
304 A
288 C
288 F

Backing 9⅜ yards
3 panels 36" x 106⅛"

Binding ¾ yard
19 strips 2" x 27"

Batting
107" x 107"

Twin Size

Quilt Size: 70½" x 94"
Block Size: 12" between seamlines
Requires: 24 X, 118 Y, 4 Z

Yardage
Ivory Print Background 5¾ yards
2 borders 2" x 72¾"
2 borders 1⅝+"* x 51⅝"
72 B
48 D
48 Dr (reversed)
96 E
48 G
260 H
4 I

Tan Print 2¾ yards
2 borders 2½" x 90½"
2 borders 2½" x 71"
126 A
288 F

Dark Prints 12 fat quarters
230 A
192 C
192 F

Backing 6 yards
2 panels 39¾" x 102"

Binding ¾ yard
16 strips 2" x 27"

Batting
79" x 102"

See rotary cutting details on pages 85–87.

**1⅝+" is halfway between 1⅝" and 1¾" rulings.*

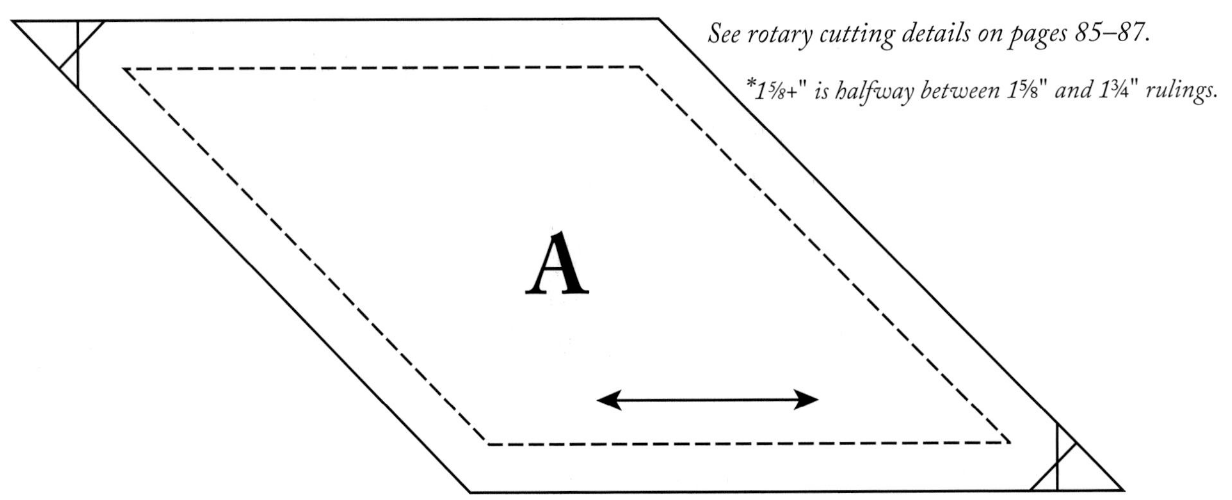

Optional Templates

E
D & Dr

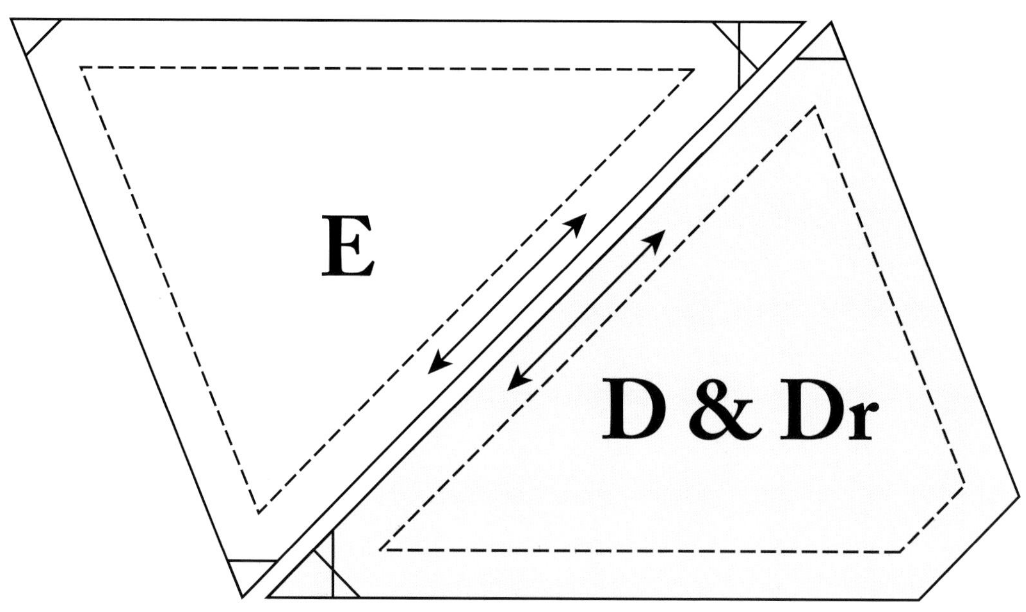

See rotary cutting details on pages 85–87.

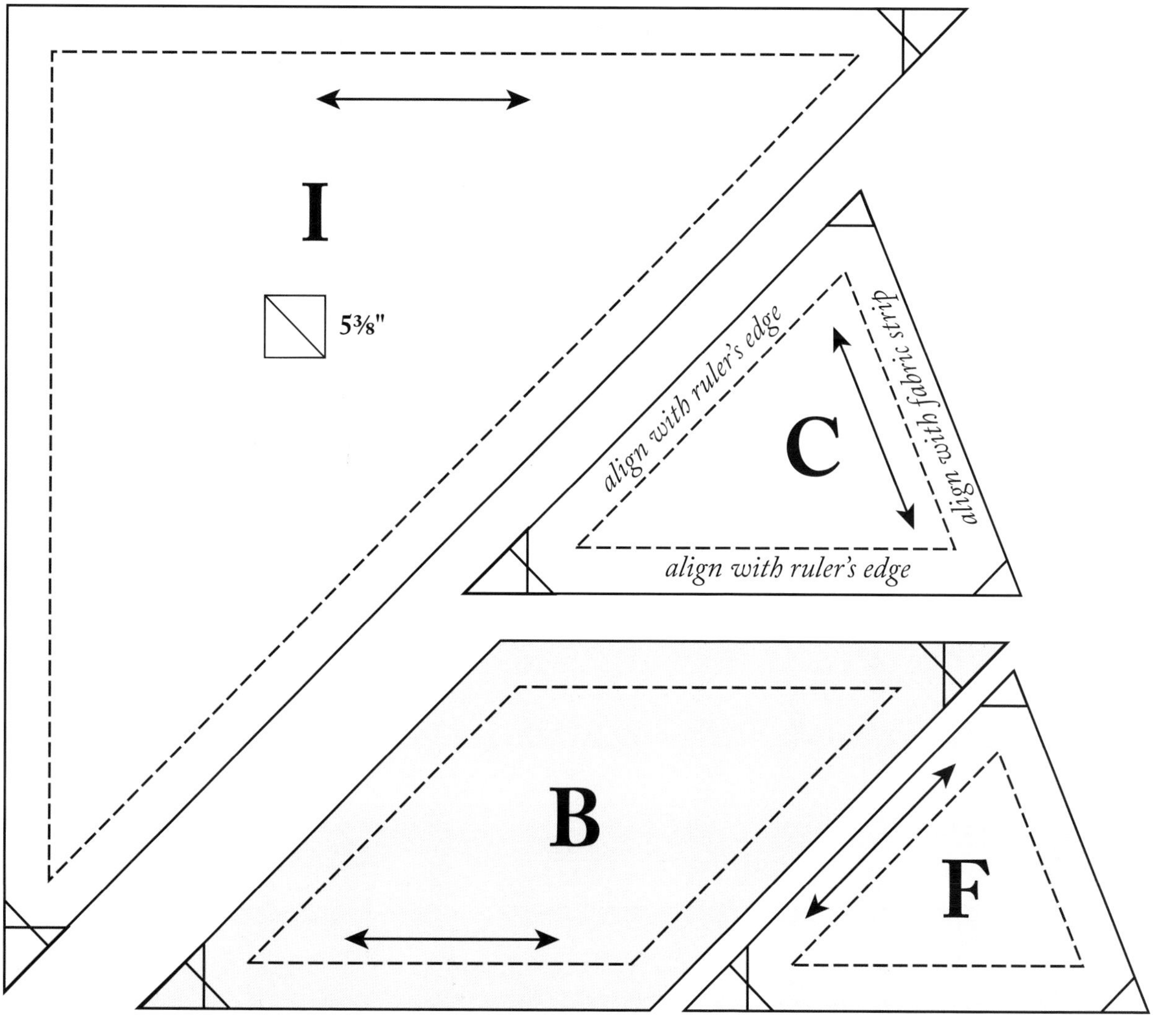

I
5⅜"
C
align with ruler's edge
align with fabric strip
align with ruler's edge
B
F

Optional Templates

align with ruler's edge

align with fabric patch

G

align with fabric patch

align with fabric patch

align with ruler's edge

align with ruler's edge

H

align with fabric strip

See rotary cutting details on pages 85–87.

Strip Cutting Layouts

It is not necessary to cut all of the patches before you start sewing. In fact, I recommend sewing a single sample block before proceeding with the rest of the cutting. This will allow you to adjust your seam allowances until the block is perfect.

If you like, do as I do: Cut enough to make a few blocks at a time, alternating cutting with sewing.

Do not cut all of the strips of a single type or patch letter from one fat quarter. Instead, cut a variety of strips and patch letters from each fabric.

Ivory 18" Strip & Patch Cutting

Number of Strips Needed for Each Quilt Size

Cut lengthwise borders first from ivory fabric. Cut remaining light yardage into 18" lengths from which to cut strips and patches.

See the Special Rotary Cutting Details on pages 86–87.

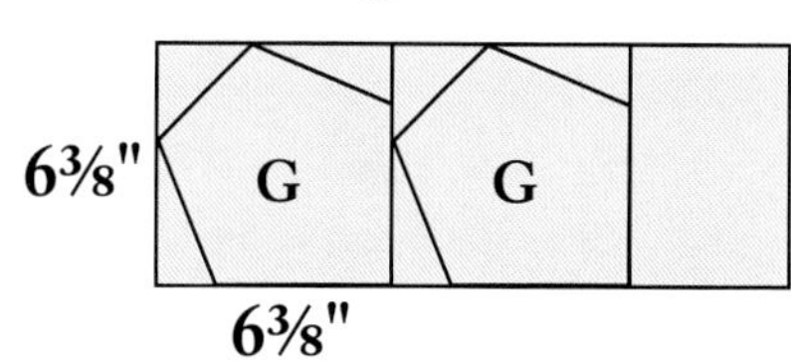

36 Queen/24 Twin

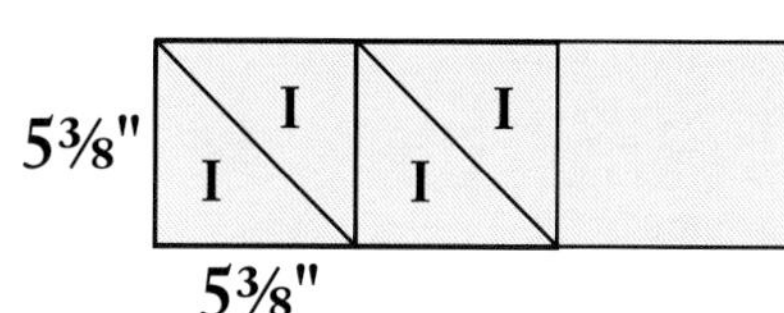

1 Queen/1 Twin

32 Queen/26 Twin

12 Queen/8 Twin

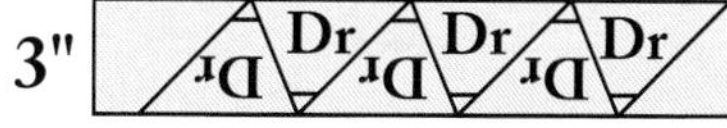

12 Queen/8 Twin

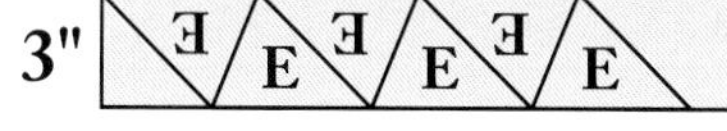

24 Queen/16 Twin

22 Queen/15 Twin

Tan 18" Strip & Patch Cutting

Cut lengthwise borders first from tan fabric. Cut remaining tan yardage into 18" lengths from which to cut strips and patches.

38 Queen/32 Twin

44 Queen/29 Twin

Dark 18" Strip & Patch Cutting

23 Queen/15 Twin

2½" — A A A A

76 Queen/58 Twin

1⅞" — F F F F F F F F F F

29 Queen/20 Twin

Special Rotary Cutting Details

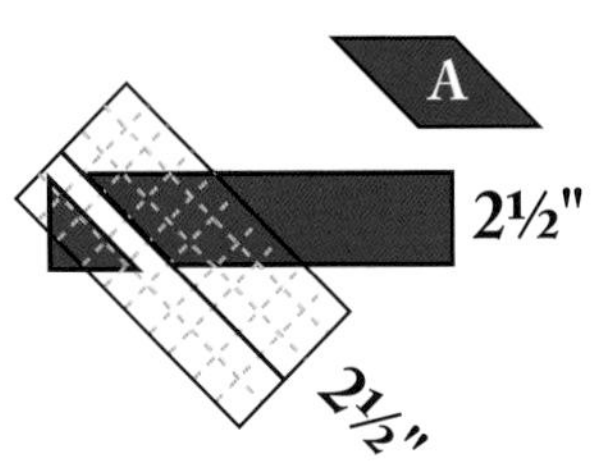

A: Cut a strip 2½" wide. Cut off the end of the strip at a 45-degree angle as shown. Align the 2½" ruling of a rotary cutting ruler with the angled end of the strip. Cut along the ruler's edge to complete an A diamond. Check your diamond against the A template in the book. Cut A diamonds down the length of the strip.

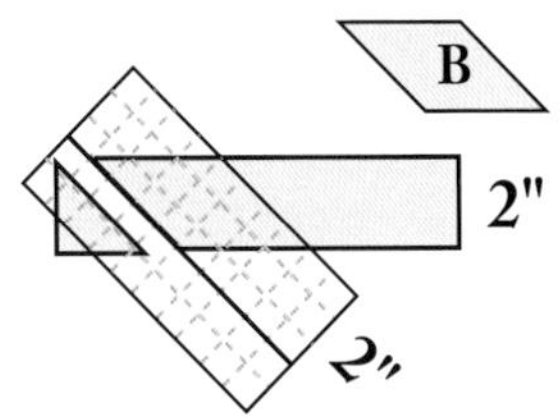

B: Cut a strip 2" wide. Cut off the end of the strip at a 45-degree angle as shown. Align the 2" ruling of a rotary cutting ruler with the angled end of the strip. Cut along the ruler's edge to complete a B diamond. Check your diamond against the B template in the book. Cut B diamonds down the length of the strip.

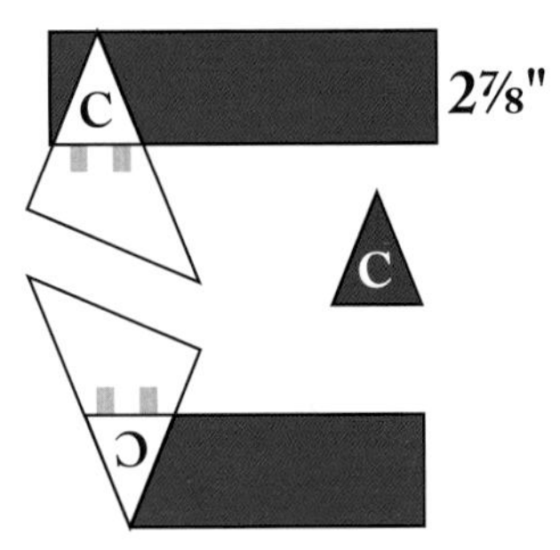

C: Cut a strip 2⅞" wide. Trace or download the template for C. Download is available at http://www.judymartin.com/templates.cfm. Be sure not to scale printing to a size other than 100%. Check template against the one in the book. Cut out and tape the C template to a triangular rotary cutting ruler that matches the 45-degree angle of the template. The 2 long sides should be on the ruler's edge, as shown at left. Align bottom of template with fabric strip as shown. Cut along the ruler's edges to complete C. Check your triangle against the C template in the book. Turn the ruler/template to cut the next C. (It is helpful to use a rotating mat.) Continue cutting C's down the length of the strip.

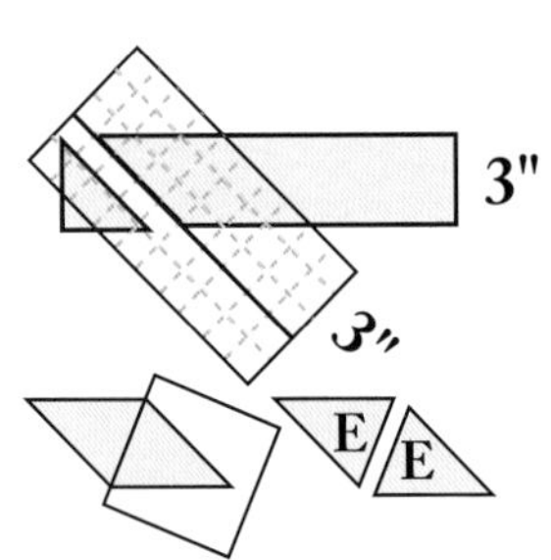

E: Cut a strip 3" wide. Cut off the end of the strip at a 45-degree angle as shown. Align the 3" ruling of a rotary cutting ruler with the angled end of the strip. Cut along the ruler's edge to complete a diamond. Lay a rotary cutting ruler's edge from corner to corner of a diamond as shown at left. Cut the diamond in half along the ruler's edge to make 2 E triangles. Check your triangle against the E template in the book. Cut diamonds down the length of the strip. Cut all diamonds in half.

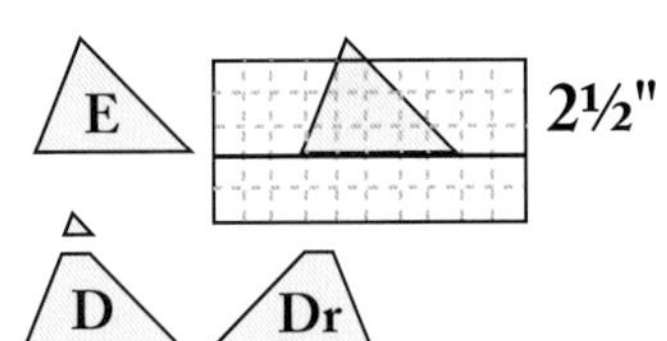

D: Start by cutting additional E patches, one for each D needed. Lay a rotary cutting ruler over one of these E's, aligning the 2½" ruling with the bottom of the patch, as shown at left. Trim off the tip of the E along the edge of the ruler to complete a D. Check your patch against the D template in the book before continuing with more D's.

Dr: Start by cutting additional E patches, one for each Dr needed. These should be cut from face-down fabric. Leaving the fabric face down, trim off the tip as you did for D to complete a Dr.

Special Rotary Cutting Details

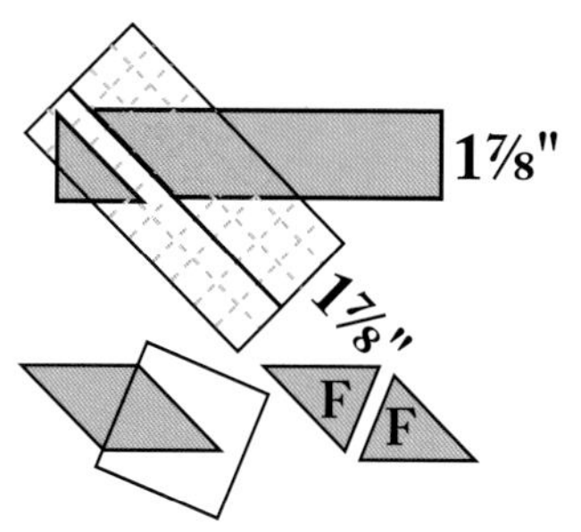

F: Cut a strip 1⅞" wide. Cut off the end of the strip at a 45-degree angle as shown. Align the 1⅞" ruling of a rotary cutting ruler with the angled end of the strip. Cut along the ruler's edge to complete a diamond. Lay a rotary cutting ruler's edge from corner to corner of a diamond as shown at left. Cut the diamond in half along the ruler's edge to make 2 F triangles. Check your triangle against the F template in the book. Cut diamonds down the length of the strip. Cut all diamonds in half.

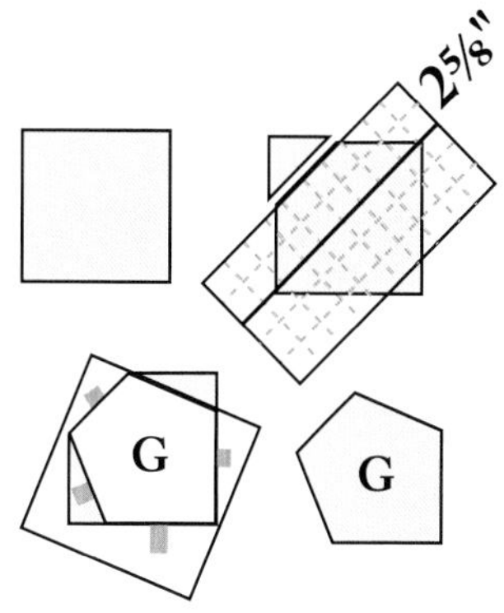

G: Cut a strip 6⅜" wide. Cut the strip into 6⅜" squares. Align the 2⅝" ruling of a rotary cutting ruler with 2 opposite corners of a square patch. Trim off a waste triangle along the ruler's edge, as shown at left. Trace or download the template for G. Template download is available at http://www.judymartin.com/templates.cfm. Be sure not to scale printing to a size other than 100%. Check template against the one in the book. Cut out and tape the G template to a rotary cutting ruler so that the indicated side is on the ruler's edge, as shown at left. Align square corner of template with fabric patch as shown. Cut along the ruler's edge. Turn fabric patch face down and trim a similar triangle from the other side to complete G. Check your patch against the G template in the book.

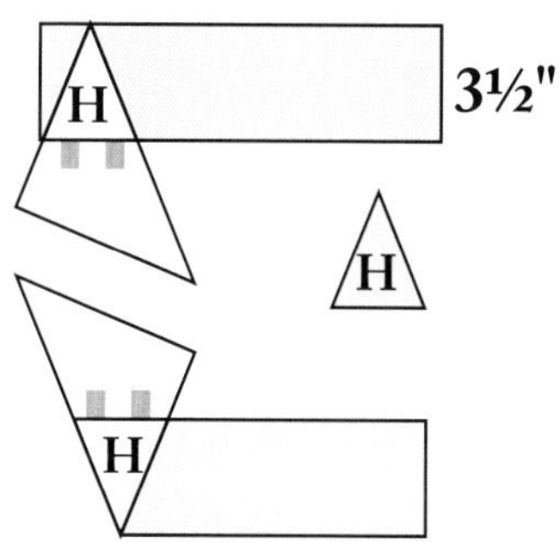

H: Cut a strip 3½" wide. Trace or download the template for H. Download is available at http://www.judymartin.com/templates.cfm. Be sure not to scale printing to a size other than 100%. Check template against the one in the book. Cut out and tape the template to a triangular rotary cutting ruler that matches the 45-degree angle of the H. The 2 long sides should be on the ruler's edge, as shown at left. Align the bottom of the template with the fabric as shown. Cut along the ruler's edge to complete an H patch. Check your triangle against the H template in the book. Turn the template on the strip, as shown, and cut another H. It is helpful to use a revolving mat so it is not awkward to cut the patches. Cut H's down the length of the strip.

Block Construction

See the Block X diagram below. Note that the tan and ivory patches are consistent, but the dark patches are cut from a multitude of colors and prints. The colors can be placed randomly within the dark placement. Start by making a strip of 3 tan F's alternated with 2 dark F's, pressing seams open. Repeat to make 4 of these. Add an ivory E to each, pressing seams toward the E's. Sew 2 of these to a G, pressing seams toward the G. Repeat.

Sew 2 C's to opposite sides of a B, pressing seams open. Repeat to make 3 of these. Sew the 3 in a row, pressing seams to the right. Sew 2 A-D-C segments and 2 A-Dr segments as shown below. Press seams away from D and toward Dr. Join A-D-C to A-Dr, pressing toward Dr. Repeat. Sew these two segments to the ends of the C-B-C segment. Press seams toward Dr's.

Attach G-F-E segments to the block's center segment. Press seams toward G's. Make the listed number of X blocks.

See the Border Y diagram. Join a tan A and a dark A; add an H to each end, as shown, pressing seams toward the bottom H. Make the listed number of Y border blocks.

See the Border Corner Z diagram. Join a tan and a dark A to an H, pressing seams toward the H. Also sew 2 H's to a dark A, pressing seams toward the H's. Join the two parts. Make a second, similar segment, as follows: join a tan and a dark A to an H, pressing seams toward the tan. Also sew 2 H's to a dark A, pressing seams toward the H's. Join the 2 segments. Join the two halves of the block. Add an I, pressing seams toward the I. This completes Border Corner Z. Make 4 of these corners.

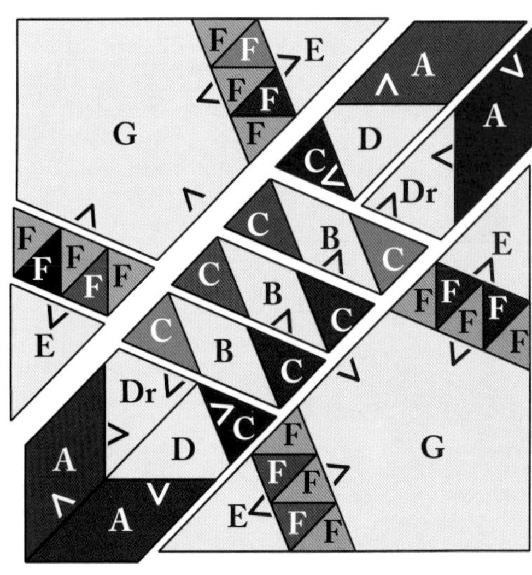

Block X
Make 36 queen
Make 24 twin

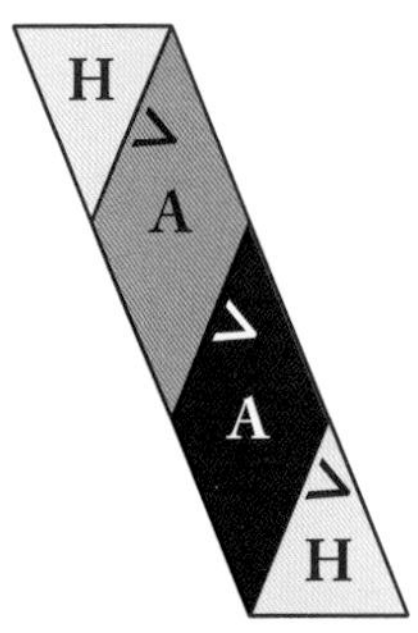

Border Y
Make 144 queen
Make 118 twin

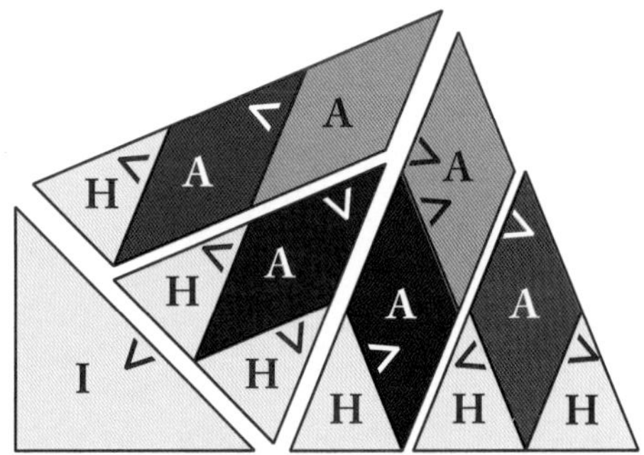

Border Corner Z
Make 4 queen
Make 4 twin

Queen Quilt Assembly

Arrange X blocks as shown below, turning them to form stars at one intersection and 4 G's at the next. Make 6 rows of 6 blocks each. Press seams to the right in odd numbered rows and to the left in even rows. Join rows.

Add the shorter ivory borders to the sides of the quilt. Press seams away from the quilt center. Add the longer ivory borders to the top and bottom of the quilt.

Join 36 Y border units. Add a border corner Z to one end to complete a pieced border. Repeat to make 4 pieced borders. Note the set-in seams indicated by pink dots. Sew one pieced border to each side of the quilt, starting and stopping ¼" in from the raw edge. Stitch the corner miters to complete the set-in seams.

Pin and stitch the shorter tan borders to the sides of the quilt. Press seams toward the tan. Pin and stitch the longer tan borders to the top and bottom of the quilt. Press seams toward tan.

Queen Quilt Diagram

Twin Quilt Assembly

Arrange X blocks as shown below, turning them to form stars at one intersection and 4 G's at the next. Make 6 rows of 4 blocks each. Press seams to the right in odd numbered rows and to the left in even rows. Join rows.

Add longer ivory borders to the sides of the quilt. Press seams away from the quilt center. Add shorter ivory borders to the quilt's top and bottom.

Join 35 Y border units. Add a border corner Z to one end. Repeat. Join 24 Y's. Add a Z to one end. Repeat. Note the set-in seams indicated by pink dots. Sew the longer pieced borders to the sides of the quilt, starting and stopping at the end of the seamline, not at the raw edge. Similarly attach the shorter pieced borders with a set-in seam. Stitch the corner miters to complete the set-in seams.

Pin and stitch the longer tan borders to the sides of the quilt. Press seams toward the tan. Pin and stitch the shorter tan borders to the top and bottom of the quilt. Press seams toward tan.

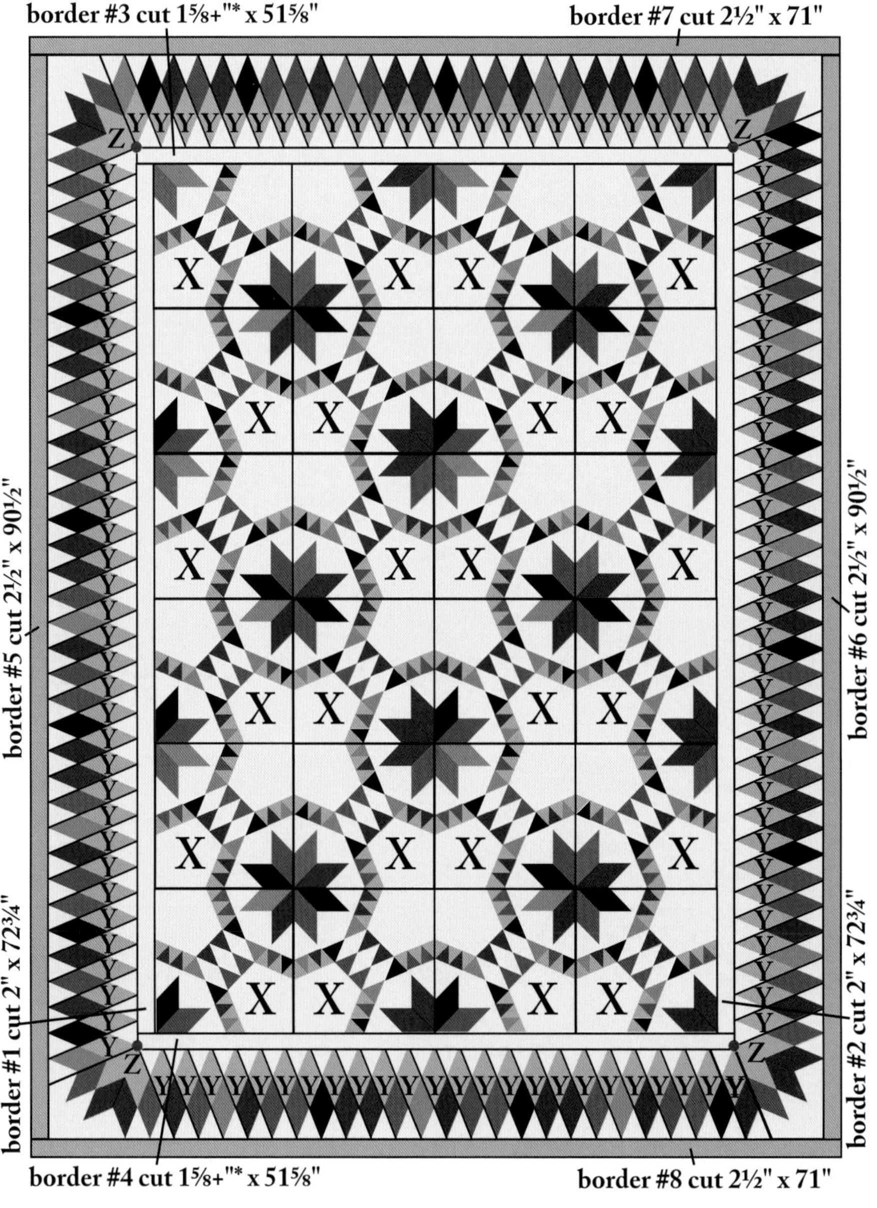

Twin Quilt Diagram

**1⅝+" is halfway between 1⅝" and 1¾" rulings.*

Quilting

Quilt in the ditch around diamond patches, along plain borders, and around rings of triangles. In the borders, quilt diagonal lines extending from the border diamonds. Quilt a feather or floral motif in the large 4-G and 2-G ivory areas. Quilt ¼" inside the seamlines of the stars.

Other Coloring Ideas

The Boston Beauty can be made in monochromatic tones, as in the blue example, below. It is also well suited to 1930s reproduction pastels (far below). Pink and black (or chocolate brown) or red, white, and blue also make striking Boston Beauty quilts, as shown on the right below.

Summer Holiday

Summer Holiday evokes the Fourth of July, whether you see bunting in the border scallops or fireworks in the star-spangled circles. It takes some time to make the many stars, but the cutting and sewing are basic.

This is an original quilt designed by Judy Martin, pieced by Doris Hareland, and quilted by Jenise Antony of Countryside Quilting.

It makes an excellent quilt for a military veteran. Gather signatures for the centers of the star circles, if desired. A strip swap is another social possibility.

Yardage & Cutting Specifications

Queen Size

Quilt Size: 98" x 98"
Block W Size: 21" between seamlines
Requires: 9 W, 24 X, 12 Y, 16 Z

Yardage
White Background 8¼ yards
144 B
288 C
180 D
9 E
36 F
36 G
24 H
16 I
36 J
4 K

Red Prints 9 fat quarters
60 A
480 B

Dark Blue Prints 10 fat quarters
64 A
512 B

Backing 9⅜ yards
3 panels 36" x 106"

Binding ¾ yard
19 strips 2" x 27"

Batting
106" x 106"

Twin Size

Quilt Size: 73½" x 98"
Block W Size: 21" between seamlines
Requires: 6 W, 17 X, 10 Y, 14 Z

Yardage
White Background 6⅛ yards
96 B
216 C
144 D
6 E
24 F
24 G
17 H
14 I
30 J
4 K

Red Prints 7 fat quarters
44 A
352 B

Dark Blue Prints 8 fat quarters
46 A
368 B

Backing 7¼ yards
3 panels 36" x 81½"

Binding ¾ yard
16 strips 2" x 27"

Batting
81½" x 106"

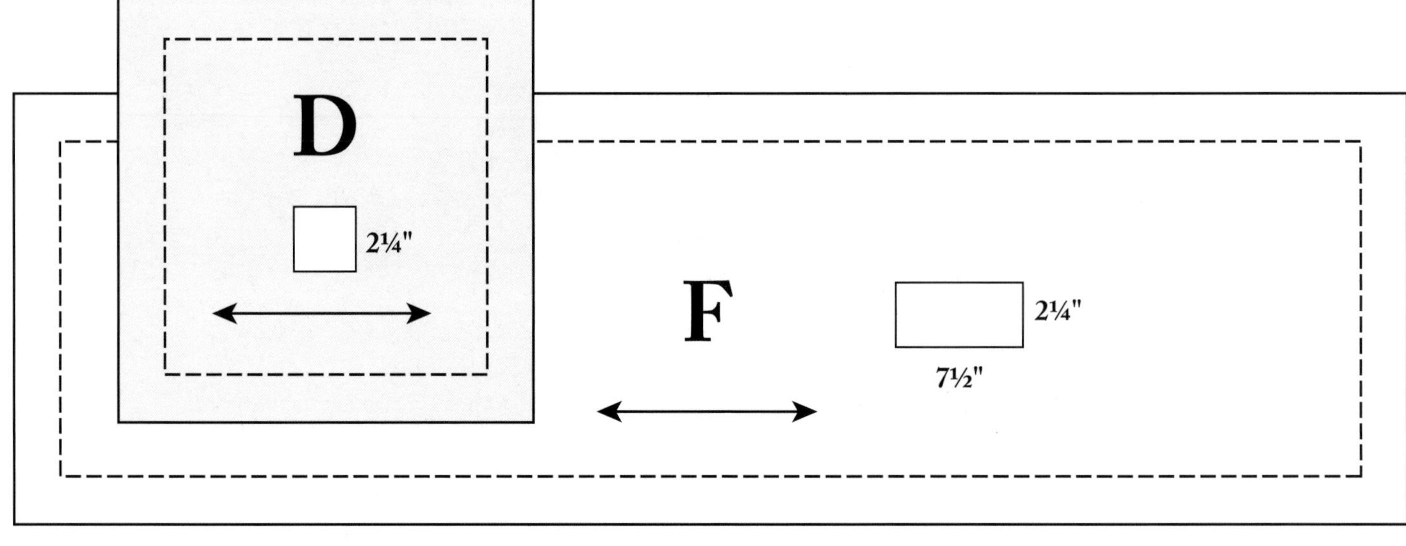

Optional Templates

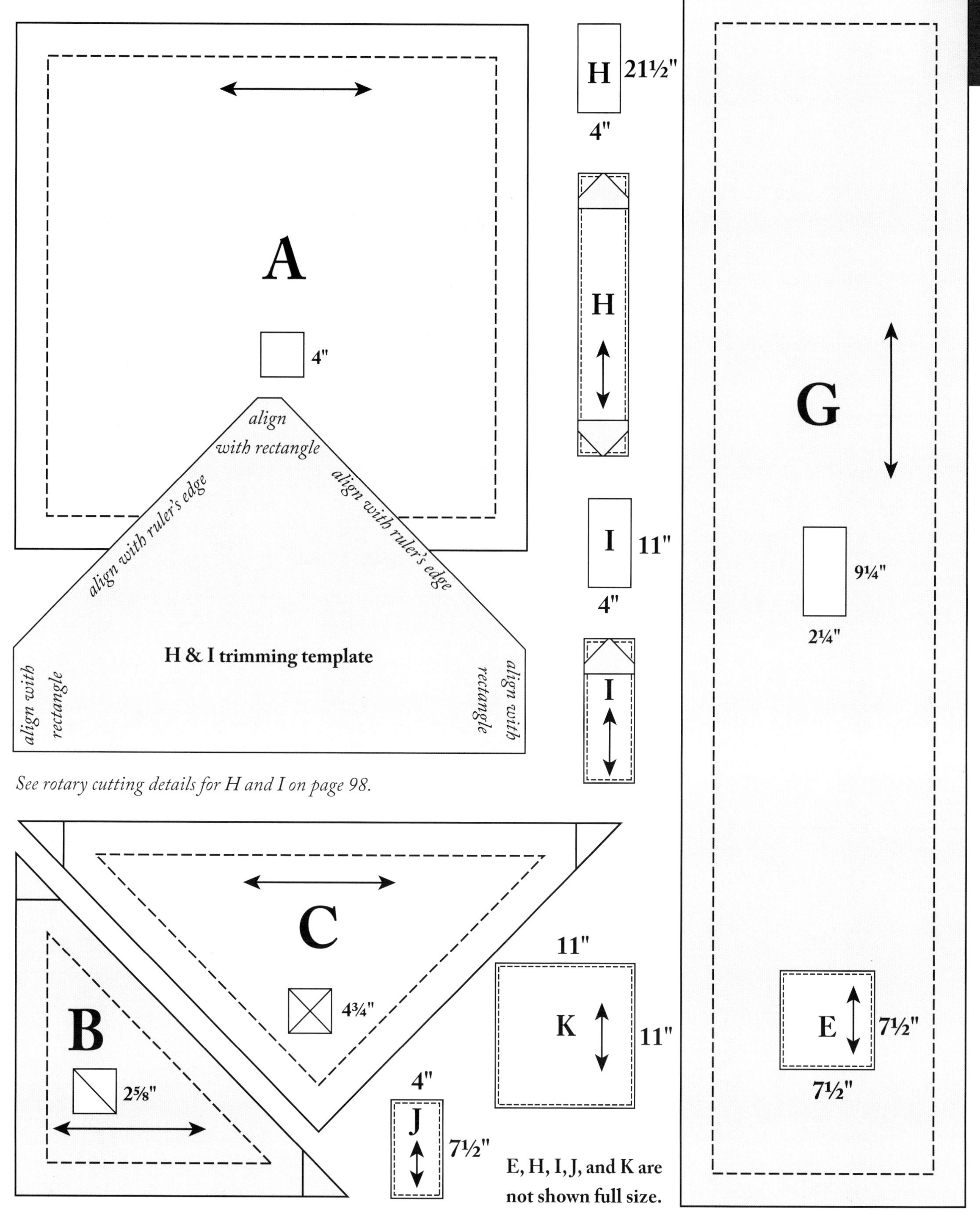

See rotary cutting details for H and I on page 98.

E, H, I, J, and K are not shown full size.

Strip Cutting Layouts

It is not necessary to cut all of the patches before you start sewing. In fact, I recommend sewing a single sample block before proceeding with the rest of the cutting. The sample block will allow you to adjust your seam allowances until the W block is precisely 21½" from raw edge to raw edge.

I get bored with the cutting, so I cut enough to make a few blocks at a time and alternate cutting with sewing.

Begin by cutting off 4 (queen)/3 (twin) lengths of 23" from the white print fabric. From these, cut the K, H, and I patches. From the remainder of the white, cut 18" lengths from which to cut E, C, J, B, G, F, and D.

For the red and blue, do not cut all of the strips of a single type from one fabric. Instead, cut a variety of strips and patch letters from each fat quarter.

See page 98 for details for cutting H and I.

White Print 18" Strip & Patch Cutting

Number of Strips Needed for Each Quilt Size

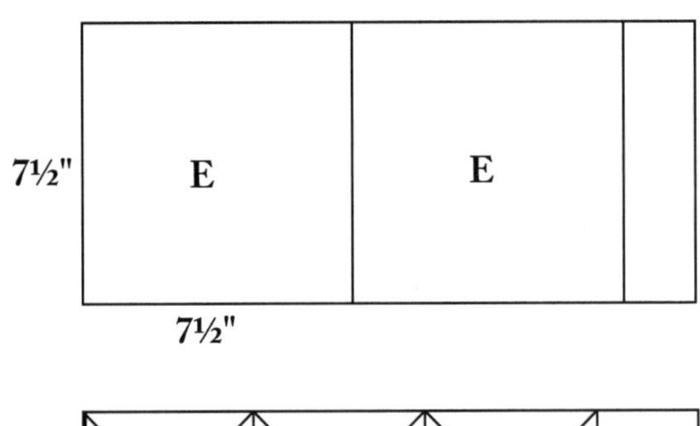

4" | J | J
7½"
18 Queen/15 Twin

2⅝" | B B | B B | B B | B B | B B | B B
2⅝"
12 Queen/8 Twin

2¼" | G | F
9¼" 7½"
36 Queen/24 Twin

2¼" | D | D | D | D | D | D | D
2¼"
26 Queen/21 Twin

For the queen quilt, cut white fabric into four 23" lengths and eleven 18" lengths from which to cut strips and patches.

For the twin quilt, cut white fabric into three 23" lengths and eight 18" lengths from which to cut strips and patches.

White Print 23" Strip Cutting

Number of Strips Needed for Each Quilt Size

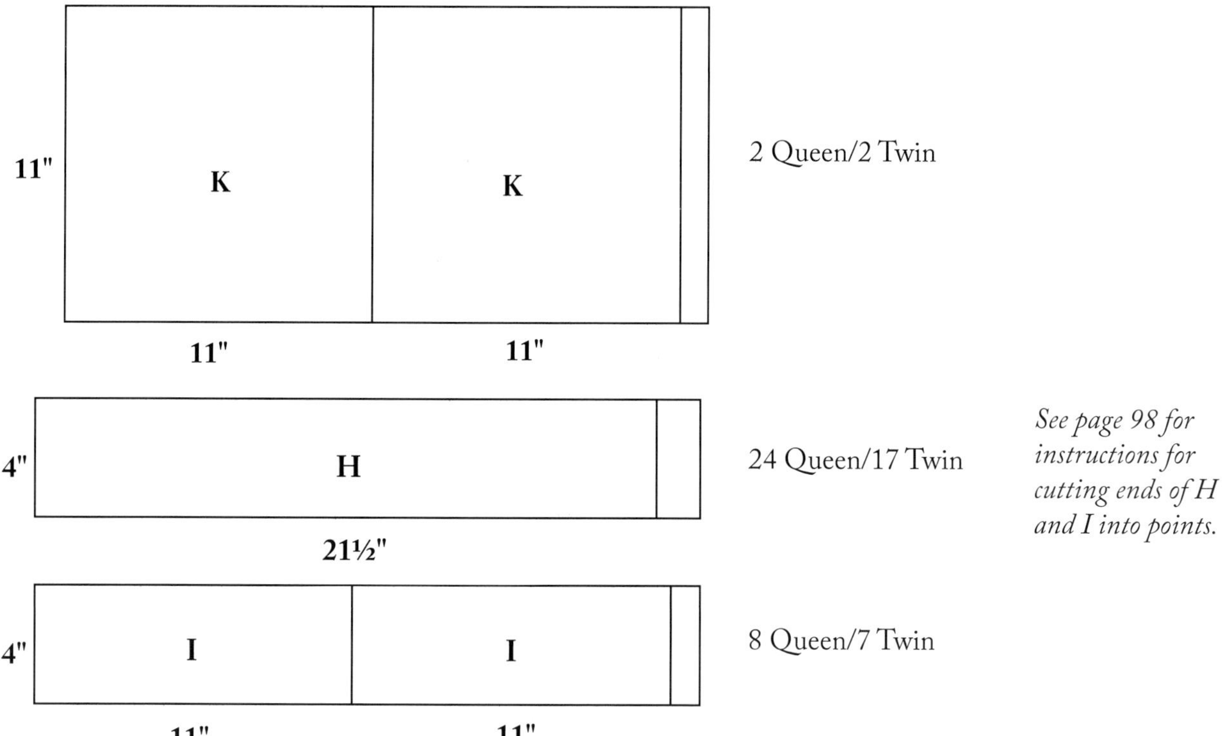

2 Queen/2 Twin

24 Queen/17 Twin

8 Queen/7 Twin

See page 98 for instructions for cutting ends of H and I into points.

Red Print 18" Strip & Patch Cutting

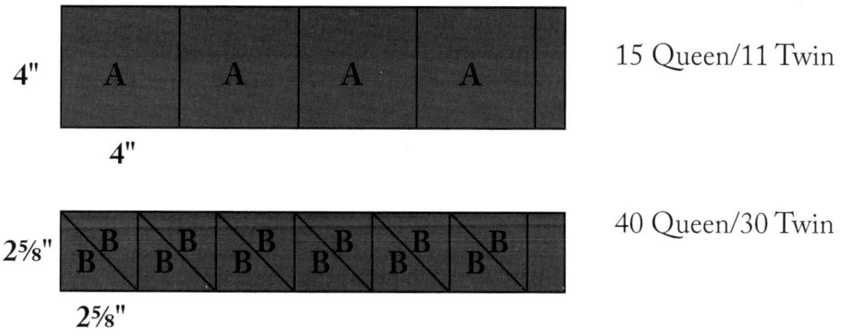

15 Queen/11 Twin

40 Queen/30 Twin

Dark Blue Print 18" Strip & Patch Cutting

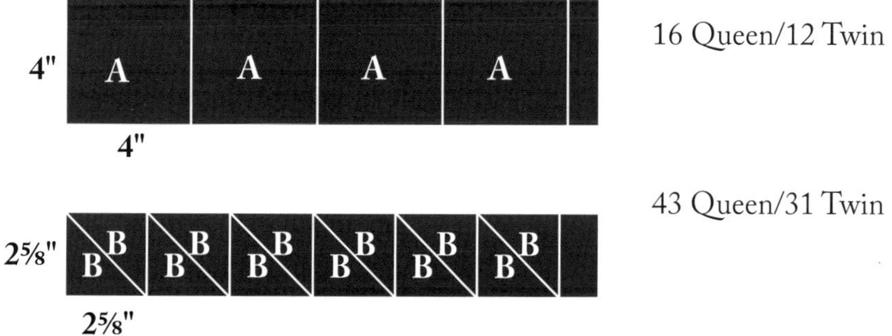

16 Queen/12 Twin

43 Queen/31 Twin

Special Rotary Cutting Details

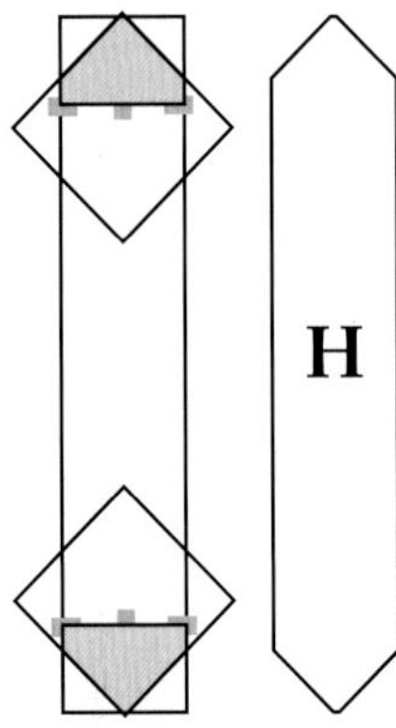

H: Trace or download the trimming template for H & I. Download is available at http://www.judymartin.com/templates.cfm. Be sure not to scale printing to a size other than 100%. Check template against the one in the book. Cut out and tape the template to a rotary cutting ruler so that the two sides are on the ruler's edge, as shown at left. Cut fabric into 4" x 21½" rectangles. Align template over fabric as shown, with top and sides of template even with end of rectangle. Cut along the ruler's edges to remove 2 waste triangles. Realign ruler to cut off 2 more waste triangles at the opposite end of the strip to complete the prism.

Note: If you use my Shapemaker 45 tool, you won't need a template to cut H and I. Simply follow the instructions in the booklet that comes with the tool.

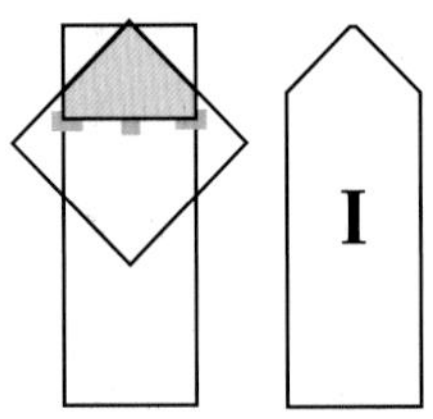

I: Use the same trimming template taped to a ruler that you used for H, above. Cut fabric into 4" x 11" rectangles. Align template over fabric as shown, with top and sides of template even with end of rectangle. Cut along the ruler's edges to remove 2 waste triangles. This completes the half prism.

Block & Unit Construction

See the block and sash diagrams below and on the next page. Start by making a sample W block. Measure to see if it comes out 21½" from raw edge to raw edge. If not, adjust seam allowances and make another sample.

Each star is made from a variety of prints in either red or blue. Start by sewing a blue B to a white B along the long edge; press seam toward blue; make 8 per W block. Similarly join red and blue B's to make 8 per W block, pressing seam toward red; and join red and white B's to make 8 per W block, pressing seam toward white. Next, make Flying Geese units as follows: sew 2 blue B's to a white C; press seams away from white; make 8 per W block and 4 per Y block. Similarly sew 2 red B's to a white C; press seams away from white; make 8 per W and 8 per Y block.

Join these parts plus 4 D, 1 E, 4 F, 4 G, 4 red A, and 4 blue A, as shown in the block W diagram. Make the listed number of W blocks.

Make X sashes by sewing a blue B to each of the 4 corners of the H patch. Make the listed number.

Use the remaining red and blue Flying Geese units, along with white D and J patches to make Y blocks as shown at right. Make the listed number.

Make the border sash Z by sewing 2 B triangles to the corners of the I patch. Make the listed quantity of border sashes.

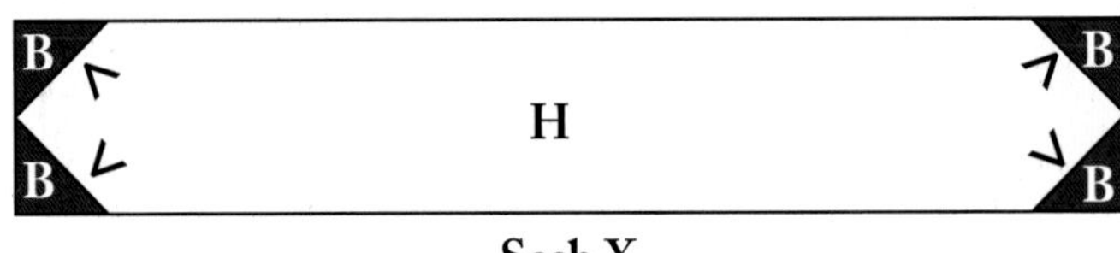

Sash X
Make 24 queen
Make 17 twin

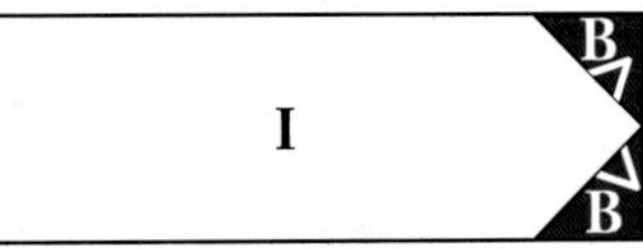

Border Sash Z
Make 16 queen
Make 14 twin

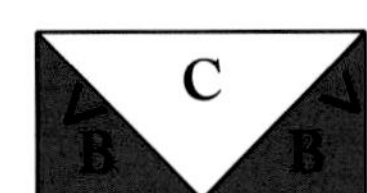

Block W Parts
Make 8 of each per W Block

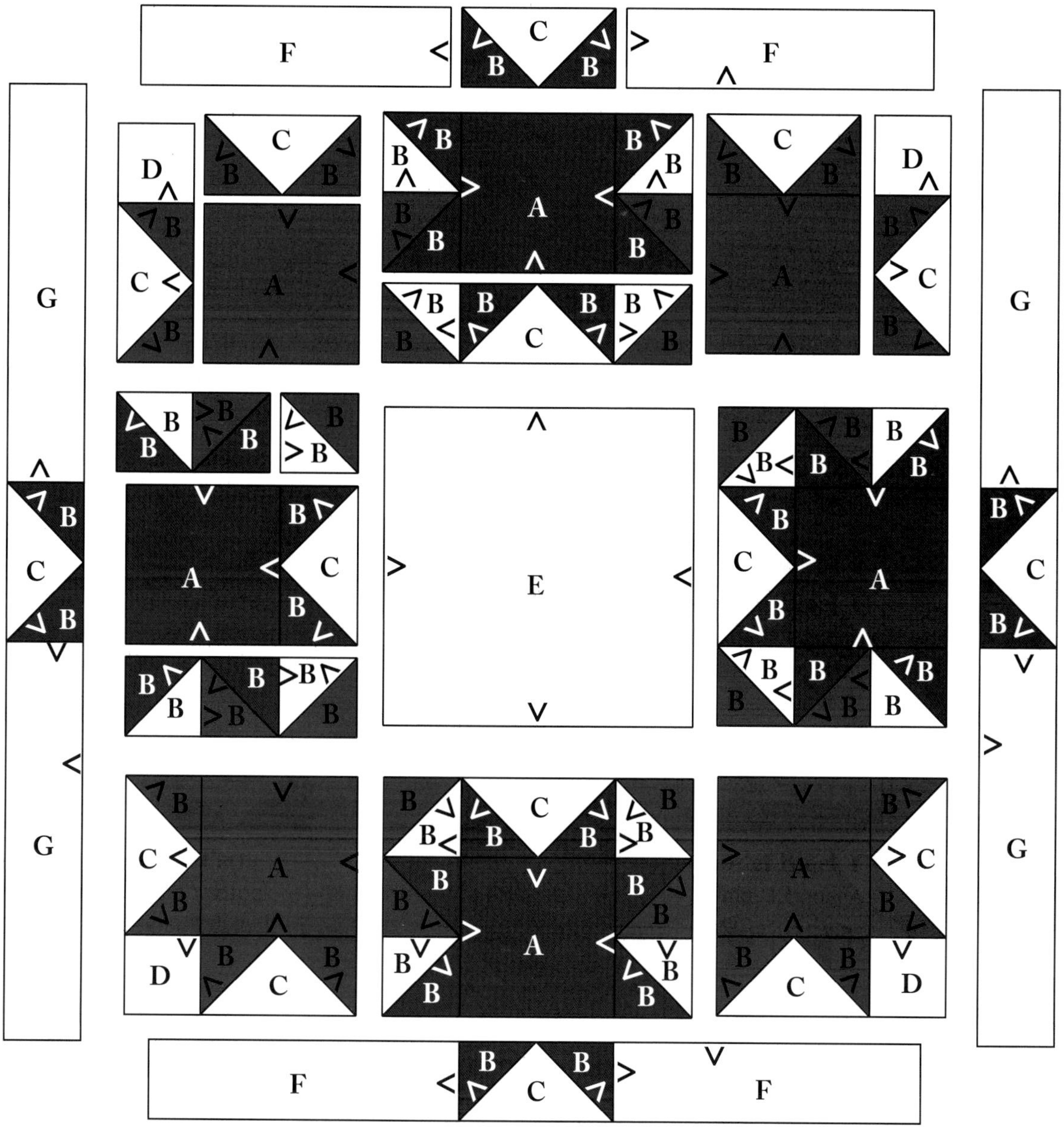

Block W
Make 9 queen
Make 6 twin

Border Block Y Parts
Red: make 8 per Y Block
Blue: make 4 per Y Block

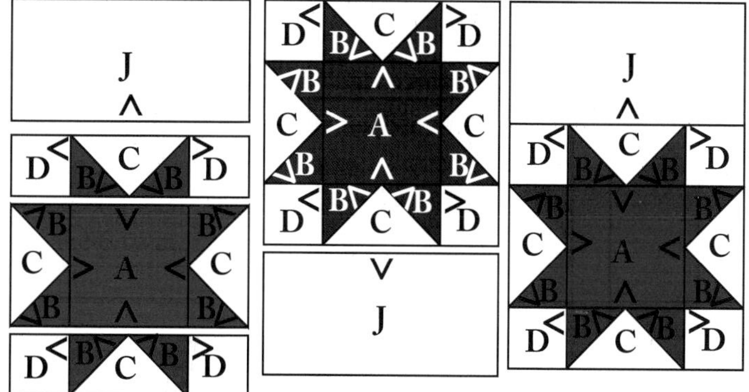

Border Block Y
Make 12 queen
Make 10 twin

Queen Quilt Assembly

Lay out W, X, Y, and Z blocks and sashes plus blue A squares and white K squares according to the quilt diagram below. For the top and bottom rows, join 4 Z alternately with 3 Y, keeping border blocks and sashes turned as shown. Add a K to each end. Press seams toward Z's.

For sash rows, join 4 blue A's alternately with 3 X's; add a Z to each end, keeping Z's turned as shown. Press seams toward blue A's. Make 4 sash rows like this.

For block rows, join four X's alternately with 3 W's. Add a Y to each end, turned as shown. Press seams toward X sashes. Make 3 block rows.

Join the 4 sash rows alternately with 3 block rows. The seams will not oppose at the joints, but this pressing distributes the bulk better. You can pin the joints with the seams opposed, then pin again, flipping seam allowances back the way they should be before stitching. Add top and bottom rows to complete the quilt top.

Queen Quilt Diagram

Twin Quilt Assembly

Lay out W, X, Y, and Z blocks and sashes plus blue A squares and white K squares according to the quilt diagram below. For the top and bottom rows, join 3 Z alternately with 2 Y, keeping border blocks and sashes turned as shown. Add a K to each end. Press seams toward Z's.

For sash rows, join 3 blue A's alternately with 2 X's; add a Z to each end, keeping Z's turned as shown. Press seams toward blue A's. Make 4 sash rows like this.

For block rows, join 3 X's alternately with 2 W's. Add a Y to each end, turned as shown. Press seams toward X sashes. Make 3 block rows.

Join the 4 sash rows alternately with 3 block rows. The seams will not oppose at the joints, but this pressing distributes the bulk better. You can pin the joints with the seams opposed for alignment, then pin again, flipping one seam allowance back the way it should be before stitching. Add top and bottom rows to complete the quilt top.

Twin Quilt Diagram

Quilting

See the quilting in the photograph below. Red and blue triangles are quilted with arcs along the seam lines. A feathered square motif is quilted in the corner K squares. A smaller version of this is quilted in W block centers and across interior sashes, as shown. A related motif fills the outer sashes and border sashes. Half feathers fill the F and G patches around the edges of the quilt.

Another option would be to quilt in the ditch around red and blue patches and quilt freehand feathers in the white areas, ignoring the seamlines joining white to white.

Other Coloring Ideas

You need not make this with a patriotic color scheme. Try three colors plus cream; monochromatic pink tones; lavender and lilac on a medium purple ground; or teal, aqua and sage.

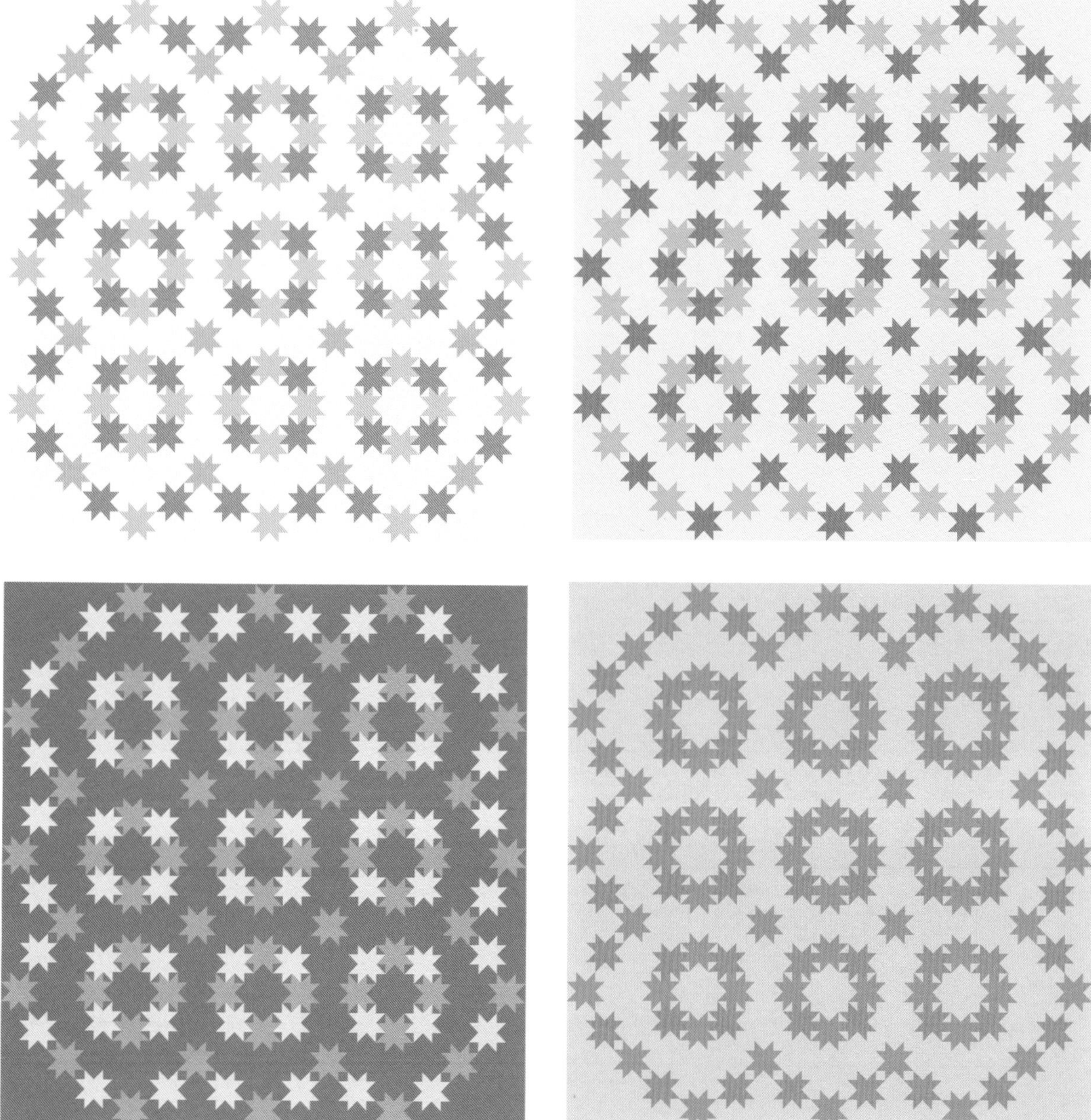

Asian Pork Balls

Makes 12 Servings

These meatballs are slightly sweet and a little spicy. They are a nice alternative to Iowa ham balls. They make a favorite family meal when served over rice. They also make an excellent potluck dish. Just transfer them to a crock pot to keep them warm for a covered-dish meal.

Meatball Ingredients

2½ lbs. ground pork
1 egg, slightly beaten
⅔ cup bread crumbs
½ teaspoon ground ginger
¼ teaspoon ground black pepper
1½ teaspoons celery salt
½ teaspoon crushed red pepper
⅓ cup orange juice
½ cup brown sugar

Meatball Method

Preheat oven to 350 degrees. In a large bowl, mix all ingredients. Shape into balls 1" to 1½" in diameter. Place close together in an ungreased jelly roll pan or two 9" x 13" pans. Bake 30–35 minutes. The meatballs should be well browned. While meatballs are cooking, make the sauce.

Sauce Ingredients

2 cans (8 oz. each) pineapple chunks in juice
2 tablespoons sherry
½ cup brown sugar
¼ teaspoon black pepper
¼ cup orange juice
¼ teaspoon ground ginger
3 tablespoons soy sauce
1 can (6 oz.) pineapple juice
½ small onion, chopped
2 medium carrots, sliced in thin disks
2 celery stalks, chopped
1 green pepper, cut in strips
2 tablespoons cornstarch
¼ cup water

Sauce Method

Wash the vegetables. Peel the carrots and remove seeds from green pepper. Cut up vegetables. Put all sauce ingredients except the cornstarch and water in a medium saucepan. Include the juice from the pineapple chunks. Boil gently for about 10 minutes or until the vegetables are tender. Scoop the vegetables and pineapple from the sauce and set aside. Mix the cornstarch with the water and stir into the sauce. Cook and stir over medium-low heat until sauce boils and thickens. Add the cooked meatballs, vegetables, and pineapple to the sauce. Serve over rice.

For a potluck, this dish can be kept warm in a crock pot and served as a side dish without rice.

Heartland Star

The Lone Star just got easier! In this new star medallion, you don't have eight points coming together, and you have simpler partial seams instead of set-in seams (Y seams). I cut and pieced Heartland Star in less than a day. The sewing is easy, though the color nuances lend complexity to the design.

This is an original quilt designed and pieced by Judy Martin and quilted by Lana Corcoran.

It is a perfect project for a class. The teacher can help you select just the right values for your fabrics and demonstrate the partial seams. A reveal party would be a fun way to celebrate the completion of your quilt.

Yardage & Cutting Specifications

Wall Size

Quilt Size: 39¼" x 39¼"
W Block Size: 4¼" between seamlines
Requires: 1 W, 8 X*, 4 Y, 8 Z

Yardage
Ivory Print 1⅛ yards
4 G
4 H

#1 Dark Purple ½ yard
8 D
8 Dr (reversed)
8 E
64 F

#2 Purple ½ yard
8 D
8 Dr (reversed)
16 E
32 F

#3 Purple ½ yard
8 D
8 Dr (reversed)
32 F

#4 Purple 1 fat quarter
8 E

#5 Lt. Purple 1 fat quarter
8 D
8 Dr (reversed)

#1 Dk. Green 1 fat quarter
8 C

#2 Green 1 fat quarter
1 A

#3 Lt. Green 1 fat quarter
8 B

Backing 2⅞ yards
2 panels 24⅛" x 47¼"

Binding ½ yard
12 strips 2" x 18"

Batting
48" x 48"

**Note that Block X totals include those used in Block Y.*

Queen Size

Quilt Size: 94¼" x 94¼"
T Block Size: 10¼" between seamlines
Requires: 8 T**, 4 U, 4 V, 1 W, 8 X*, 4 Y, 8 Z

Yardage
Ivory Print 3½ yards
4 H
56 I
64 J
4 K
12 L
8 M
4 N
4 O
4 P

#1 Dark Purple 1 yard
128 C
8 D
8 Dr (reversed)
8 E
64 F

#2 Purple ½ yard
8 D
8 Dr (reversed)
16 E
32 F

#3 Purple 5 yards
2 borders cut 10½" x 94¾"
2 borders cut 10½" x 74¾"
128 B
8 D
8 Dr (reversed)
32 F

#4 Purple 1 fat quarter
8 E

#5 Lt. Purple 1 fat quarter
8 D
8 Dr (reversed)

#1 Dk. Green 1 fat quarter
8 C

#2 Green 2¼ yards
2 borders cut 3½" x 74¾"
2 borders cut 3½" x 68¾"
17 A

continued on next page

**Note that Block X totals include those used in Block Y.*
***T Blocks are used to make U and V Blocks.*

Optional Templates

Queen Size Continued

#3 Lt. Green 1 fat quarter
8 B

Backing 9 yards
3 panels 34½" x 102¼"

Binding ¾ yard
18 strips 2" x 27"

Batting
103" x 103"

See rotary cutting details on pages 109–111.

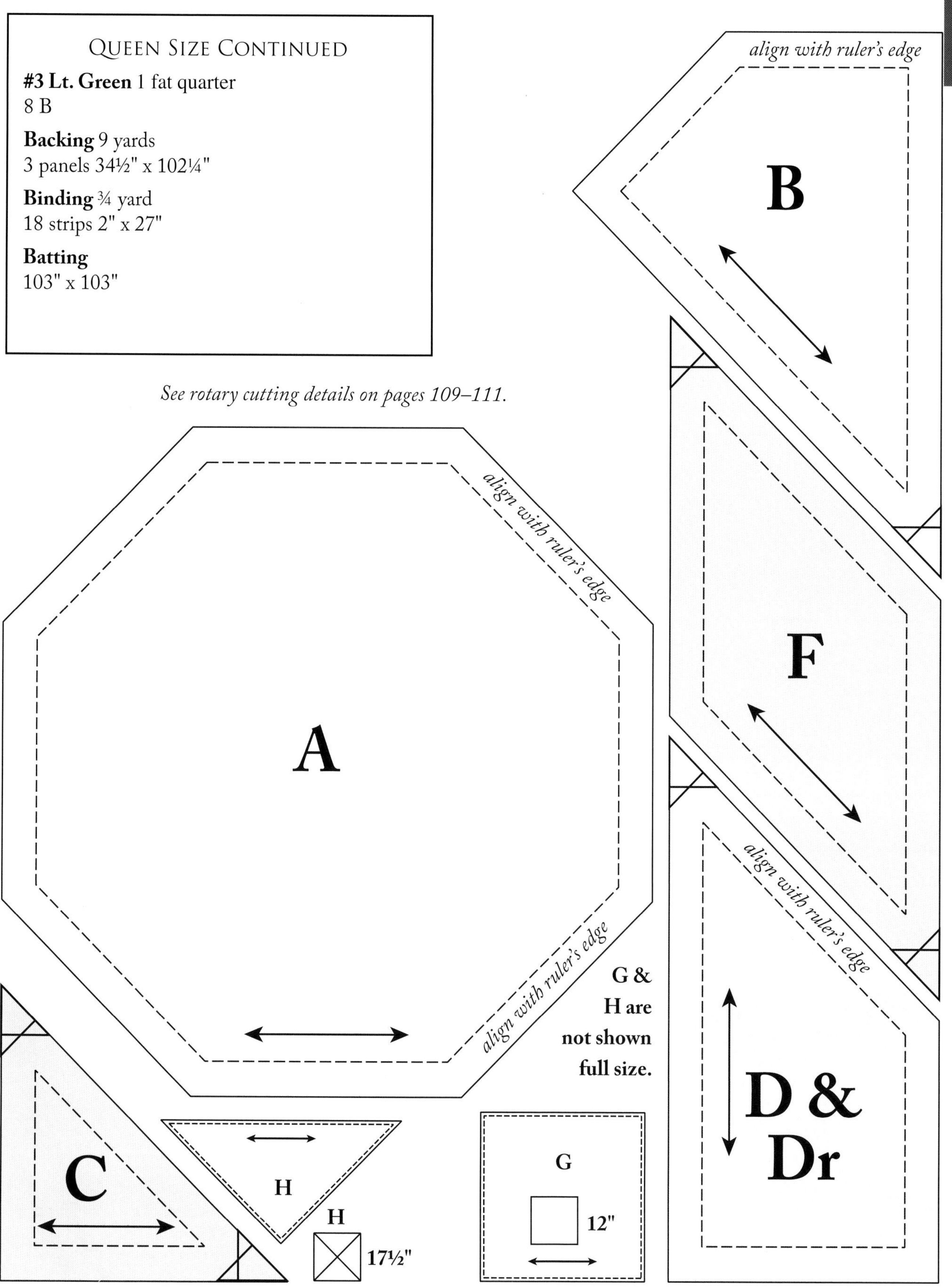

Optional Templates

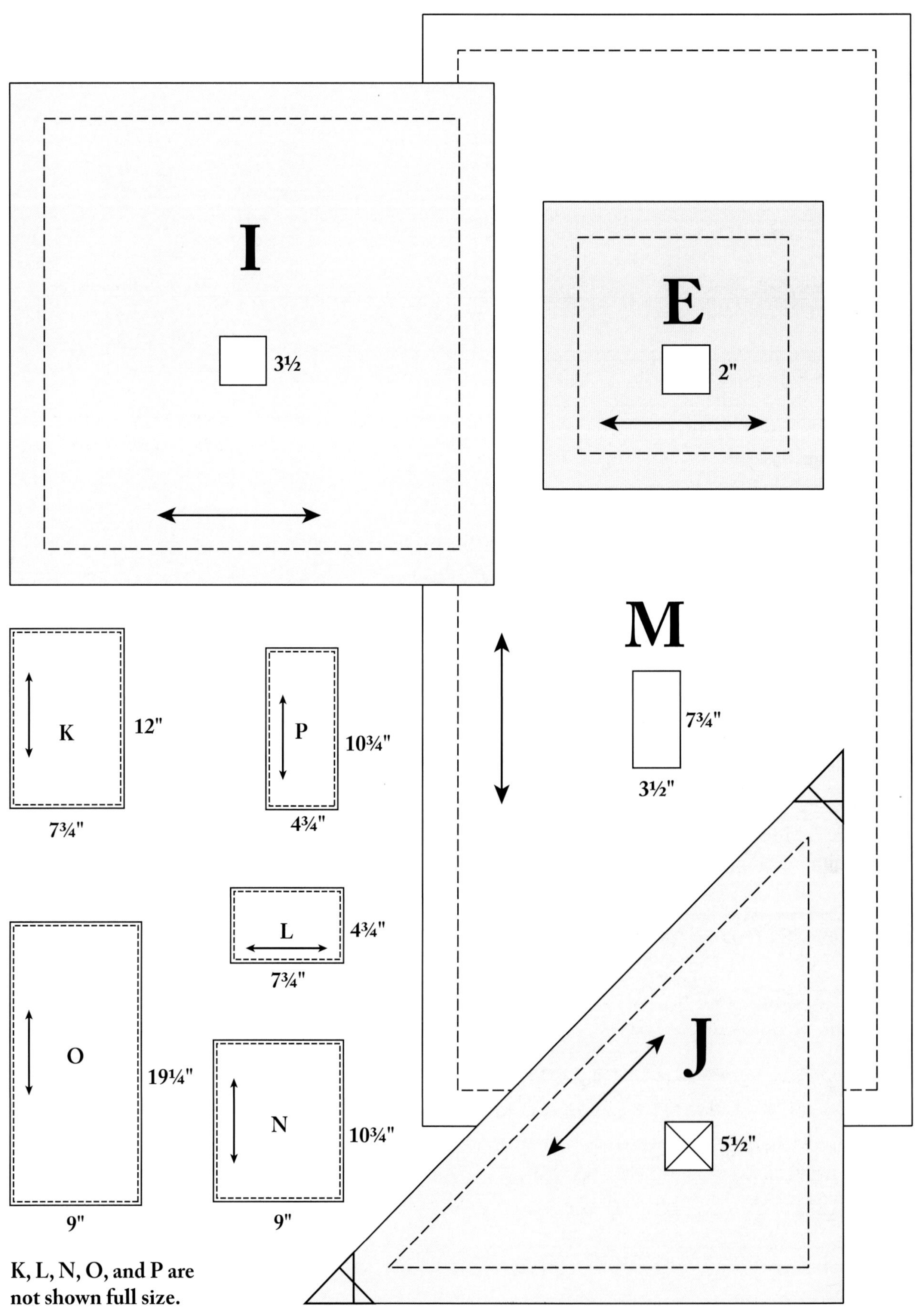

K, L, N, O, and P are not shown full size.

Strip Cutting Layouts

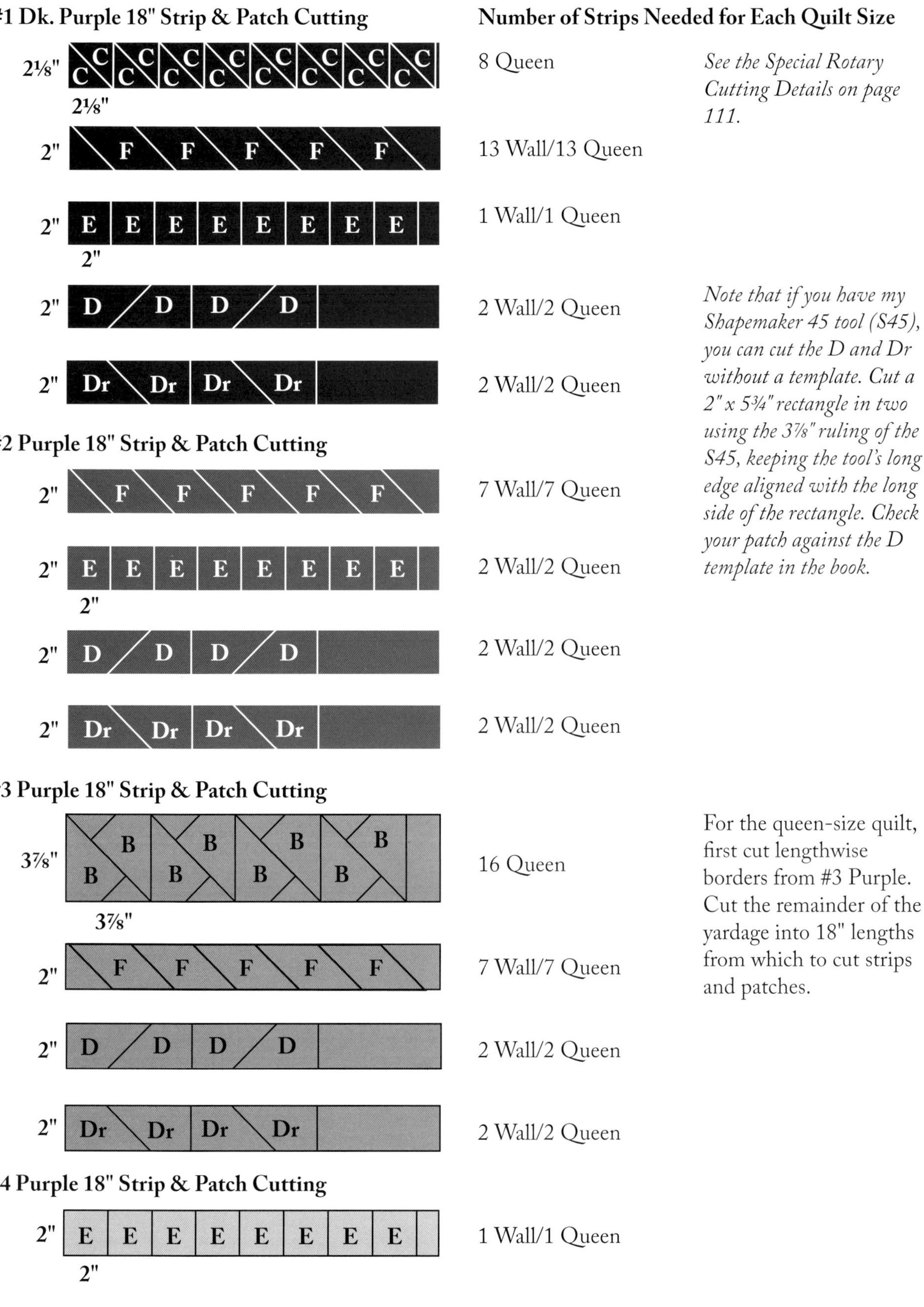

Number of Strips Needed for Each Quilt Size

#1 Dk. Purple 18" Strip & Patch Cutting

8 Queen

See the Special Rotary Cutting Details on page 111.

13 Wall/13 Queen

1 Wall/1 Queen

2 Wall/2 Queen

2 Wall/2 Queen

Note that if you have my Shapemaker 45 tool (S45), you can cut the D and Dr without a template. Cut a 2" x 5¾" rectangle in two using the 3⅞" ruling of the S45, keeping the tool's long edge aligned with the long side of the rectangle. Check your patch against the D template in the book.

#2 Purple 18" Strip & Patch Cutting

7 Wall/7 Queen

2 Wall/2 Queen

2 Wall/2 Queen

2 Wall/2 Queen

#3 Purple 18" Strip & Patch Cutting

16 Queen

For the queen-size quilt, first cut lengthwise borders from #3 Purple. Cut the remainder of the yardage into 18" lengths from which to cut strips and patches.

7 Wall/7 Queen

2 Wall/2 Queen

2 Wall/2 Queen

#4 Purple 18" Strip & Patch Cutting

1 Wall/1 Queen

Strip Cutting Layouts continued

#5 Lt. Purple 18" Strip & Patch Cutting

Number of Strips Needed for Each Quilt Size

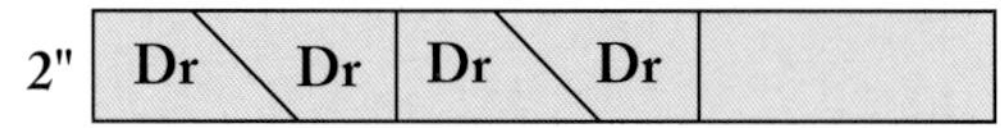

2 Wall/2 Queen

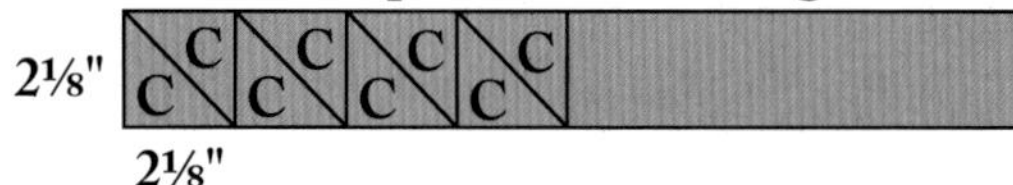

2 Wall/2 Queen

#1 Dk. Green 18" Strip & Patch Cutting

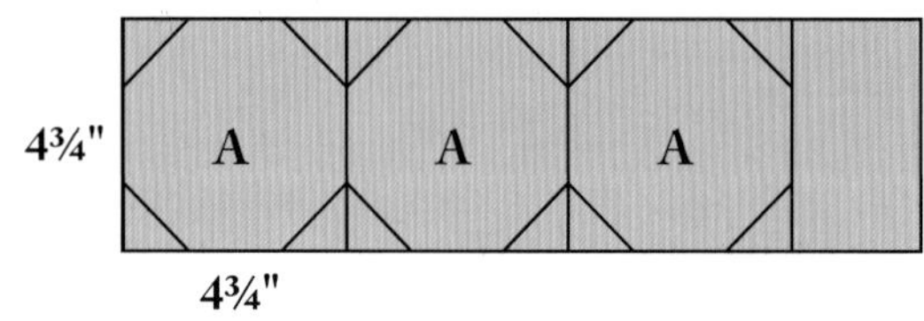

1 Wall/1 Queen

1 Wall/6 Queen

For the queen-size quilt, first cut lengthwise borders from #2 Green. From the remainder of the yardage cut two 18" lengths from which to cut strips and A patches.

#3 Lt. Green 18" Strip & Patch Cutting

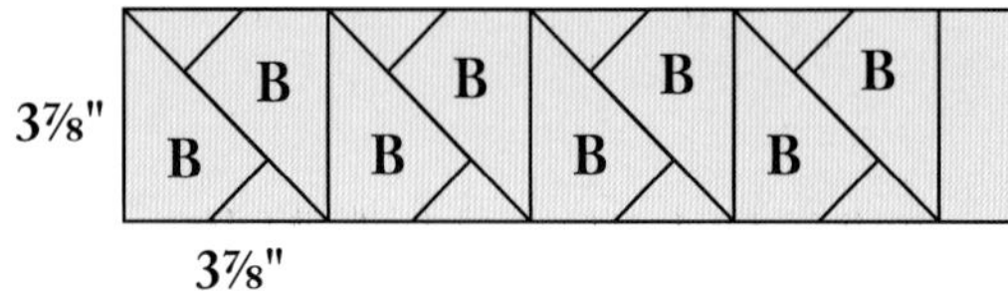

1 Wall/1 Queen

Ivory Yardage Cutting Layout for Wall Quilt

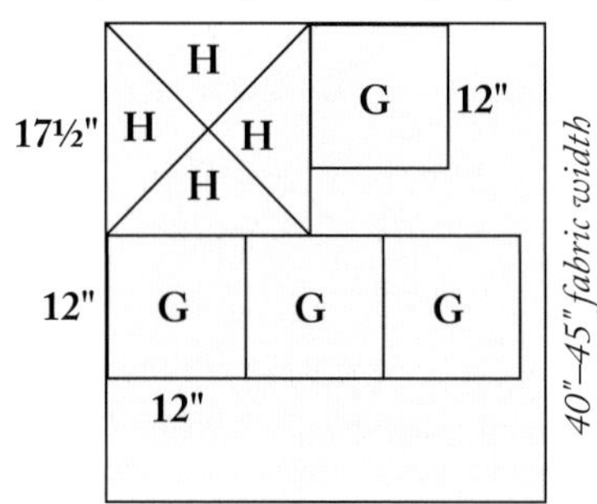

Note that Ivory layouts are not drawn to the same scale as the other fabrics.

Ivory Yardage Cutting Layout for Queen Quilt

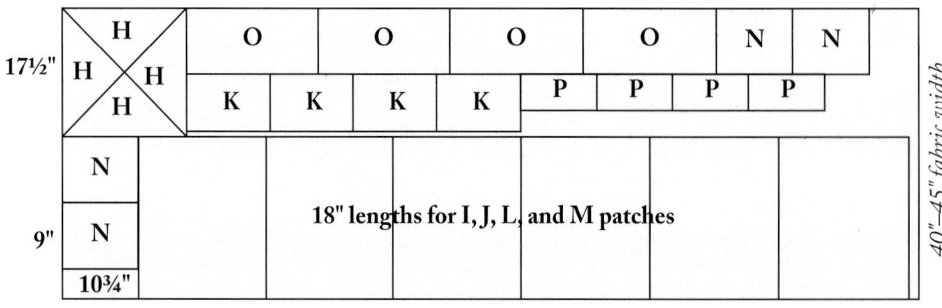

Cut G 12" x 12".
Cut H 17½" x 17½".
Cut K 7¾" x 12".
Cut N 9" x 10¾".
Cut O 9" x 19¼".
Cut P 4¾" x 10¾".

Strip Cutting Layouts continued

Ivory 18" Strip & Patch Cutting

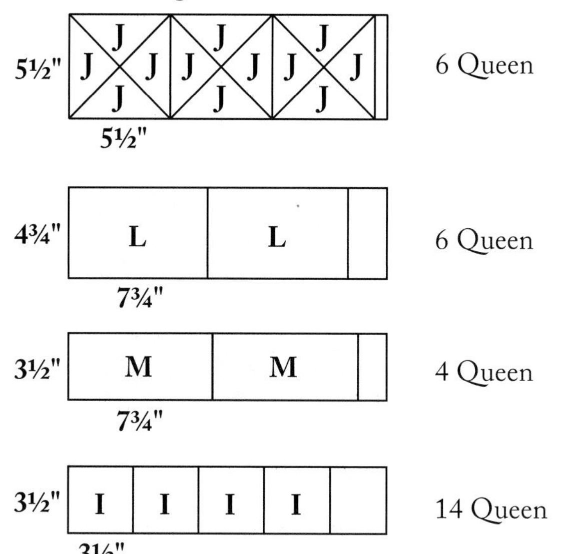

For the queen quilt, first cut large patches from Ivory fabric. Cut the remainder of the yardage into 18" lengths from which to cut strips and patches as shown at left.

Note that Ivory layouts are not drawn to the same scale as the other fabrics.

Special Rotary Cutting Details

Note: Downloads for templates A, B, and D are available at http://www.judymartin.com/templates.cfm. Be sure not to scale printing to a size other than 100%. Check templates against the ones in the book.

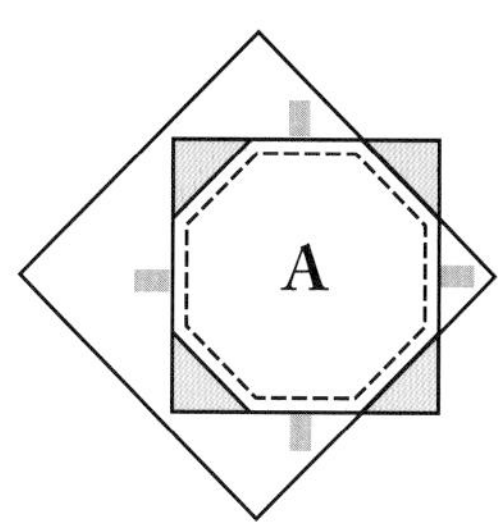

A: Trace or download A template. Cut out and tape the template to a rotary cutting ruler so that two sides are on the ruler's edges, as shown at left. Cut fabric into 4¾" squares. Align template over fabric as shown, with four sides of template even with four sides of square. Cut along the ruler's edges to remove 2 waste triangles. Realign ruler to cut off 2 more waste triangles to complete the octagon.

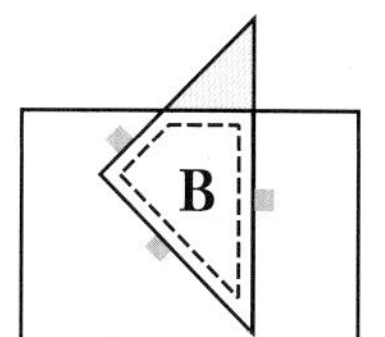

B: Trace or download B template. Cut out and tape template to a rotary cutting ruler so that one short side is at the ruler's edge as shown. Cut 3⅞" fabric squares in half to make triangles. Align template with a triangle as shown. Cut off the part that extends beyond template.

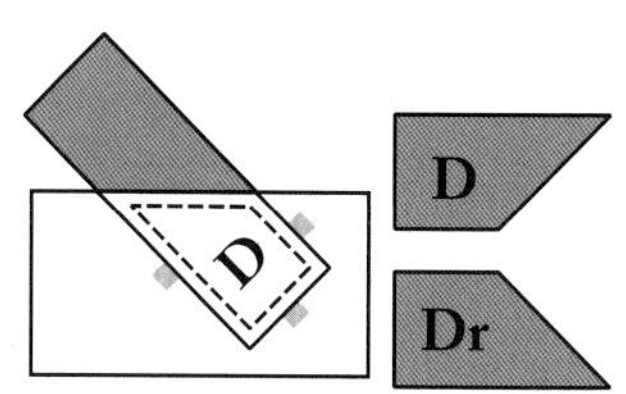

D: Trace or download D template. Cut out and tape the template to a rotary cutting ruler so that the angled side is at the ruler's edge as shown. Cut 2" x 5¾" rectangles of fabric. Align template with one end of a rectangle as shown. Cut along the ruler's edge to make 2 D patches.

Dr: For Dr, use the D template as described above, but place the fabric rectangle face down on the cutting mat.

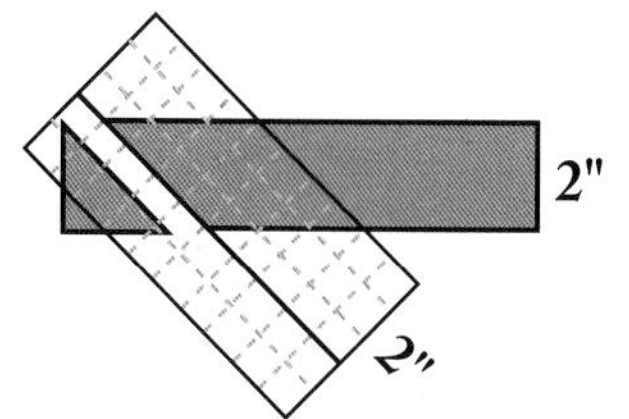

F: Cut a 2" wide fabric strip. Cut off one end at a 45-degree angle, leaving a waste triangle, as shown. Align the 2" ruling of your rotary cutting ruler with the angled end of the strip. Cut along the ruler's edge to make an F diamond. Check your diamond against the F template in the book. Continue down the strip cutting F diamonds in this fashion.

Block Construction

See the W block diagram below. Sew 4 dark green C's to an A octagon. Press seams toward the triangles. (Note: pressing is indicated by arrows.)

See X diagrams below. Patches are shown in the Block X diagram, and the piecing order is shown to the right of that. Sew the patches in numerical order, first sewing same-numbered patches to each other, then sewing them to the block in steps numbered 1–8. Note that the first seam is a partial seam. Stitch only between the pink dots, leaving the right end of the seam unstitched. Later, when you add H and G patches or U blocks, you will stitch these first to the left side of Block X. Then you can complete the partial seam. Make 8 X blocks for either quilt size.

See the Y diagram. To 4 of the X blocks add a light green B. Sew a second light green B to a dark green C. Add one of these to each of the 4 blocks. This completes the 4 Y blocks.

See the Z diagram below, noting pressing arrows particularly. Sew a #1 purple F to a #3 purple F to a #1 purple F to a #2 purple F. Also sew a #3 purple F to a #1 purple F to a #2 purple F to a #1 purple F. Sew this to the right side of the first F segment. Sew a #1 purple F to a #2 purple F to a #1 purple F to a #3 purple F. Attach to the right side of the Z block. Also sew a #2 purple F to a #1 purple F to a #3 purple F to a #1 purple F. Sew to the right side of the Z to complete the block. Make 8 Z blocks.

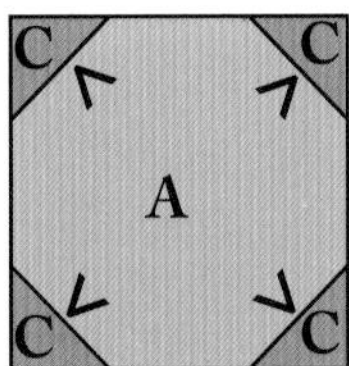

Block W
Make 1 wall
Make 1 queen

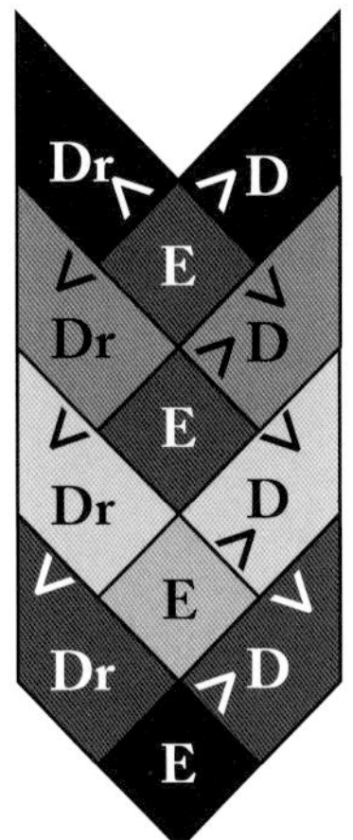

Block X
Make 8 wall*
Make 8 queen*

**Note that Block X totals include those used in Block Y.*

X Piecing Sequence
Join same-number pairs before attaching in numerical order. Sew #1 to #2-2 with a partial seam where indicated between pink dots. This will avoid a set-in seam when attaching background H triangles and G squares or U blocks.

Block Y
Make 4 wall
Make 4 queen

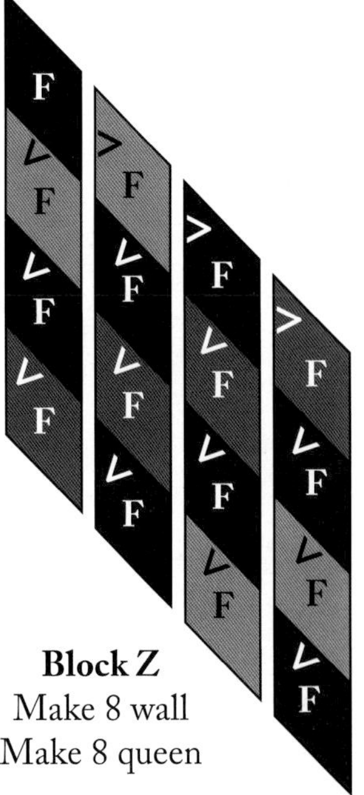

Block Z
Make 8 wall
Make 8 queen

Wall Quilt & Queen Center Assembly

Arrange blocks as shown below. Pin and stitch 2 Z's to each X. Sew 2 Y to a W. Sew a Y between 2 Z-X-Z segments. Repeat. Pin and stitch these to opposite sides of the Y-W-Y. See the Partial Seam Detail diagram at the bottom of the page. Sew the left side of an H to the star, as indicated in green. Then complete the partial seam on the right side of H, as indicated in pink. Attach 4 H's this way. For the wall quilt only, attach 4 G's in a similar fashion. This completes the wall quilt.

Wall Quilt Diagram

Note that the queen-size quilt does not use the G squares.

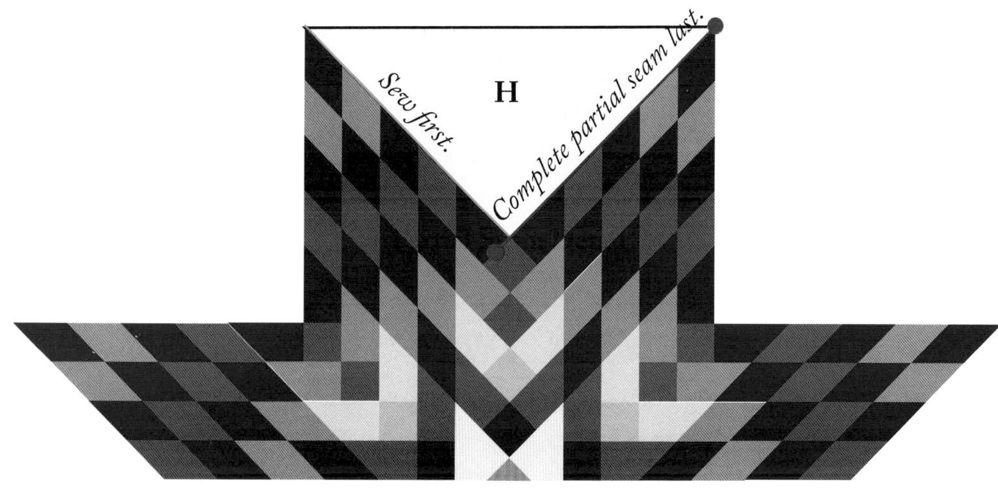

Partial Seam Detail

Additional Queen Block Construction

See the T block diagram below. Sew an ivory J to a #3 purple B; press seams toward the B. Sew a #1 purple C to a #3 purple B. Press seams toward B. Join the two segments; press seam toward B-C. Repeat to make 4 star points segments.

Sew 4 #1 dark purple C triangles to a #2 green A octagon. Press seams toward the triangles. Pin and stitch star point segments to opposite sides of the octagon. Press seams away from the octagon. Sew 2 I squares to each of 2 remaining star point segments. Press seams toward I's. Pin and stitch these to top and bottom of the block. Press seams away from the octagon. Make 8 T's. In a similar fashion, make 8 Unit 1's and 8 more star point segments for the V blocks.

Use T blocks, K, L, N, and O patches, and Unit 1's to make 4 U blocks as shown below. Press seams away from blocks and units where possible.

Use T blocks, I, M, and P patches, and star point segments to make V blocks as shown, again pressing seams away from T's. (Press seam allowances toward M, I, and P patches, as shown.)

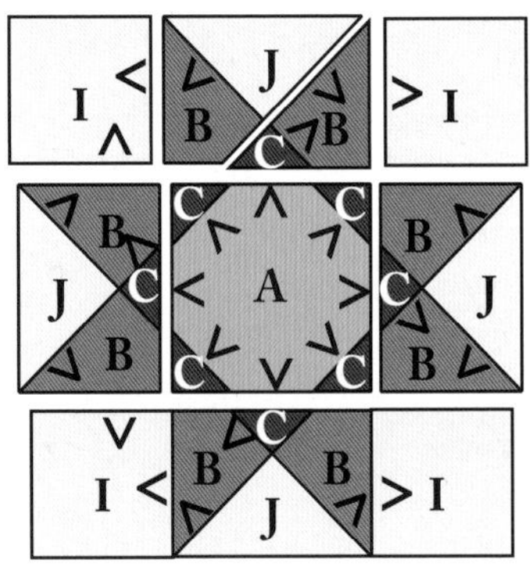

Block T
Make 8 queen

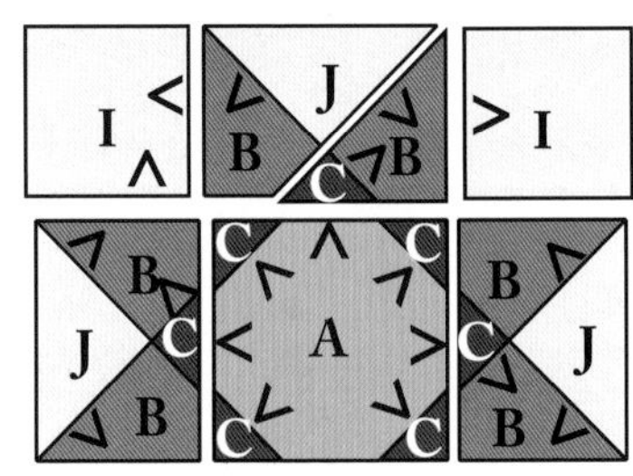

Unit 1
Make 8 queen

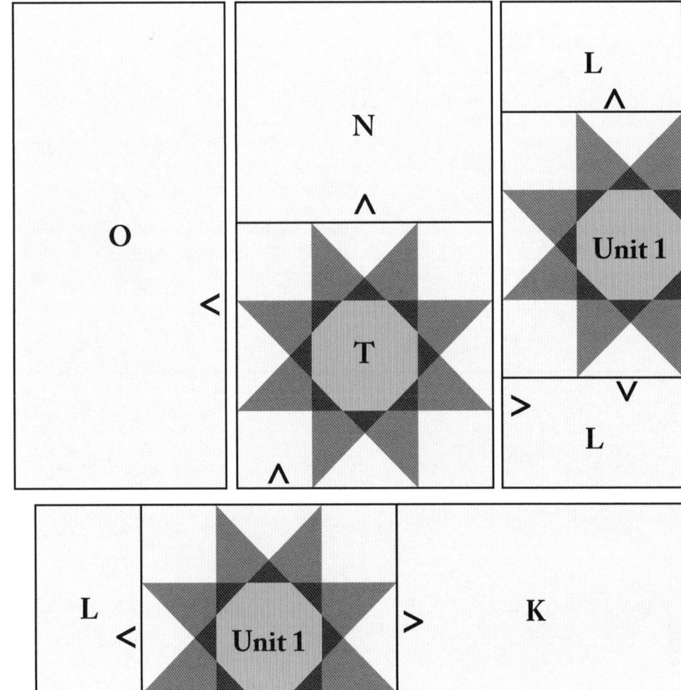

Block U
Make 4 queen

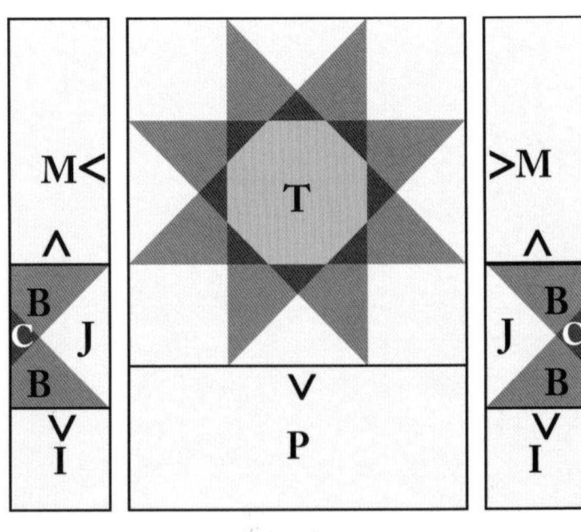

Block V
Make 4 queen

Queen Quilt Assembly

The queen quilt begins with a central star that is like the wall quilt (page 113) minus the 4 G squares in the corners. Sew a V to each H of the central star, keeping V's turned as shown below. Sew a U to each corner, stitching the partial seam last. Keep the U's turned as shown below.

Pin and stitch the shorter green borders to the top and bottom of the quilt. Press seams away from the quilt center. Pin and stitch the longer green borders to the sides of the quilt. Press seams away from the quilt center.

Pin and stitch the shorter purple borders to the top and bottom of the quilt. Press seam allowances away from the quilt center. Pin and stitch the longer purple borders to the sides of the quilt. Press seam allowances away from the quilt center.

Queen Quilt Diagram

Quilting

For either quilt size, quilt in the ditch around all patches, and quilt a small motif in the octagon. For the wall quilt, quilt a large, square motif in G, and quilt half of one of these in each H. For the queen quilt, quilt freehand feathers in the ivory background, ignoring the seamlines between ivory patches. Quilt a simple cable in the green border. Quilt feathers in the wide purple borders.

Other Coloring Ideas

Heartland Star can be colored with a bright, light, or dark background. Stars can be monochromatic or not. Diamonds can blend in some places and contrast in others for totally different looks.

Pear Cobbler Recipe

Makes 8-12 Servings

Serve this treat at your reveal party to celebrate the completion of your quilts. It is especially good topped with a dollop of vanilla ice cream. If you prefer, you may substitute canned peaches for the pears.

Ingredients

¼ cup (1 stick) butter
1 cup flour
1 cup granulated sugar
½ teaspoon salt
1 tablespoon baking powder
¾ cup milk
30 oz. (2 cans) pears in heavy syrup
12½ oz. (1 can) almond cake and pastry filling

Method

Turn on the oven to 350°. Cut cold butter into 8 pieces. Put butter in 2 quart casserole dish or the removable ceramic insert to your crock pot. Put the casserole dish in the oven to melt the butter. The butter will probably be melted before the oven reaches 350°, so keep an eye on it.

In a separate bowl, mix the flour, sugar, salt, and baking powder. Stir in milk. Pour this batter over the butter in the baking dish. Do not stir.

Remove pears from cans, reserving juice. Slice pears into bite-sized pieces. Dump the pear slices into the baking dish. Do not stir.

Measure 1¼ cups of reserved pear juice and add it to the baking dish. Do not stir.

Arrange almond filling over the top of the cobbler in spoonfuls.

Bake for 45 minutes until deeply golden on top and pulling away from the edges.

Remove from oven and cool somewhat on a wire rack. Serve warm. To keep the cobbler warm, put the still-warm insert in your crockpot and set the temperature on low. If the cobbler is completely cooled before you put it into the crockpot, heat it on high, then turn down to low.

Apple Slaw Recipe

Makes 6 Side Servings

If you like cilantro, you'll love this! Serve it as a wholesome side dish or as a condiment on chicken or pork tacos or pulled pork sandwiches. Apple slaw is best served shortly after making.

Ingredients

1 Gala or Fuji apple
1 Pippin or Granny Smith apple
3 scallions (green tails and white tips only)
⅓ bunch of fresh cilantro
1 dash of salt
black pepper to taste
½ teaspoon olive oil
½ teaspoon balsamic vinegar

Method

Wash and cut apples and scallions into chunks. Wash and remove stems from cilantro. Put apples, scallions, and cilantro in a food processor or chopper to cut them into small pieces.

Scoop the chopped ingredients into a medium-sized serving bowl. Stir in the salt, pepper, olive oil, and balsamic vinegar. Serve shortly after making.

Rainbow's End

Rainbow's End began as a border idea. I developed a block to complement the border. Designed and pieced by Judy Martin and quilted by Lana Corcoran, 2011.

The block is elementary, but the border gets into triangles so it is a bit more difficult. I think the border adds a great finishing touch, but if you want the easiest of projects, choose the twin size, which I present with a plain border rather than the pieced one..

This quilt block has a plain center square perfect for a signature or friendship quilt. You can double the variety in the brights by splitting and swapping fat quarters. The quilt also lends itself to strip exchanges.

Yardage & Cutting Specifications

Queen/King Size

Quilt Size: 104½" x 104½"
Block Size: 14" between seamlines
Requires: 25 Z

Yardage
White Print 8 yards
4 mitered borders cut 1½" x 105¾"
4 mitered borders cut 11¾" x 93¾"
200 A
125 C
312 D

Red Orange Prints 4 fat quarters
76 A
76 B

Yellow Orange Prints 4 fat quarters
76 A
76 B

Yellow Green Prints 4 fat quarters
76 A
76 B

Blue Green Prints 4 fat quarters
76 A
76 B

Blue Violet Prints 4 fat quarters
76 A
76 B

Red Violet Prints 4 fat quarters
76 A
76 B

Backing 9⅞ yards
3 panels 38" x 112½"

Binding ¾ yard
20 strips 2" x 27"

Batting
113" x 113"

Twin/Long Twin Size

Quilt Size: 70" x 98"
Block Size: 14" between seamlines
Requires: 24 Z

Yardage
White Print 4¾ yards
2 borders cut 7½" x 84½"
2 borders cut 7½" x 70½"
192 A
120 C

Red Orange Prints 3 fat quarters
48 A
48 B

Yellow Orange Prints 3 fat quarters
48 A
48 B

Yellow Green Prints 3 fat quarters
48 A
48 B

Blue Green Prints 3 fat quarters
48 A
48 B

Blue Violet Prints 3 fat quarters
48 A
48 B

Red Violet Prints 3 fat quarters
48 A
48 B

Backing 6¼ yards
2 panels 39½" x 106"

Binding ¾ yard
16 strips 2" x 27"

Batting
78" x 106"

Optional Templates

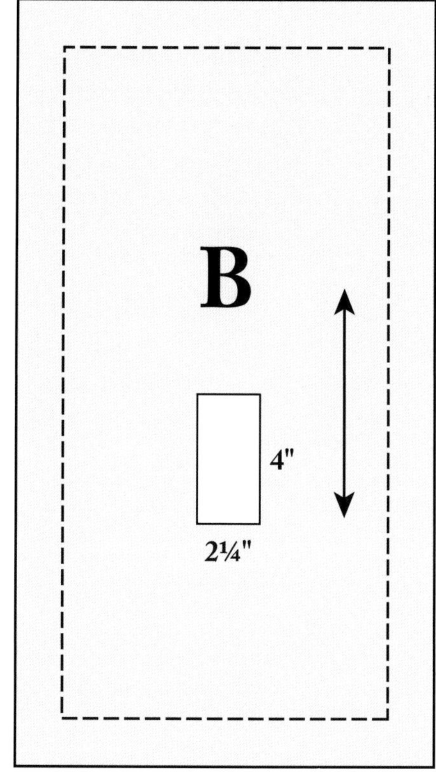

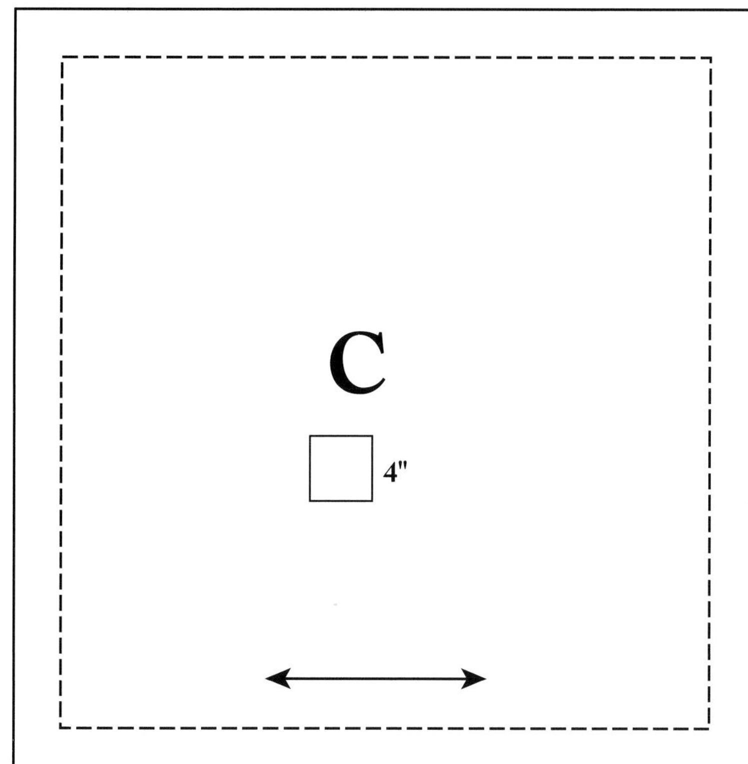

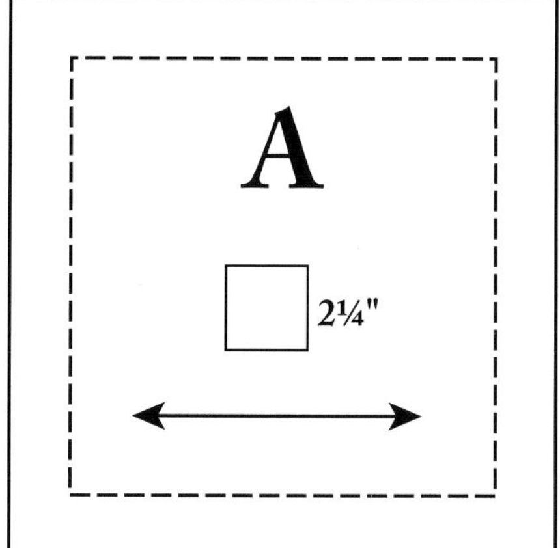

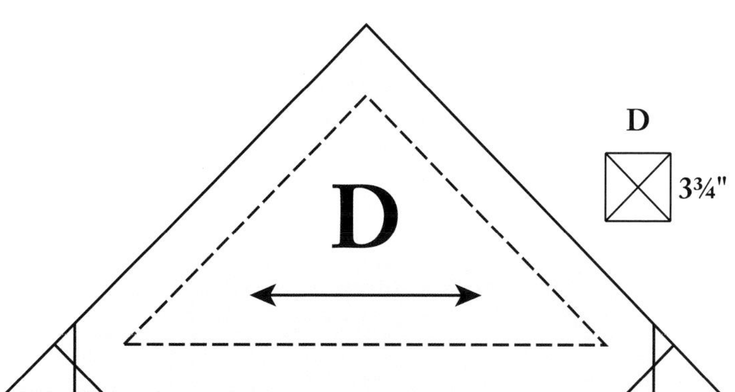

Strip Cutting Layouts

Number of Strips Needed for Each Quilt Size

First cut lengthwise borders from white print. Cut the remainder of the yardage into 18" lengths from which to cut strips and patches.

White 18" Strip & Patch Cutting

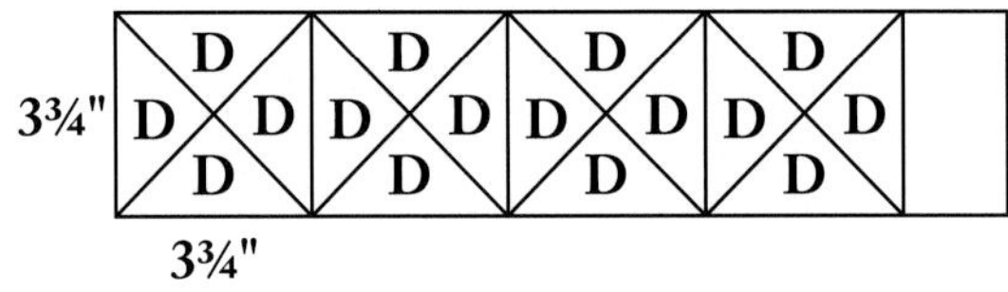

32 Queen/30 Twin

20 Queen

29 Queen/28 Twin

Red-Orange 18" Strip & Patch Cutting

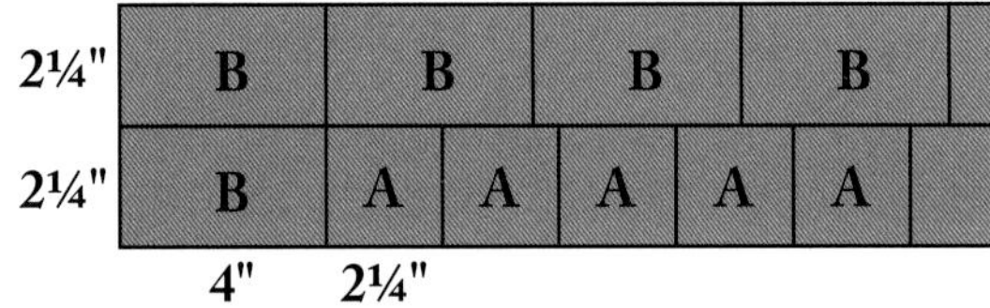

16 Queen/10 Twin

Yellow-Orange 18" Strip & Patch Cutting

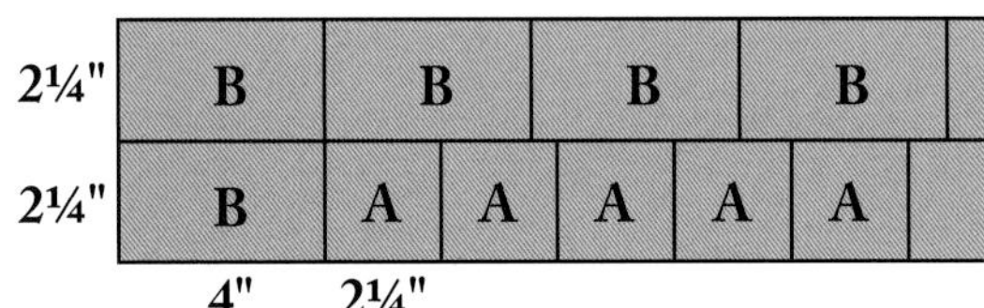

16 Queen/10 Twin

Yellow-Green 18" Strip & Patch Cutting

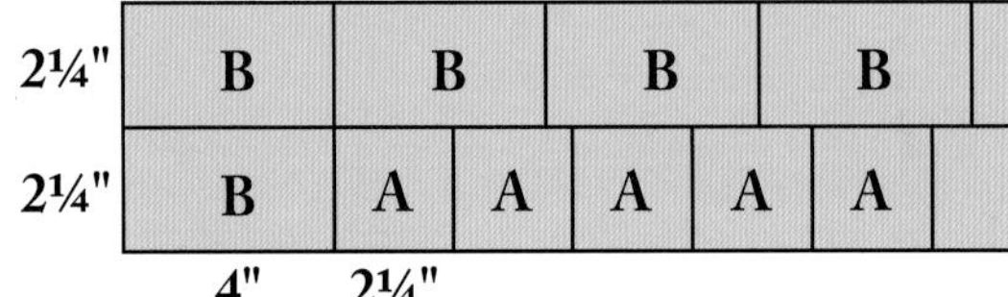

16 Queen/10 Twin

Blue-Green 18" Strip & Patch Cutting

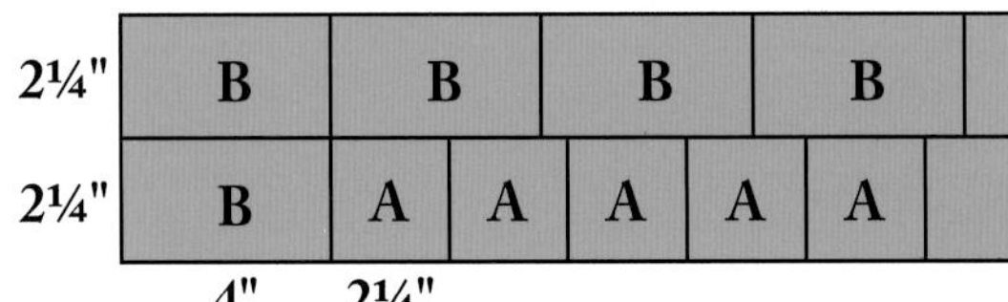

16 Queen/10 Twin

Blue-Violet 18" Strip & Patch Cutting

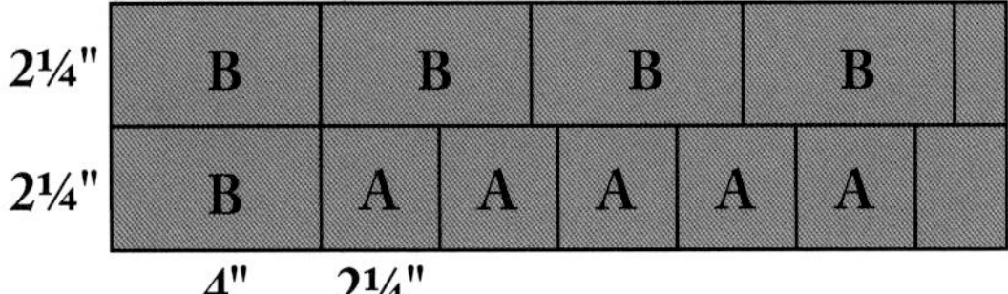

16 Queen/10 Twin

Red-Violet 18" Strip & Patch Cutting

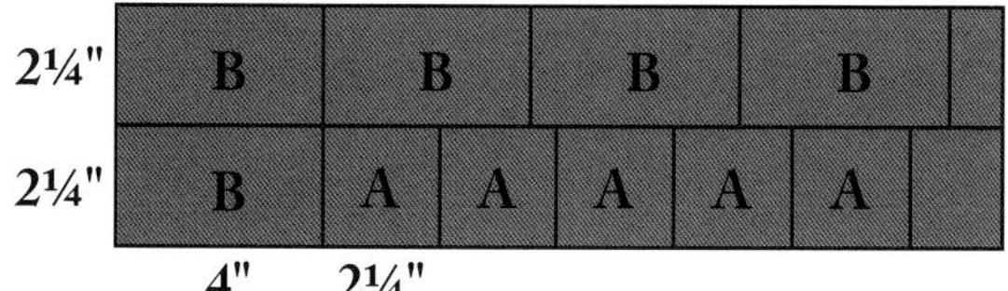

Number of Strips Needed for Each Quilt Size

16 Queen/10 Twin

Block Construction

After cutting, keep the matching A and B patches together. Lay out a block at a time, with matched A-B pairs touching. Sew a white A square to each end of a yellow-green B rectangle. Press seams toward B. Next, sew a blue-green B, a yellow-green A, and then a yellow-orange A end to end. Press seam allowances toward the yellow-orange end. Sew these two segments together and press seam toward the yellow-green B. Add a white C to each end; press seam allowances toward the white C patches.

Sew the following end to end: white A, blue-violet B, blue-green A, yellow-orange B, red-orange A, and white A. Press all seams toward the blue-violet B, as shown below. Pin and stitch this strip to the blue-green edge of the other segment. Press seam toward the yellow-orange B. Repeat to make a similar segment for the bottom of the block.

Now make the middle segment, joining red-violet B to blue-violet A and red-violet A to red-orange B as shown below. Join the two A-B strips for one side. Press seam allowances toward the red-violet B. Repeat for the other side. Add a white C between the two segments, pressing seams toward C. Pin and stitch the three segments together to complete the block. Press seam allowances away from the center segment. Make the listed number of blocks for your quilt size.

For the queen quilt border, keep track of matching patches. Make the border corners first in exactly the colors shown. Stitch 1 D, then another, to A, pressing the first seam toward A and the second toward D. Sew D to B; press seam toward B. Stitch this to A-D-D. Sew A-B-D, pressing seams toward A. Attach to complete Border Corner, pressing seams to the right.

Next sew remaining patches into Unit 1's of the six colorings shown below. Press seam allowances toward the squares and away from the triangles. Make 22 border blocks out of Unit 1's, all in the same color sequence shown. Press seams to the right. You will have some Unit 1's left over for now. See the queen quilt diagram and the narrative on the next page to see how to join border units, corner units, and remaining Unit 1's to make borders. Attach borders as directed on the next page.

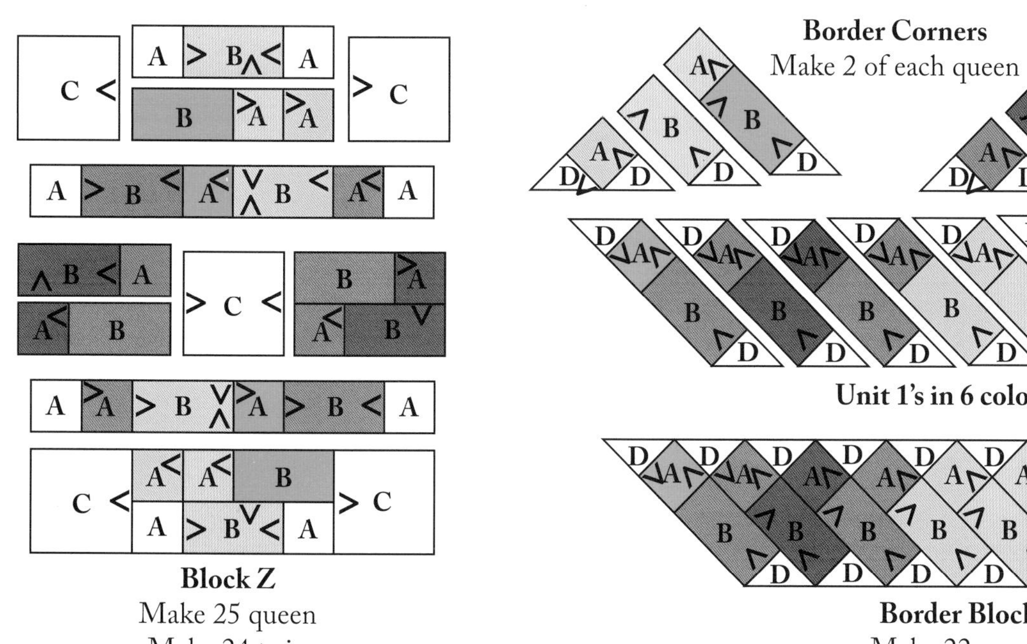

Block Z
Make 25 queen
Make 24 twin

Border Corners
Make 2 of each queen

Unit 1's in 6 colorings

Border Block
Make 22 queen

Queen Quilt Assembly

Join five Z blocks in a row, turning every second block so that yellow-green touches red-violet. Make five rows, starting odd-numbered rows with red-violet at the top of the left-most block and even-numbered rows with yellow-green at the top. Press seams to the right in odd rows and to the left in even rows. Join rows to complete the quilt center. Press seams toward the bottom of the quilt.

Cut the corners off of the 8 plain border strips to miter them. Set aside.

For the pieced border, make the border corners first, as shown on the previous page. Sew the remaining patches into 148 Unit 1's in the six color combinations shown. Join these to make 22 border units, leaving some leftover Unit 1's. Sew six border units together for each side border. Sew five border units end to end for each top or bottom border. To the border ends, add Unit 1's and border corners in the color sequence shown below. Press seam allowancess to the right.

Pin and stitch the plain borders to the pieced border strips. Press seams toward the plain borders.

Note the set-in seams indicated by the pink dots. Pin and stitch borders to quilt center, starting and stopping ¼" in from raw edges; stitch the miter. Press seams away from the quilt center.

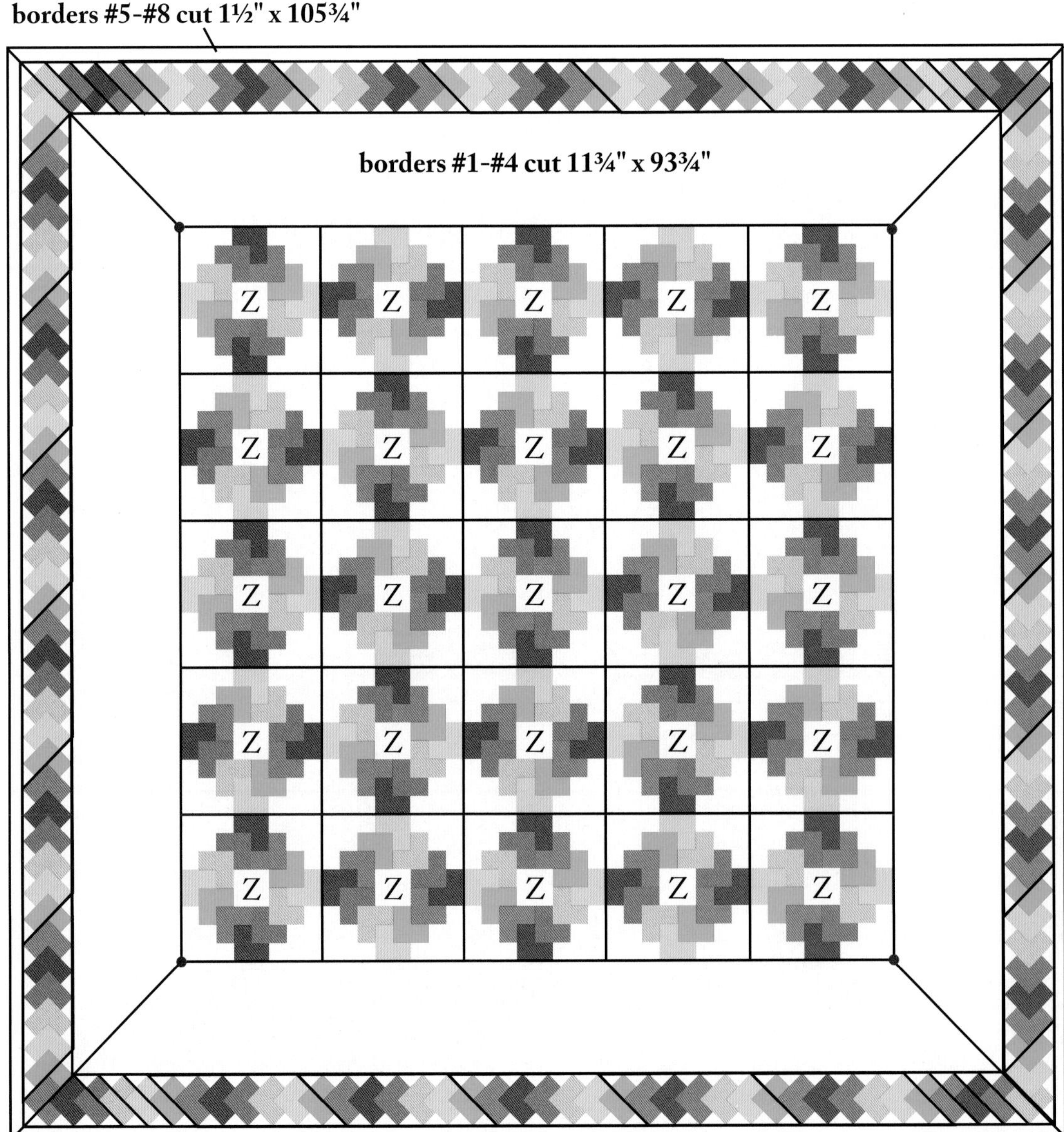

Queen Quilt Diagram

Twin Quilt Assembly

Join four Z blocks in a row, turning every second block so that yellow-green touches red-violet. Make six rows, starting odd-numbered rows with red-violet at the top of the left-most block and even-numbered rows with yellow-green at the top. Press seams to the right in odd rows and to the left in even rows. Join rows to complete the quilt center. Press seams toward the bottom of the quilt.

Pin and stitch the longer plain borders to the sides of the quilt center. Press seam allowances toward the plain borders. Pin and stitch the shorter plain borders to the top and bottom of the quilt center. Press seams toward the plain borders. This completes the quilt top.

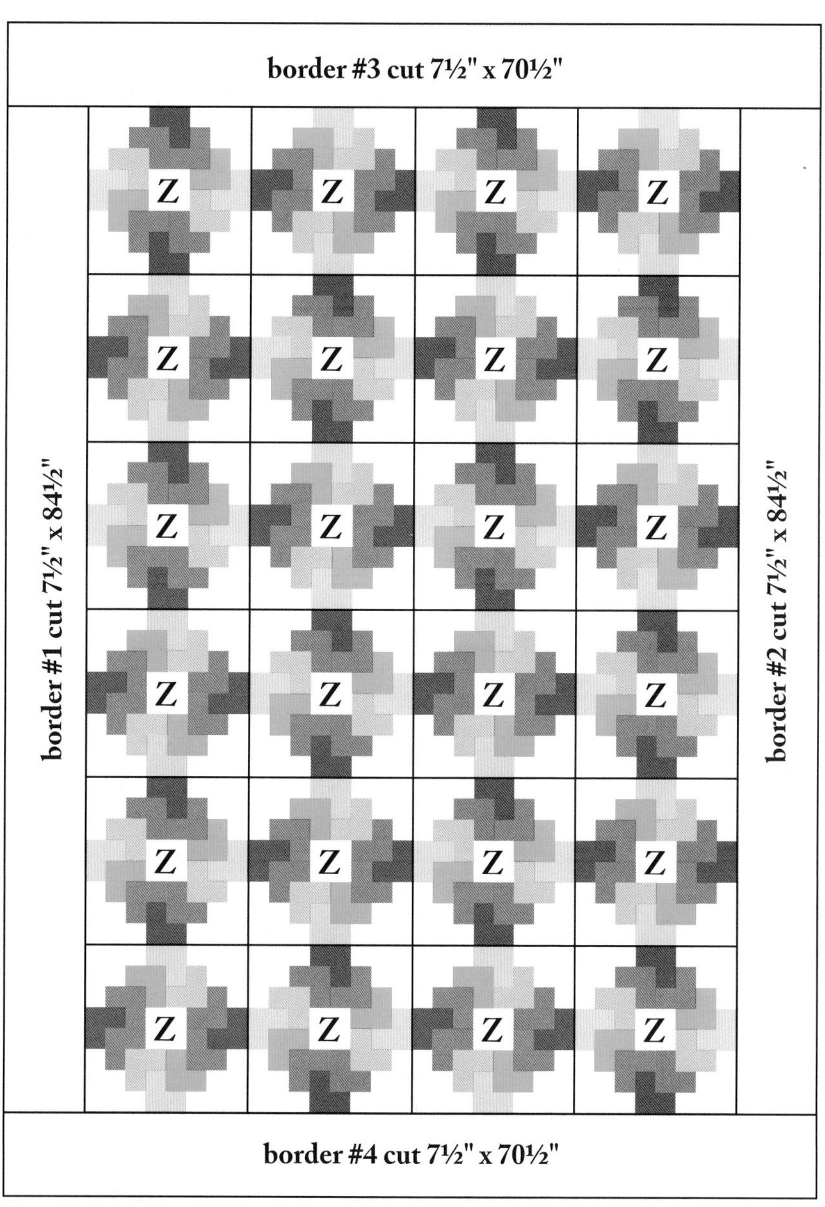

Twin Quilt Diagram

Quilting

Quilt in the ditch between white and colored patches. Quilt a feather motif in the white space at the block corners. Quilt freehand serpentine feathers in the wide white borders. Quilt pumpkin seeds as shown in the colored patches. Quilt a four-teardrop motif in each white block center. In the outer white border of the queen size, quilt a narrow pumpkin-seed-and-diamond motif.

Other Coloring Ideas

The example immediately below utilizes 12 colors in rainbow sequence for the blocks and 6 rainbow colors for the border. Below that is a version in six rainbow colors against a black background.

To the right of that example is one in 6 shades of blue. Above the blue quilt is a version in 6 analogous colors: yellow-green, green, blue-green, blue, blue-violet, and violet.

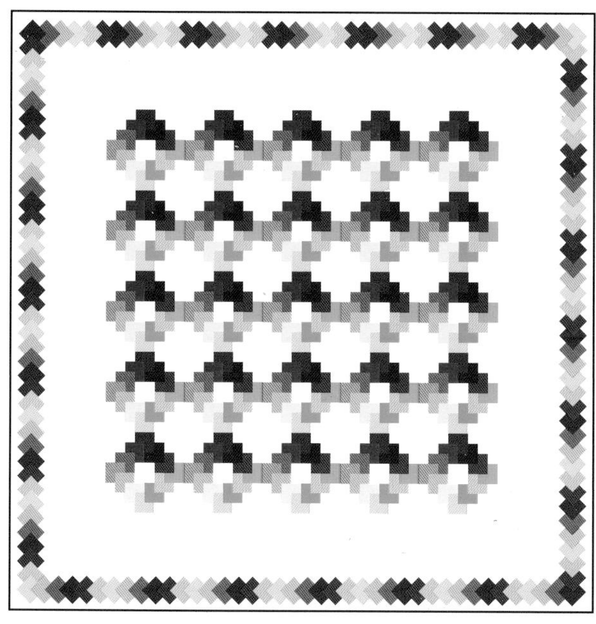

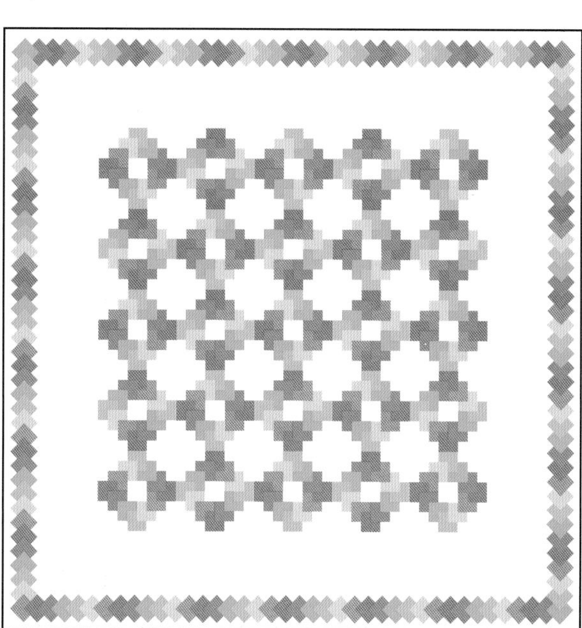

Other Books & Products by Judy Martin

Stellar Quilts, 2010, 128 pages. 13 patterns for outstanding star quilts in multiple sizes. Includes additional colorings for each. "Your quilts are fabulous. *Stellar Quilts* took my breath away." –Mary V., Lincoln, NE "Judy designs quilts like no other....complex looking, but not necessarily complex in construction."–*American Quilt Retailer*

Judy Martin's Log Cabin Quilt Book, 2007, 128 pages. 16 Log Cabins and exciting variations are presented in multiple sizes. This lavishly illustrated book has 150 color photos, 100 setting plans, 50 log borders, charts, and more. "As usual, Judy's instructions are precise, complete and easy to follow."
–Helen Weinman, Heartbeat Quilts, Hyannis, MA

Scraps, 2006, 128 pages. 16 original quilts are presented in multiple sizes. Learn all about scrap style, with tips from one of the foremost authorities on the subject. "*Scraps* is wonderful!!! It has wonderful patterns and easy-to-follow instructions." –Martha S., Frankfort, KY

Piece 'n' Play Quilts, 2002, 96 pages. Complete patterns for 12 new and easy Drunkard's Paths, Log Cabins, and more. First you follow the pattern and piece the blocks. Then you play with their arrangement until you find the look YOU want. "*Piece 'n' Play Quilts* is a great book for beginners as well as the more experienced quilter."
–Patricia T., Pahoa, HI

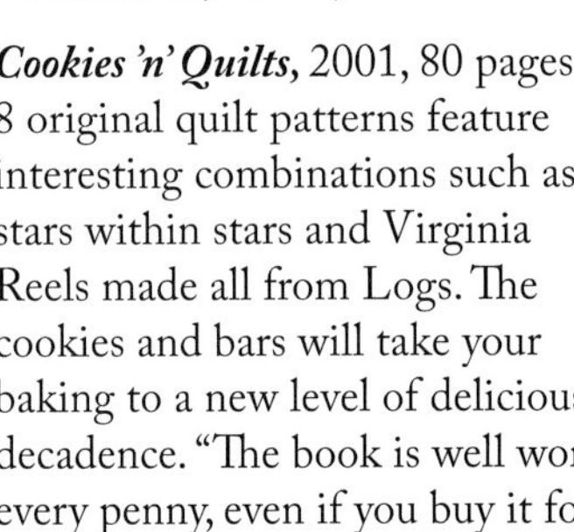

Cookies 'n' Quilts, 2001, 80 pages. 8 original quilt patterns feature interesting combinations such as stars within stars and Virginia Reels made all from Logs. The cookies and bars will take your baking to a new level of delicious decadence. "The book is well worth every penny, even if you buy it for the quilt patterns alone." –Sophie Littlefield, QuiltersReview.com

The Creative Pattern Book, 2000, 176 pages. This book has it all–27 complete quilt patterns (12 quilts and 15 wonderful variations). Find out what Judy was thinking when she designed each quilt. Learn all her secrets for dealing with bias, partial seams, handling fabric, and so much more! "*The Creative Pattern Book* is the best quilt book I own, period."
–Gloria J., Crandon, WI

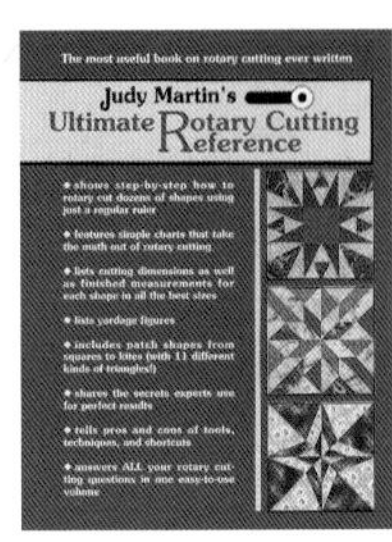

Judy Martin's Ultimate Rotary Cutting Reference, 1997, 80 pages. You'll find charts and instructions for cutting 52 shapes in countless sizes, plus detailed information on tools and techniques. "*Judy Martin's Ultimate Rotary Cutting Reference* will show you how to make the most of the rotary cutting rulers and tools you already own to cut shapes you didn't think were possible to rotary cut."
–Liz Porter, "Love of Quilting"

Point Trimmer Tool, 1996. The Point Trimmer is the easiest way to pre-trim points, helping you align neighboring patches and reducing bulk in your quilt. "The Point Trimmer is one of the greatest tools ever." –Barbara L., Lancaster, PA

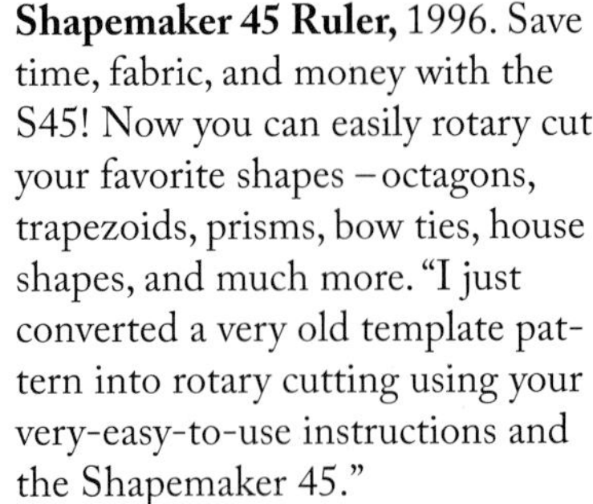

Shapemaker 45 Ruler, 1996. Save time, fabric, and money with the S45! Now you can easily rotary cut your favorite shapes –octagons, trapezoids, prisms, bow ties, house shapes, and much more. "I just converted a very old template pattern into rotary cutting using your very-easy-to-use instructions and the Shapemaker 45."
–Karen M., Littleton, CO

Quilt Show Game, avail. June '12. Have fun with family and friends playing Judy's prize-winning game. Collect fabric cards and use them to "make" blocks and quilts. Enter your quilts in the quilt show and see if you can earn the most prize money—and win the game!

See all of Judy's books and products at www.judymartin.com